THE TANTRIC
MYSTICISM
OF TIBET

1. Vajrasattva Buddha

THE TANTRIC MYSTICISM OF TIBET

A Practical Guide

By John Blofeld

translator of the *I Ching*

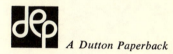

A Dutton Paperback

NEW YORK

E. P. DUTTON & CO., INC.

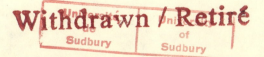

SBN 0-525-47270-3

First published 1970 by E. P. Dutton & Co., Inc.
All rights reserved. Printed in the U.S.A.

FIRST EDITION

Copyright © 1970 by George Allen and Unwin Ltd.

Dedicated to the Lamas and their pupils at Samyé Ling, Scotland, and to John Driver

The Vajrayana or Adamantine Vehicle is the school of Mahayana Buddhism prevalent in Tibet and Mongolia. A highly practical form of mysticism, it affords precise techniques for attaining that wisdom whereby man's ego is negated and he enters upon the bliss of his own divinity.

For more than a thousand years, these techniques—developed at Nalanda University in India at the time of the Roman occupation of Britain—were handed down from teacher to disciple and carefully guarded from outsiders. A few years ago, tragedy struck Tibet sending its people fleeing in thousands across the frontiers. Since then, the Lamas have come to recognize that, unless their homeland is recovered within a generation, the sacred knowledge may decline and vanish. Hence they are eager to instruct all who sincerely desire to learn. In this one respect, Tibet's tragic fate has been the world's gain.

Mysticism, or the search for divine truth within the mind, has always existed among small groups everywhere; but the Tantric mystical techniques have few parallels in other religions or in other schools of Buddhism; many of them are virtually unique. Besides being of absorbing interest to students of Buddhism (especially Zen) and of psychology, a study of them will reward everyone who seeks to lift aside the veil of appearances and penetrate to the very source of all divinity and wisdom.

The way of the Vajrayana is the Way of Power which leads to the mastery of good and evil. It is also the Way of Transformation whereby inward and outward circumstances are transmuted into weapons by the power of mind. It goes without saying that progress in conjuring so vast a transformation is not easy and not to be accomplished by liturgies and sacred formulas. Here as everywhere, Mind is the King. Who, without adamantine strength of will, can attain the stature of a god in this very life? The whole of the adept's being, experience and environment—good and evil—must be harnessed to his purpose.

The first requirement is indomitable resolution; the second

9

is a teacher who teaches not only from sacred texts but also from experience and an illumined mind. In the West, such men are scarcely more plentiful than Wish-Fulfilling-Gems; but among the Tibetan refugees who have poured into India, Sikkim and Nepal are enlightened Lamas from the great monastic seats of learning and accomplished yogins driven from their mountain fastnesses. Of these, a handful have made their way to Europe and America to work in universities or to found gompas in lonely places that will become centres of meditation. Already, Samyé Ling, a small gompa on the Scottish moors, has attracted a band of Lamas and more students than it can accommodate.

Once these Lamas have mastered European languages, books like this one will be outmoded. We may expect from their pens authoritative works setting forth the teaching more openly than was ever done in Tibet because already they have come to realize that maintaining the ancient safeguards would be to threaten the Vajrayana with extinction. Not all their pupils will be Buddhists, for others may find it fruitful to adapt the Tantric techniques to their spiritual life. In the meanwhile, it behoves us Western followers of the Vajrayana to introduce the subject as best we can. Hence this book. I hesitated over writing it for some ten years, feeling that my knowledge is inadequate and knowing that it is usually best to be silent until our spiritual progress fits us to speak with authority; my decision to write it was taken at last, despite insufficient progress, because I believe there is a growing interest in the Vajrayana and it is certainly high time to clear up the grotesque misunderstandings about Tantric Buddhism to which the traditional secrecy has given rise.

In Tibet, the vital oral teachings without which Tantric works are enigmas are accompanied by an injunction not to speak of them without permission. To allow a half-fledged medical student to practise as freely as a qualified doctor would be less dangerous than to permit novices to set themselves up as the teachers of techniques able to revolutionize, not merely thought, but the mind itself. Wrongly applied, they could lead to madness and worse than madness.

This book barely touches upon the history, development and present status of the Vajrayana, and upon the different schools and sects. It is chiefly concerned with Tantric *method*—the means of achieving the extraordinary results that flow from mind control and the negation of the ego. The idea that Tantric techniques could be adapted for use outside the Buddhist fold dawned on me and has grown as the outcome of two circumstances—the separate visits of an English and an American Benedictine abbot to Bangkok who were eager to study Buddhist meditational methods, and my chancing to learn of several Catholic dignitaries engaged in similar studies. Moreover, in Australia, one or two Quakers I met expressed deep interest in the Vajrayana. I have as yet no idea of how much can be gained by practising Vajrayana techniques outside their Buddhist context and I should prefer to see the entire Dharma accepted together with the techniques. Nevertheless, spiritual progress and attainment are no one religion's prerogative; they are open to all men of vision and determination.

Believing the Vajrayana to be one of the loveliest flowers of man's spiritual achievement, I am sure I have failed to do it justice. A description of the sky's immensity by a frog peering at the stars from the bottom of a well is bound to be deficient.

JOHN BLOFELD

Bangkok 28/12/68

CONTENTS

PART II   PRACTICE

ILLUSTRATIONS

17

colour, but occasionally white, as here. The position
of the hands identifies him. Symbolizing boundless light
and (in this Amitayus form) longevity, he holds a vial
of the nectar of immortal wisdom. (A valuable Mongolian painting.)

5. *A Grand Initiation Mandala* 102A

This was painted on the floor of a temple in Hangchow
in the 1930s to serve for initiations conducted by the
Panchen Lama when (during his previous incarnation)
he visited east China. It is similar to the mandala described in this book, except that the deities are represented by signs instead of figures and that its core is
not in the usual fivefold form, but ninefold, i.e. ⊞.
Moreover at the very centre is a circular tower which,
like those on the outer rim, is not painted but stands
upon the painting. (Photograph supplied by Mr Gerald
Yorke.)

6. *The Wheel of Life* 120A

The profound symbolism of this pictorial representation
of the Sacred Doctrine is described in the appropriate
section. (Painted by the palace artist of Sikkim.)

7. *A Chorten* 122A

The unusual history of this reliquary tower is related
in the footnote at the end of Part I, chapter 4. (A beautiful example of Tibetan metal-work from Lhasa.)

8. *Maha Arya Tara (The Green Drölma)* 178A

The Green Tara (or Drölma), a beneficent 'deity' very
widely adopted as a Yidam. She embodies compassion
and protection. (Painted by the palace artist of Sikkim.)

9. *Yamantaka (The wrathful form of Manjusri* 178C
Bodhisattva)

The wrathful form of Manjusri, embodiment of wisdom.
Widely adopted as a Yidam by those with fierce passions
to cleanse, he is also one of the Guardians of the Gelugpa

sect. His body is blue (wisdom); the severed heads and corpses represent evil propensities conquered by wisdom. (Painted in Kalimpong.)

10. *Ritual implements*   184A

To the left is a vajra-sceptre and vajra-bell, to the right a pot of the nectar of wisdom. In the centre are three butter-lamps and seven offering-bowls. At the back is an oblong incense-burner. (The pot, lamps and water-bowls are silverware from Sikkim.)

11. *A visualization diagram*   208A

Such diagrams are used when teaching a sadhana to beginners. In the Arya Tara sadhana, a white *Bham* appears and changes into a white lotus, from which rises a white *Ah*. This becomes a moon-disk on which a green *Dham* appears and changes into a blue lotus with a shining green *Dham* in its calyx. (Drawn in Kalimpong.)

12. *Three Guardians of the Nyingmapa sect*   250A

These are the principal Guardians of the Nyingmapa sect, whose duty it is to uphold the Dharma and dis-courage breaking of the Samaya-pledge. Before their conversion to Buddhism, they may perhaps have been awe-inspiring daemonic forces.

DIAGRAMS

(All the diagrams are fully described in the text)

Part I

BACKGROUND AND THEORY

CHAPTER I

THE VAJRAYANA

Mystical Intuitions

There are moments during life when a startling but marvellous experience leaps into mind as though coming from another world. The magic that calls it forth—as though someone had accidentally whispered the 'open sesame' that rolls the stone back from the hidden treasure—is often so fleeting as to be forgotten in the joy of the experience. It may be a thin cadence of music: a skylark bursting into song, the plash of a wave, a flute played by moonlight. It may be a grand harmony of sound, peaceful or awe-inspiring: the murmurous voices of a summer's afternoon or the fateful shrieking and drumming of a mountain storm. It may be something seen: a lovely smile or the curve of an arm; a single gesture, form or hue of compelling beauty; a familiar scene transformed by an unusual quality of light; a majestic panorama of interweaving colours splashed across sea or sky; a cluster of rocks suggestive of enormous beings imbued with life. Or the spell may be wrought by a sudden exaltation springing directly from the mind and jerking it, so to speak, into an unknown dimension.

That the experience is not a passing fancy but an intimation of something profoundly significant is recognized in a flash, but understanding of its significance does not always follow. A curtain hitherto unnoticed is suddenly twitched aside; and, though other veils intervene, for a timeless moment there stands partially revealed—a mystery. Then the curtain falls in place and at least a measure of oblivion descends.

'Mystery' is not a satisfactory term, but what else can be said of it? It has a hundred names, all of them inapt. It has been called the Good, the True, the Beautiful and all of these together. Philosophers term it the Absolute or Ultimate Reality.

23

To Christian mystics it is known as the Godhead and to Christians in general as God. It is the Brahma and Para-Atma of the Hindus, the Beloved of the Sufis, the Tao or Way of the Taoists. Buddhist names for it vary with the context: Nirvana, the Womb of Dharmas, Suchness, the Void, the Clear Light, the One Mind. In the words of the Chinese sage Lao-tzê, 'The Way that can be conceived of is not the Eternal Way; the Name by which it can be named is not its Eternal Name.' Of late, some psychologists have displayed an awareness of it by suggesting the need for 'integration' with something reaching far beyond ourselves. William James spoke of it obliquely. Were it not that frequent and clear visions of it engender a compassionate urge to communicate the bliss, it would be best to use no name at all.

Names set bounds. Unfathomable by the keenest scientific probing, the mystery can be intuited but never grasped, how then named?

Mystics and poets are supremely fortunate in that visions of it sometimes dawn on them unsought; hearty extroverts, if they glimpse it at all, are shocked into fears for their sanity. Uncomfortably they dismiss it as a mental aberration—or run for the doctor!

Attempts to define it succeed no better than the search for a name. To say that it exists is to exclude from it the non-existent and limit it to what speaker or hearer means by existence. To say that it does not exist involves the other side of the dilemma. Both concepts are too crude to describe its subtle nature. To say, as many do, that it is pure mind is well enough in certain contexts, but it ought not to be set apart from matter with which it is inseparably united. To say that it is at once material and otherwise is to play with words.

However, man's consciousness cannot easily divest itself of symbols. Accomplished mystics tend to describe it in terms of the qualities lent to it by the filter of their senses: Clear Radiance, Immaculate Void, Ecstatic Bliss, Infinite Love, All-Embracing Unity.

Clear and profound intuitions of the mystery are not limited to any period, region, kind of person or religious faith. Knowledge of it has come from widely varied sources: the Egyptian and Greek mystery cults, the Druids (so it is said), the tribal peoples of the two Americas, people with no particular religious faith and followers of all the world's great religions. On the whole, however, religious *authorities* seem to fear it. Mysticism has seldom been encouraged (and sometimes savagely repressed) by the Catholic and Protestant Churches, by orthodox Muslims —that is to say non-Sufis—and by the Confucians, although each of these communities has produced some notable mystics. The reason for this attitude seems to be that mystics, intoxicated with their vision, no longer care for conventional forms; like artists, they offend against propriety. The Christian Orthodox Church of Greece and Russia seems less hostile, but even there exoteric, liturgical religion prevails. The Taoists, once mystics *par excellence*, have by and large turned to magic. The Hindus, to their everlasting credit, allow freedom for every sort of religious belief and practice, but even among them true mystics are a minority.

Buddhism is perhaps the one widespread religion which, in theory at least, is wholly mystical, for it recommends to all its followers the practice of mind control and the attainment of intuitive wisdom. Even so, among Buddhists, people *actively* engaged in the sublime search are less common than might be supposed except for a few schools and sects of which the Vajrayana is one.

Confirmation of the genuineness of the mystical experience is to be found in the high degree of unanimity observable in the attempts to describe its nature. Descriptions by people widely separated in time and place are strikingly similar, especially if allowance is made for four diversive factors; the impossibility of accurately describing an experience that transcends all concepts for which words exist; the pious tendency to reconcile all religious experience with cherished doctrines; the prohibition in some societies against expressing views not in accord with the prevailing doctrines; and the need to make descriptions intelligible and acceptable to others. The underlying unanimity which characterizes the mystical writings of all faiths is well brought out in Aldous Huxley's *Perennial Philosophy*. If, as the cynics would have it, the mystical experience is sheer illusion, the stuff of dreams, it is strange that men and women belonging to widely different environments have, throughout the centuries, suffered the same delusions and dreamed the same dream.

No one who has had several intense or prolonged mystical experiences doubts their validity, but what is intuited is so hard to communicate that the mystics' virtual unanimity is the only evidence that can be offered to the world at large. Nor is the value of these experiences easy to demonstrate. Indeed, from the point of view of society, they must seem detrimental, for a mystic can no more subscribe to mundane values than unicorns can behave like bees or ants. Nevertheless, the people concerned regard them as the most worthwhile happenings in their lives: they are tormented by a thirst to regain them and prolong the bliss for ever. The possibility of attaining to unexcelled beauty, truth and ecstasy makes it natural to re-nounce all other goals.

Unhappily modern life is not conducive to the spontaneous dawning of the experience; people are so used to filling their leisure with gay distractions that the surface of their minds is seldom placid. Scholars are too preoccupied with investigating details of the outward flux to pay much heed to those who speak of a sublime truth discoverable within; but it must be said that their unwillingness to experiment with the techniques affirmed to lead to that discovery ill accords with their spirit of scientific enquiry. No doubt, the reason is that the techniques demand prolonged exertion to achieve a goal of which they doubt the very existence.

The Need for the Sacred Quest

There are a fortunate few to whom powerful intimations of the sacred mystery come unsought and others who, accepting the affirmations of accomplished mystics, have faith in its reality. For them it would be unthinkable not to seek the source and there dwell for ever. For the rest, the conclusions forced on us by an unprejudiced examination of the human lot *ought* to be shattering enough to make us eager to try every means of transforming it into something less inherently tragic. With the passing of youth, life's rainbow glitter soon wears off; one by one the shining bubbles burst and the 'shades of the prison house' close in.

Even those who escape great physical distress in the form of disease, hunger, want or back-breaking toil find happiness elusive. True, in the more advanced countries, crushing poverty is becoming rare; few women die in childbirth or needlessly lose their babies for want of care; unshod waifs are no longer seen upon the streets; no hordes of children grow up sickly for lack of nourishment; no corpses lie by the wayside to be devoured by dogs and flies; musicians no longer cough away their lives in icy garrets; no children singe their flesh against the bricks of soot-filled chimneys or drag heavy loads up forbidding flights of stairs. Yet, even if we dare ignore the three-quarters of the human race who still toil like buffaloes for the means of bare subsistence, who can say that life brings more joy than discontent? Whereas hunger is always hunger, cold always cold and pain always pain, pleasures diminish with repetition; real satisfaction is less familiar to the gourmet than is pain to the human donkey sweating away his life in an Eastern sugar mill. Moreover it now appears that, where wealth abounds, want and insecurity have been replaced not by happiness but by mounting boredom and frustration. Blindly accepting the views of Darwin and his heirs, including Marx, we have reposed all our faith in material progress. With what result?

That the need for a radical readjustment of our aims is desperate can be deduced from the unprecedented rise in the incidence of nervous maladies, from the motiveless crimes perpetrated by well-fed, well-educated children, from the hideous examples of mass cruelty carried out by civilized nations on a scale worthy of Attila or Genghis Khan, and from the terrifying speed with which we are rushing towards the abyss of world destruction.

What a joy if we could come upon some means of lasting satisfaction that would give meaning to our existence and sweep away cruelty and frustration! Aesthetic and intellectual satisfactions are subject to the same law of diminishing returns

27

as the cruder forms of sensual pleasure. Organized religion too often resembles a bone-dry vessel from which the water of life has long been drained away. How good if men would heed the precious counsel 'Look within' and embark on the sacred quest!

No doubt most thoughtful people will agree that the tremendous social and scientific advances of this century have, even in the most privileged communities, added far less to the sum total of human happiness than was expected, besides creating new dangers. They will readily see the need for a fresh approach, but not many are likely to have patience with someone who offers an Eastern religion as the remedy. The day has passed when missionary-minded folk could raucously proclaim that they and their fellows were the sole custodians of the divine will and that whoever thought differently would roast throughout eternity. By and large people have rejected religious solutions to life's unsatisfactoriness and regard those who propose them as crackpots, bigots or both.

What is proposed in these chapters is not necessarily a return to religion in exotic oriental guise, but a return to the wisdom that antedates all religions and has been distorted, overlaid and hidden by centuries of misguided religiosity. That this wisdom, or the means of achieving it, has been presented in accordance with Tibetan tradition is because, owing to a combination of geographical and historical circumstances, knowledge of the road to it has been preserved in Tibet more fully than elsewhere. Tibet, as it was up to the recent Communist invasion, was the one living link with the ancient world that still remained—if we exclude the pockets of rather primitive culture found here and there in inaccessible places. Tibet's culture, though ancient, is far from primitive. True, there are Tibetan nomads and mountain tribes living in conditions as close to natural as any in the world, but the learning preserved until recently in Tibet's great monasteries is, in the main, of a highly sophisticated kind.

In reading about Tibetan mysticism, a clear distinction has to be made between what is essential and what is fortuitous. The ancient wisdom has naturally been preserved in a form suited to Tibet—a country where demigods and demons are accepted by most people as being no less real than eagles and scorpions. In presenting my material, I have seldom ventured to separate aspects which seem to me of principal value from those whose worth strikes me as dubious, because I feel unqualified to draw the dividing line. I have written as one who, having been accepted as a disciple by several outstanding Lamas, naturally tries to follow their teaching in all respects. Yet I do not for one moment suppose that it is all equally precious.

My purpose can be understood from an analogy. Suppose that the ancient wisdom is a treasure locked in a vast mine to which only one entrance remains open. I have tried to describe that entrance and the passageways leading into the mine as I saw them. I believe implicitly in the inestimable value of the treasure; I do not, however, take it for granted that the approach revealed to me is the only one or necessarily the best one. If others can find another approach more consonant with their dispositions, so much the better—so long as it reaches the treasure and does not leave them groping in the darkness of the mine. Until such a way is found, we had best make do with the present one, altering it perhaps to suit our special needs.

The Choice of a Path

In most well-to-do communities, disillusion with the results of material progress has already become widespread and the number of people turning to mystical oriental faiths, though still not great, has grown astonishingly. In England and the United States especially, there are flourishing meditation centres which have to turn away students for lack of accommodation. Buddhist and Brahminist groups flourish in places where twenty years ago such a development could not be imagined and the number of books written to instruct the devotees of these religions rather than for the sake of scientific or general interest has increased by leaps and bounds. The rise of mysticism in these exotic forms results from the feeling that the established religious bodies in the West have, in their eagerness to conform with modern values, gradually lost contact with spiritual realities. Another reason is mysticism's emphasis on spiritual *experience* and its freedom from formalism and dogma. The mystic is less concerned with doing and believing than with *being* or *becoming*.

Of the great world religions, Buddhism is the one which most clearly defines the goal in terms acceptable to mystics and provides a detailed, practical guide to mystical attainment. Hitherto the branches of Buddhism most prevalent in the West have been Zen and Theravada, of which Zen is more wholly mystical. The Tantric methods of the Vajrayana are just beginning to arouse interest. The Vajrayana is perhaps unlikely to achieve Zen's widespread appeal, because it may be thought altogether too exotic; but certain kinds of people will find in it a powerful means of arousing the latent forces of their minds and coming face to face with the reality within.

Zen owes its popularity in the West to a number of causes. It provides very direct methods for piercing the veils of illusion, negating the ego and encouraging the influx of intuitive wisdom. It emphasizes the necessity for by-passing the intellect. It is not concerned with metaphysical speculation and its freedom from complex rituals makes it especially attractive to people reacting from the liturgical formalism of their Christian and Jewish forebears. Moreover Zen accords well with the modern scientific spirit; although Zen adepts, seeking truth within themselves, are not concerned with the details of the world about them, they share with scientists a preference for clear-cut objective methods and an impatience with woolly-mindedness. White-overalled scientists who have no sympathy with richly apparelled priests hovering amidst points of flame and clouds of incense smoke may recognize in the barely appointed cell of the black-gowned Zen adept a laboratory for the investigation of psychological processes.

However, though Zen is austere, it is very far from simple. It is an almost perpendicular path leading up towards a lofty peak and the adept has to dispense with climbing aids. *Those fully qualified for the ascent* will, after five, ten or twenty years of unremitting toil, suddenly emerge in the dazzling snow and

30

gaze down with astonishment at the narrow valleys they had once taken for the universe. Forgetful of the rigours of the climb, they will shout with glee in the exhilaration of their new-found freedom; but, when they look around for their companions, they may find few in sight.

Now, despite enormous external differences, the Vajrayana is essentially close to Zen. Its goal is the same—Enlightenment *here* and *now*—and its approach no less direct; but, unlike Zen, it relies on an abundance of aids. For the many people who, not being spiritual giants, conscientiously practise Zen or some other austere form of mysticism over the years without notable results, meditation becomes more of a burden than a joy. Some of these may be glad to attempt the cloud-girt peak again with skilful devices to help them. They may at first be troubled by Tantric Buddhism's lavish use of rites and symbols; but once it is understood how far the sublime purpose of the rituals is removed from mere liturgical pomp, they will perceive their value and perhaps welcome them. Then the Vajrayana will awaken a deep response and lead to the achievement of results that eluded them before. The point is not that the Vajrayana is superior to Zen; no one intimately acquainted with Zen could doubt the excellence of its methods; what is more doubtful is the ability of most of us to employ them successfully.

The Tantric Way

In its general purpose, the Vajrayana does not differ from other forms of Buddhism or from any religious endeavour aimed not at personal survival but at negating the ego and attaining a state of unity transcending 'I' and 'other'. This goal has been envisaged by people of many creeds ever since the first arising of the urge to leap through the enchanting rainbows and terrifying thunder-clouds of illusion which veil the still, clear void beyond. What is unique about the Tantric method is its wealth of techniques for utilizing all things good and evil to that end. As with judo, the adept learns to use the antagonist's weight to his own advantage. Obstacles are transmuted into instruments for providing the tremendous momentum

31

needed. Most other spiritual paths require a turning away from dark to light, whereas Vajrayana yogins welcome both demons and angels as their allies. Transcending good and evil, they transmute them both back into that pure essence from which the universe's whirling phantasmagoria is mentally created.

Manipulation of the forces of good and evil provides the power. Wisdom and compassion are the means. The adamantine jewel enfolded by the lotus is the symbol. The Liberation of ourselves and all sentient beings is the goal. Perfect at-onement with pure undifferentiated Mind, a synonym for the stainless Void, is the fruit.

Naturally such a goal is not lightly won. The victory entails a shattering revolution of consciousness, progressive diminution of cherished egos and, ultimately, the burning up of the last vestiges of self. It would be folly to embark upon so perilous a quest without the guidance of a teacher who, having progressed far along the path, speaks from an illumined mind, though he need not actually have attained Liberation.

Of the activities and lines of conduct normally associated with a religious life, Tantric Buddhists extol faith as the most essential—not blind faith, nor faith in dogmas, but faith that the goal exists; for without it no one would choose to undergo the rigours of the path. Good works, as such, are not of main importance, though compassion is enjoined as an essential means for negating the ego and attaining wisdom. Whereas Buddhists of other sects are often much concerned with piling up stocks of merit, Vajrayana adepts perceive that, unless great care is taken, engrossing oneself in good works tends to inflate the ego by engendering complacency. As to prayers (or their Buddhist equivalent) and rites, these play a large part in the Vajrayana, but their significance is different from that accorded them by other religions; they are not thought of as 'pleasing to the gods' but as means of leading the mind to higher states of consciousness; they are no more than aids to the very important mental practices loosely covered by the term 'meditation'.

The conduct of a Vajrayana adept is likely to be unorthodox; intent upon employing *everything* in life as a means to achievement, he does not except such animal processes as sleeping, eating, excreting and (if he is not a monk) sexual intercourse. The energy of passions and desires must be yoked, not wasted. Every act of body, speech and mind, every circumstance, every sensation, every dream can be turned to good account.

This aspect of Tantric Buddhism has led to the great error of confounding it with libertinism. Though *all* things are employed as means, they must be *rightly* used and their right use is far removed from sensual gratification. The possible use of drugs such as mescaline which produce psychedelic effects provides a good example. Suppose a medieval traveller had been about to undertake an arduous journey through burning deserts and icy mountains in search of some fabled city, and someone had shown him an authentic picture of the place; his will to endure the terrible hardships involved would have been enormously strengthened. At least he would have been freed from gnawing doubts as to whether the city really existed. Similarly, mescaline does in many cases imbue the users with an absolute conviction of the existence of a spiritual goal of the kind postulated by mystics. Therefore using it once or twice, with proper preparation and under suitable conditions, might benefit newcomers to the path; on the other hand, its continued use would be disastrous—bliss so easily attainable would be likely to reconcile them to life as it is and induce them to be content with drug-induced experiences instead of actually treading the path. Fingering a picture of a city is no substitute for going to live there. If the path were abandoned, the effort to negate the ego would be abandoned with it and unutterable loss sustained.[1]

The danger of confounding Tantric practice with, or using

[1] During my one experience with such a drug, I was plunged into a state of ecstasy in which dawned full awareness of three great truths I had long accepted intellectually but never experienced as being self-evident; now, all of a sudden, they became as tangible as the heat of a raging fire. There was awareness of undifferentiated unity embracing perfect identification of subject and object; logic was transcended and I beheld a whirling mass of brilliant colours and forms which, being several, differed from one another and yet were *altogether the same* at the moment of being different! The concept 'I' had ceased to be; I was at once the audience, the actors and the play! Secondly I recognized the unutterable bliss I was experiencing as the *only* real state of being, all others amounting to no more than passing dreams. Thirdly came awareness of all that is implied by the

it as an excuse for, libertinism cannot be stressed too strongly. Already certain Western converts to Zen have fallen into grave error by misinterpreting a doctrine Zen shares in common with the Vajrayana. They have used the facile argument that, since pairs of opposites are two sides of the same coin and good and evil ultimately identical, it follows that one may indulge in all kinds of crimes and excesses without departing from the state of holiness. It is true that good and evil are identical (or, rather, that they cease to be) at the level where delusion is transcended, but how many of those self-styled Zen followers are within a billion billion miles of that level?

Among other causes which have led to misunderstandings regarding Tantric Buddhism are: the secrecy which has traditionally surrounded the inner core of doctrine; the sexual symbolism employed in Tantric texts and iconography; and the appalling misrepresentations put about by certain Christian missionaries, of whom a prime example was Waddell, the first person to write at length on Tibetan Buddhism in English. The reasons for secrecy and for the choice of symbolism are discussed in later chapters. For the present it is enough to say that the secrecy prevents the misuse of powerful mind forces that would be dangerous to employ without expert guidance; and that the sexual symbolism results from a frank acceptance of sex as the most powerful of the forces motivating sentient beings, human and animal. Putting aside prudery, what apter symbols can there be of the union of opposites—the doctrine upon which the entire Tantric system is based? Or by what vivid pictorial representation could the indomitable force which moves the universe be better symbolized?

Among scholars there are some who hold Tantric Buddhism

Buddhist doctrine of 'dharmas' (see Elements of Being in chapter II), namely the doctrine that all objects of perception are alike devoid of own-being, mere transitory combinations of an infinite number of impulses. I experienced the rising of each impulse and the thrill of culmination with which it ceased to be, waves mounting and dissolving in a sea of bliss. That experience, which, since it was almost too intense for flesh and blood to bear, I have no desire to repeat, gave me an incomparable insight into the true meaning of what I had learned from my Lamas. Undoubtedly I benefited as the traveller in my analogy would have benefited from the picture of the city, but I am no nearer Liberation than before; therein lies the limitation of the drug-induced experience.

to be an offspring of Tantric Hinduism. However, as the Lama Govinda, Dr Benoytash Bhattacharya and other authorities have now demonstrated, several of the Buddhist Tantras were composed at a very early date and, by the third century A.D., the Vajrayana had already crystallized into a definite form. No doubt the two systems have interacted upon each other, but it now seems probable that the earliest Tantric Buddhism antedates Tantric Hinduism (though not, of course, Hinduism itself). The situation is confused by the Vajrayana's wide use of Hindu deities to symbolize universal forces; and, unfortunately, the degenerate practices of some Hindu Tantric sects in Bengal have, owing to this confusion, led to unmerited aspersions upon the Vajrayana.

It has also been suggested by travellers in the Tibetan border regions that the Vajrayana is a decadent form of Buddhism owing more to the ancient Bön religion of Tibet, to shamanism and animism than to the Buddha Dharma. As the next chapter will show, the Vajrayana, far from being decadent, is the ultimate flowering of Mahayana doctrine. Buddhism, never aggressive, has in all Buddhist countries absorbed numerous vestiges of earlier religions and, at the popular level, is generally intermixed with non-Buddhist elements. This is as true of Thailand and Ceylon as of China and Tibet. It is this which is responsible for a good deal of local colour which makes the differences between Buddhism in one country and another seem much greater than they are. In essentials, the underlying unity of all Buddhist schools and sects is remarkable, despite some fairly wide differences between the two principal branches: the Mahayana of northern Asia and the Theravada of the south. Tantric Buddhism is a logical outcome of the teachings of the Vijnanavadins and the Yogacharins[1] who respectively developed the philosophical and practical aspects of the Mahayana. It has added no new principals but has developed some very effective *methods* of its own. Those who deplore developments of any kind in Buddhism should refresh their memories as to the Buddha's own definition of true Dharma:

[1] Both these sects arose from the ancient Madhyamika school which was the progenitor of almost all branches of Mahayana Buddhism.

'Of whatsoever teachings you can assure yourself thus: These doctrines conduce not to passions but to dispassion; not to bondage but to detachment; not to the increase of worldly gains but to their decrease; not to greed but to frugality; not to discontent but to content; not to company but to solitude; not to sluggishness but to energy; not to delight in evil but to delight in good; of such teachings you may with certainty affirm: These are the Norm, these are the Discipline.'

In spiritual matters, a purely historical approach is often pointless. Common sense tells us that no system of teaching can be effective unless it is adaptable to time, place, and local characteristics. A perfectly rigid system would soon become a dry husk, a worm-eaten remnant, interesting only to historians. In practice, Buddhists have always treated the Buddha Dharma as something adaptable to circumstances; it is a living, fluid tradition which fits effortlessly into different surroundings.

Seekers after truth do well to accept whatever assists their progress. Proof of spiritual progress is not easily communicable, but the adept can gauge his own by the facility with which he achieves successively higher states of consciousness that bring him closer to the immaculate, all-pervading mind. Efficiency not orthodoxy is the test.

The Vajrayana in Tibet

The terms Vajrayana or Tantric Buddhism are often used loosely of Tibetan Buddhism as a whole. Properly speaking, Tibetans and Mongols are Mahayana Buddhists of whom many but not all observe the Vajrayana practices derived from a special additional section found only in the Tibetan Buddhist canon.[1] Otherwise, that version of the canon contains the usual vinaya (rules of conduct), sutras (discourses) and the equivalent of abhidharma (advanced doctrines). The part played by the Tantras in Tibetan spiritual life varies. Lamas of the Gelugpa (Yellow Hat) sect are expected to spend twenty years on sutra and scholastic study before starting on the Tantras; many of

[1] Translated from the Sanskrit canon, much of which is no longer extant in the original.

them do not get that far and never become Tantric adepts. At the opposite extreme are the Nyingmapas (one of the Red Hat sects) who are initiated into the Tantras early and spend little time on other sacred studies. However, it is true to say that all Tibetan Lamas, and most laymen too, do follow some degree of Tantric practice, even if it amounts to no more than the visualization which is attached to the mantra *Om Mani Padme Hum*.

Buddhism was introduced into Tibet some twelve hundred years ago in a form which included the Vajrayana. The first Lamas were Indians and Tibetans who had studied at northern India's great University of Nalanda, which then had some thirty thousand students. That this form of Buddhism has persisted in Tibet and neighbouring Mongolia until today, despite Chinese rather than Indian influence on other aspects of their cultures, is because mountains and deserts offer admirable soil for the cultivation of the flowers of the Vajrayana.

The most striking characteristic of those two countries is the cruel inhospitality of their terrain. Tibet consists of high plateaux scourged by icy winds and of range upon range of mountains where frightful thunderstorms and murderous hail seem like the manifestations of demons athirst for blood. Mongolia's wideflung deserts are strewn with bleached bones and its grasslands are comfortless wastes where nomads roam. Children reared in those frightful windswept regions soon learn that life is a battle against remorseless nature. People there live in close proximity to disaster and sudden death. Being constantly menaced by danger, they have developed admirable courage and are easily moved to gaiety, but there is no shrinking from recognition of life's inherent bitterness. Man's spiritual thirst arises from two causes: intimations of a splendidly luminous, quiescent state lying beyond the weaving mists and murky clouds of the cosmic flux; and a longing to escape from an existence compounded of fleeting joys intermixed with inevitable boredom and suffering. Dwellers in a wilderness are brought face to face with both of these. They have a more intense awareness of the contrasting splendours and terrors of the universe than city dwellers pent within walls and living in cushioned ease; and, in Tibet especially, intimations of an all-encompassing glory are of almost daily occurrence, as when the sun god dances upon pinnacles of snow; or when the traveller, after fighting his way through blizzards howling amidst slippery crags and echoing caverns, crosses the pass and gazes down upon a lake flashing turquoise and emerald amidst the shining rocks of the sunlit valley.

At those high altitudes and in that pure air, the richness of nature's colours is marvellously enhanced; so, also, man's perceptiveness. Intuitions of the dazzling reality which is their source are doubly welcome on account of present pains and terrors, which include labouring from dawn till eve to wrest a meagre harvest; seeing the ripening crops flattened to the ground by hailstones large enough to smash a man's skull, floundering amidst the ruins of homesteads toppled by earthquakes or torrential rains, and knowing that loved ones while yet within a bowshot of home may be devoured by famished beasts or perish miserably in a blizzard.

Thus, in Tibet, all conditions are fulfilled for naked displays of violent contrasts between the forces of good and evil which elsewhere, though just as active, are less visible. The Vajrayana's vivid symbolism marvellously depicts the interplay of contrasting forces. Strangers entering a Tibetan milieu may be inclined to doubt the loftiness of a religion in which rites and symbols play so great a part. They may carry away impressions of temples overstocked with images and sacred pictures, of people fingering their rosaries and whispering mantras even when window-shopping, of old women twirling their prayer-wheels and intoning *Om Mani Padme Hum* while riding in buses, and of processions of monks striding along to the thunder of mighty horns. There is seldom anyone at hand who can properly explain the significance of these things in English. How are they to know that the benign and nightmarish figures in the sacred pictures, unlike gods and demons elsewhere, are recognized by the faithful as the products of their own minds, as symbolic representations of the phantasmagoria that haunts the threshold of human consciousness, and as personifications of the forces of passion called into being by the everlasting play of mind?

38

The symbols are often of great beauty, especially the tankas (religious paintings). The artists take great pains, grinding their own colours from mineral substances and performing the brush-work with infinite skill and patience. The mountings of the tankas are of rich brocade and the rollers tipped with heavy ornaments of silver filigree. Besides these, the many ritual objects and some personal and household articles are fashioned with exquisite artistry.

The reason why so many of the figures of 'deities' and other symbols are reminiscent of the Hindu and Tibetan Bön religions is that, in the old days, Buddhists used the outward forms of local faiths to make the transition to Buddhist concepts easier. This has always been the way. If Buddhism had spread through medieval Europe, we should have had Bodhisattvas and Arahans looking like Christian saints. The borrowing of externals to suit local needs does not involve any departure from Buddhist principles. In the early centuries of the Catholic Church, the same method was used. Christmas and at least one of the festivals connected with the Virgin Mary are celebrated on days that were once the feasts of pagan divinities; and in Italy one sometimes sees depictions of the Virgin with several attributes of the Goddess Diana: a sickle moon, a stag and so forth.

Of special interest to Western scholars is the faithfulness with which the system of instruction formulated at Nalanda in the early centuries of the Christian era has been preserved in Tibet. Right up to the Chinese occupation a few years ago, the courses given at Lhasa's monastic universities in such subjects as Buddhism, metaphysics, astrology, grammar, logic and medicine, as well as the manner of student debating, remained much the same as they had been at Nalanda fifteen centuries earlier. The world provides no example of another teaching system continued for half as long. The content of the courses should be of profound interest to students of India's and mankind's past.

Advanced degrees from Lhasa's universities were not recklessly bestowed. The Geshé (Doctor of Divinity) degree took some twenty years and there were others that took even longer. Years of study principally devoted to methods of mind control resulted in the development of remarkable powers of extrasensory perception, of which telepathy is so common as to excite no comment in Tibet. Such powers, though deemed unimportant by-products of Buddhist meditational and yogic practices, do provide a kind of evidence of the efficiency of the Vajrayana techniques. (I have more than once had cause to redden on discovering that the Lama I was talking to had an all too accurate knowledge of my thoughts!)

For a deep study of Tibetan Buddhism, some knowledge of the different 'lineages' of the Lamas, or sects, is important; here, a brief note will suffice, all the more so as differences among the sects are not doctrinal but largely a matter of what emphasis each gives to certain aspects of the Vajrayana teaching. Of the four main sects, three are grouped together as Red Hats; the fourth and largest is nicknamed the Yellow Hat sect.

Of the Red Hats, the Nyingmapa—to which most of my teachers belong—is the oldest and the most faithful to the ancient traditions. Its spiritual lineage is traced back through Padma Sambhava, who was the first great Nalanda scholar to reach Tibet, where he arrived (A.D. 747) a few years after King Sron Tsan Kampo had been converted to Buddhism by his Chinese and Nepalese wives. On this account, he is venerated by all Tibetans as Guru Rimpoché, the Precious Teacher. Nyingmapas are expert Tantrists, but less well-schooled in Mahayana scriptural studies. Few of the Nyingmapa Lamas take monastic vows; they wear a special habit, but are married clergy, not monks. (The supposition that Lama means monk has led to the charge that there are in Tibet 'married monks'—an absurd contradiction in terms. The word for monk is 'gelung'; Lamas may be gelung or married clergy or laymen; gelungs of course observe their monastic vows.)

The Kargyupa sect traces its spiritual lineage back through Milarepa, Tibet's poet-hermit-saint, and through him to the Lama Marpa (eleventh century A.D.) and his Indian teacher Naropa. Many of its members pass much of their lives in lonely caves absorbed in Tantric meditations. Kargyupas tend generally to be austere; they adhere more strictly to the Buddhist rules of discipline (vinaya) than do the Nyingmapas and often

2. Guru Rimpoché in mature guise

practise a type of meditation that is almost identical with that of Zen.

The Sakyapas trace their lineage back through Atisa, an Indian sage who spent his last years in Tibet (died A.D. 1052). At one time, this 'reformed' sect exercised temporal power in the kingdom. Of the Red Hat sects, it is nearest to the Gelugpa.

The Gelugpas trace their spiritual lineage back through Tsong Kapa (fifteenth century A.D.) and beyond him to Atisa. Tsong Kapa was a reformer who gave the sect its present form. It encourages monastic discipline and learning, postponing the Tantras until the end of a long course of study. Most of its Lamas are monks. Since A.D. 1640, its leader, His Holiness the Dalai Lama, has been King as well as Pontiff of Tibet and the Gelugpa sect corresponds to the 'established church'. In Mongolia, almost everyone is a Gelugpa. The sect's admirers point to the excellence of its discipline and learning; but there are some who fear that the Venerable Tsong Kapa, in his zeal to put down existing abuses, may inadvertently have cast out some hidden jewels—as generally happens with zealous reformers everywhere. In any case, his reforms were beneficial and no real loss occurred, as Tibetans have free access to the teachers and teachings of all the sects.

A rare phenomenon peculiar to Tibet and Mongolia is the prevalence of Tulkus—the *recognized* incarnations of departed dignitaries. Elsewhere even Buddhists find this strange; all of them accept the fact of reincarnation as a matter of course, but that a child can be recognized as the incarnation of a particular individual strikes them as debatable. The Tibetans hold that a Lama far advanced along the path is able to choose the circumstances of his next incarnation and, before his death, foretell where his rebirth will take place—not with great accuracy but with enough detail to enable his colleagues to discover his new incarnation at the age of about four or five. Many tests have to be applied before the new incarnation is accepted and invested with the deceased Lama's titles and functions. For example, some thirty objects are placed before a child who seems likely to be the one for whom a search is being made; of these, half once belonged to the late Lama and half to strangers. If the child unerringly picks out the right objects and rejects the others, a high degree of probability is established and other tests follow until no doubt remains. Then he is publicly recognized and conveyed to his own monastery where he will remain under the care of tutors until he is old enough to govern its affairs again. Child Tulkus are remarkable boys, generally exceedingly good-looking, cheerful and intelligent. Receiving the very best teaching available, they soon become outstanding scholars, which makes it difficult to judge how much of their talent has descended from the previous incarnation.

The Dalai and the Panchen Lamas are the most famous of the three hundred-odd Tulkus. In Chinese and English, the word Tulku is sometimes translated Living Buddha. This is a misnomer. However, in the case of the Dalai and Panchen Lamas, it has some cogency as both of them are held to be the reincarnations of beings who in the distant past were respectively emanations of Avalokitesvara and Amida Buddha.

The Vajrayana for the West

I have suggested that the Vajrayana may not achieve Zen's popularity in the West because many of the people attracted to oriental forms of mysticism do not care for ceremonial usages. Though the Vajrayana does include paths wholly free from set forms of any kind, by and large it makes elaborate use of rites because the power generated by emotion and by aesthetic satisfaction is a force too valuable to waste. The rites have a tremendous psychological value and this may in time become more fully appreciated by those temperamentally not fond of ritual. Meanwhile, it is likely that some people will from the first find the Vajrayana's colourful techniques a boon to their spiritual practice and that even some non-Buddhists may wish to adapt them—especially the technique of visualization—for use in the context of their own religions. Though prayer-wheels may never turn in Madison Square or prayer-flags flutter from the roofs of Westminster, already there are lovely Tibetan-style shrinerooms tucked away in private houses.

The varied rites and meditative practices within the Vajrayana afford to widely different kinds of people means to still the monkey-like leaping of their thoughts, develop their latent powers and, by entering ever-deepening states of consciousness, to be flooded at last by the dazzling light of wisdom. Concurrently, they develop an enviable attitude to life, learn to transmute ugliness into beauty, become expert in harnessing the energy of their passions and presently discover that their own nature soaringly transcends man's highest conception of divinity. The choice between Zen and the Vajrayana is not a choice of goal but of method and even the methods are alike in that both deal with the mind at a level that transcends conceptual thought; but the Vajrayana caters to people who find it easier to use symbols and concepts as the very weapons with which to do away with concepts, instead of trying to banish them from the first. With Zen we start, so to speak, at the Ph.D level; with the Vajrayana, we may enter the path at any level from kindergarten to professor.

For a long time to come, the main impediment will be finding a suitable teacher. Few accomplished adepts from Tibet are really proficient in a Western language; of the Tibetans young enough to have acquired the language proficiency necessary for the task, not many have advanced far enough along the path to teach the sacred practice. What can be hoped for is that the older non-English speaking Lamas will be able to continue training their disciples at places of refuge in the Himalayan foot-hills on the Indian side of the frontier and that these disciples will acquire a fluent knowledge of one or more Western languages.

Meanwhile, another great obstacle is being removed. The Lamas, to ensure that the teaching is transmitted before the older generation passes away, are making everything as easy as possible by relaxing the precautionary rules as far as can be safely done. Advanced teaching is sometimes given to Westerners who have not completed the all-important preliminary training, on the understanding that they will do so before proceeding with the main practice. Were this condition to be ignored, the relaxation would defeat its object, as the advanced techniques of visualization cannot be successfully used without sufficient preparation of the mind.

There is likely to be a rather unfortunate division of effort. Some Lamas have been attracted to universities which have the means to pay their passages from India, support them and buy whatever texts are needed for building up good Tibetan libraries. Their services will naturally be utilized for scientific purposes and their students will seldom be people who intend to put the teachings into practice. On the other hand, those Lamas who found small gompas for teaching purposes will be short of money for acquiring texts of which few copies are available outside Tibet; moreover, many of their Western pupils will not be able to spend more than a few days or weeks at a time away from their ordinary work, with the result that the teaching will have to be of a very elementary or general kind. Unless this problem can be overcome, treasures of wisdom lovingly preserved throughout the centuries will be lost to the world or fossilized in scholarly works unconnected with mystical practice.[1]

[1] Those who are truly concerned lest knowledge of this wisdom perish can help to preserve it by sending a cash contribution to the newly established Tibetan National Library, c/o the Council of Cultural and Religious Affairs of His Holiness the Dalai Lama, Gangchen Kyishong, Session Road, Dharamsala, Himalpradesh, India.

Chapter II

THE MAHAYANA SETTING

The Roots of the Vajrayana

Of the two great schools of Buddhism, the Mahayana is prevalent in Tibet and all the Buddhist countries except those in
south-east Asia, where the Theravada holds sway. The Tantras
are embodied in a final section of the Mahayana canon which
the Tibetans received from India and translated with great
care and exactness into their own language. They are based on
teachings propounded by the ancient Madhyamika sect, one
of whose basic tenets was that truth is attained by adhering to
the middle path between belief in (or craving for) permanent
existence and extinction, since the real nature of ultimate
reality is so subtle that it can neither be said to exist nor not to
exist. From the Madhyamika other sects arose, of which the
Vijnanavadins and Yogacharins each contributed to the doctrines
and practices of the Vajrayana. Tantric Buddhism particularly
emphasizes *method* as opposed to mere piety or scholarship. The
very word Tantra, being connected with a Sanskrit root meaning
'to weave', suggests activity.

To understand the Tantras, it is important to know something of the history of Indian Buddhist development, which can
be divided into four distinct periods: (1) the early centuries
during which the original teachings of Sakyamuni (Gautama
Buddha) formed the main substance; (2) a period of expanding
the teachings to embrace philosophy, during which a rational
systematization took place; (3) a period of reaction in favour of
less rigid views with emphasis on the compassionate Bodhisattvas, beings who renounce Nirvana so as to assist others to
reach it; (4) a period of counter-reaction. Very early Pali works
and early Sanskrit works (preserved in Chinese and Tibetan)
suggest that the emphasis was originally on final attainment

in this life. The Great Discourse on the Foundations of Mind-fulness (Bhaddekavatta Sutta, Magjhima Nikaya) goes so far as to say that from seven years down to as little as seven days is sufficient for an earnest man to attain Enlightenment. In the second period, attention was devoted more to scholarship than to meditation practice, with the result that the teachings became too theoretical and metaphysical. During the period of reaction, meditation was at first re-emphasized, but later the idea grew up of a would-be Bodhisattva's requiring aeon upon aeon of effort coupled with the achievement of almost incredible degrees of virtue in order to attain Enlightenment. When people thought in these terms, the urge towards immediate attainment by frequent meditation declined. In the fourth period, there was a strong reaction in favour of the original ideal of practice and attainment in this life.[1] Like Zen, the Vajrayana became very much concerned with the Short Path to speedy attainment. Meditation came back into its own.

Tantric Buddhism is so much an integral part of the Mahayana that its special techniques cannot be understood apart from the Mahayana background. What follows is a bare outline of the basic assumptions underlying the whole fabric of Buddhist and therefore Tantric belief and practice.[2]

Buddhism is not a revealed religion depending upon a divinely inspired book like Judaism, Christianity and Islam. Its founder, Sakyamuni (Gautama) Buddha taught his followers not to put blind faith in his teachings but to test their validity. It does not follow that *no* faith is required. Indeed, it is taught that: 'Of the ten evils, the greatest is lack of faith.' While there are no special articles to which Buddhists are obliged to sub-scribe, they must have some spiritual belief or they would never set foot upon the path of attainment. Perhaps the really essential belief could be defined as 'belief in the existence of a supramundane alternative to the wretchedness of life as we know it'. Some misinformed Western writers have castigated

[1] I owe this conception of four periods to the Ven. Bhikkhu Khantipalo of Bangkok.

[2] For a short but excellent book with sections on all forms of Buddhism, I recommend Dr Edward Conze's *Buddhism*.

Buddhism as being pessimistic; of course it is not, for its whole purpose is to point the way to the permanent destruction of suffering and, unlike Christianity with its grim doctrine of eternal hell, Buddhism postulates that ultimately every sentient being will attain to the bliss that is called Nirvana.

Metaphysical speculation is discouraged. Even in the unlikely event that scientists could provide us with an irrefutable explanation of the universe's origin, what difference would that make to our conduct or to our happiness? We all face the problem: 'Here am I in the world; what am I going to do about it?' Certain knowledge that the universe was evolved from a gas or that it was created by one or more divine beings would be of little practical use. This example illustrates the orthodox Buddhist attitude to metaphysical questions, but in practice Buddhists do share a set of common views about the universe—views derived from three sources. They are: (1) the cosmological and metaphysical beliefs of the Buddha's contemporaries; (2) relevant passages gleaned from the Buddha's own teaching and that of later generations of monks; (3) intuitions of the nature of reality which dawn on adepts during meditation. The following notions have almost the force of dogmas, though no Buddhist is compelled to subscribe to them.

It is held that the universe is not the work of a supreme god—indeed, not a creation at all. Rather it is a delusion, part and parcel of the delusion which makes each being suppose that he has a separate ego, a genuine self-contained entity. This conviction leads to self-love, which serves in turn to solidify the ego-consciousness and immure us in the virtually endless round of birth and death known as Samsara. Thus we are governed by Avidhya—primordial ignorance or delusion. How it arose in the first place is not very clearly explained, although its workings are classified into what is called the Twelvefold Chain of Causality. The illusory existence that results from Avidhya takes place in Samsara, a universe of dimensions so vast that, in comparison, our world is like 'one grain of sand to all the sands in the Ganges river'.

Clinging to the false notion of its permanency, the wretched ego suffers successive rounds of death and rebirth, aeon upon

aeon, during which it fashions its own rewards and retri-
butions; every thought, word and action produces karma, a
force which brings results exactly consonant with their causes.
Whatever tends to diminish the ego-illusion loosens the grip
of karma; whatever strengthens it draws tight the bonds. None
of the infinite number of states in Samsara is altogether satisfactory; progress lies not in trying by good works to achieve
rebirth, say, among the gods; even the gods have dissatisfactions
to put up with and, when their good karma is exhausted, they
will have to descend to more painful states. The remedy lies
in freeing oneself from Samsara forever by destroying the last
shreds of egohood.

Within Samsara everything is transient, everything subject
to duhkha (suffering in the sense of every kind of dissatisfaction, from mild to agonizing) and nothing has a true own-
being, since it cannot exist independently of others even for a
moment. This picture of a universal flux filled with illusory
entities, mingling, separating and reforming, seems contradictory to the notion of rebirth; but it is not so. The so-
called beings who are born to die and who die to be reborn are
in fact not beings but waves of being. At sea we can watch the
arising of a wave, see it grow big, diminish and cease to be.
We think of it as an individual wave, but we know that the
water composing it is changing all the time and that it is in fact
inseparable from the sea. Only the motion is real.

It should not be thought that the universe, any more than
the wave in our analogy, is wholly unreal. In a sense, everything
exists, but our perceptions lie in giving us an impression of
individual objects. The concept of the universe's reality is
important. Were it but a dream, we could wake up (or die)
and put an end to it. As it is, karmic accretions enclose our false
ego like a turtle's shell and hinder its dissolution. These
accretions, in the form of instincts, desires, longings, tendencies,
facets of character, ways of thought and so forth, must be
shattered. The ego must be negated.

Of the three universal characteristics—transience, duhkha
(suffering) and absence of own-being—the Buddha selected
duhkha as the starting-point of his teaching. Dissatisfaction and

suffering in their innumerable forms are largely caused by tanha (which embraces both desire and aversion) or longing for things to be other than they are. If we cultivate profound equanimity, although illness, old age and death will still be with us, most of suffering's other manifestations will vanish. Thereafter we can proceed further towards Liberation by means of restraint, compassion and insight, all of which are powerful weapons for negating the ego and thereby fully emancipating ourselves from Samsara.

In pursuing the goal, we have to depend on our own efforts. It is believed that there are invisible divine beings in the universe, but they too are creatures of Samsara and unable to assist us, unless perhaps by doing us mundane favours which, by slightly alleviating our lot, are likely to weaken our resolution to be quit of Samsara once and for all. A Buddhist knows that his vessel will sail or sink in accordance with his skill in steering it and his resolution in not letting go the rudder. What he requires are restraint, compassion, self-awareness and wisdom. Restraint does not involve self-mortification, but avoidance of excess and mastery over the senses and emotions. Compassion involves the negative virtue of avoiding harm to others and the positive virtues of helpfulness, generosity and ready sympathy. Self-awareness includes scrutinizing our actions and motives, sitting back, as it were, to watch our passions and greedy desires in action, observing the thoughts slip through our minds and making a careful study of our bodily functions such as muscular movements (walking, standing, sitting, lying, etc.) and the pulsing of our blood, the process of breathing and so forth. Awareness helps us to come to realize the illusory nature of the ego. Wisdom means the intuitive wisdom that dawns when the mind is stilled. It is acquired by physical and mental exercises which start with simple feats like breath control and achieving one-pointedness of mind, from which the adept is led forward into the more difficult kinds of meditation and, in the case of Tantrists especially, visualization. All of these help to negate the ego and promote the unimpeded flow of divine wisdom from within the mind.

Compassion and wisdom interact upon each other. Compassion, besides making us good to others, is very beneficial to ourselves. Gifts of thought, time, energy, goods or wealth are all expended at the cost of the ego, which diminishes accordingly. With the diminution of the ego, wisdom arises; and, with wisdom's dawning, compassion increases; for the clearer it becomes that distinctions between I and other are unreal, the more natural it is to be compassionate. Few people choose to rob or violate themselves. The radiant wisdom that gradually manifests itself in the stillness of a peaceful mind is in fact the first gleam of ineffable wisdom which in its fullness is the Enlightenment of a Buddha.

As to Nirvana, the goal of all this effort, the Buddha never spoke of it except to say what it is *not*, thus conveying that it fits no category conceivable by the human mind. However, certain things are tentatively said of it—not based on speculation but on intimations received during meditation. Theravadin Buddhists hold that it is a state beyond, and thus outside, Samsara. Mahayanists believe it to be Samsara as seen when the veils of delusion have fallen. It has been described by means of analogies deduced from the mystical perception that arises in meditation. The descriptions of it include radiant light, ecstatic bliss, infinity, wholeness, eternity, reality, shining void, the union of opposites, boundless compassion, immaculate undifferentiated mind and many, many more. Although radiant, it is said to be colourless and without form or substance; for which reason, I have sometimes called it the non-substance of reality. Christian and Sufi mystics ascribe similar attributes to God. Doubtless they have experienced the same reality, but there are important differences between the Buddhist and the ordinary Christian or Moslem *interpretations* of what is experienced. Buddhists do not equate this shining reality with a creator of the universe; they hold Nirvana to be not the presence of God, nor a heaven inhabited by individual souls, but a state of being beyond duality in which all beings are one with one another and with Nirvana itself. This accords with the Buddhist concept of a middle path between belief in permanent existence and extinction. No being is ever extinguished but, when his false ego has been negated, nothing remains of which it could be said 'he exists'. So, to use Sir Edwin Arnold's lovely phrase, 'the dewdrop slips into the shining sea'; only it should be added that strictly speaking there is no slipping into, for sea and dewdrop have never been separate except in appearance; nor is the sea a sea in the sense of a substance in which the many are absorbed into the one; it is a non-substance which has the marvellous quality of being the one and the many simultaneous y. This is something which can be understood in mystical sta es of consciousness in which dualistic logic is transcended.

Some points in this outline need further elaboration.

The Concept of No God

To many people, the idea of a religion without God seems extraordinary, so they are apt to equate Buddhism with atheism as ordinarily understood, although in fact they have no affinity. True, the various kinds of supernatural beings recognized by Buddhism are regarded as devoid of saving power and the existence of a supreme god is categorically denied; but it is not really the concept of a creator god which unites all those countless people who, since the beginning of the world, have sought a spiritual antidote to the miseries of existence. On the contrary, rigid theism has been a diversive factor responsible for a great deal of unnecessary hostility between the followers of different religions. The real distinction between Christians, Jews, Moslems, Hindus, etc., and the followers of religions not based on the doctrine of a supreme deity (Taoists, Platonists and Buddhists) is largely a verbal one; what is more, the mystical sects among Christians and Moslems hold views that make them in some respects closer to the Buddhists than to their co-religionists.

Buddhists, despite their firm faith in the existence of what for the moment we will call a supernatural order of being, eschew the word 'God' for three reasons: (1) being non-dualists, they cannot conceive of a supreme being and of other beings as more than provisionally separate; (2) their conception of ultimate reality is impersonal; (3) they look upon the

51

universe not as a creation of divine reality but as a delusion in men's minds, or rather, as we shall see later, they equate it with divine reality as seen in the distorting mirror of the senses— it is not the universe itself but our perception of it that con- stitutes the delusion. Mystics of other religions who take the term 'God' to mean ultimate, divine reality—uncreate, sublime, omnipresent, immaculate, void of duality and the source of infinite compassion, but nevertheless impersonal—come very close to the Buddhist position. Theravadin Buddhists might be inclined to dispute this, but I believe it would be a dispute over words rather than over what they signify. As with what Christian mystics call the Godhead, Buddhists think of divine reality not as a *person* to be adored but as a *state* to be attained. They regard delusion (i.e. the universe as we see it now) not as a creation of divine reality because it does not proceed from a divine source but from our own ignorance.

Mahayana Buddhists have no one name for divine reality. It is so exalted and so subtle that any name must demean it since all names imply the limitation 'this but not that' and because things named are usually held to exist whereas we are now considering what is above the categories of existence and non-existence. However, for convenience sake, various names are given to it in different contexts. As a state to be attained, it is Nirvana; as the source of everything, One Mind, as the 'container' of everything, the Womb of Dharmas, as the condition of one who has attained it, the Dharmakaya; as the principal of Enlightenment, Bodhi or Buddha; as the source of Enlightenment, the Buddhatathata; as free from characteristics, the Void; and so on. There is not a hair's breadth of difference among them. The word 'God' which might conveniently have been used to embrace them all would have given rise to two errors—the concept of a personal deity and the concept of a creator forever distinct from his creation. In my own view, the ideal Buddhist name for divine reality is Tathata or Suchness.

It follows that the aim of Buddhists is union with this state or, to be more accurate, conscious experience of a union that has never ceased to be. This is called Enlightenment and, in the sense that it frees us from the shackles of our egos and the need to be reborn, Liberation. Indeed, when full perception dawns 'with the brilliance of a thousand suns', men become so free that the limitations 'I' and 'other' vanish; then each perceives that he contains the entire universe within himself—that he *is* the entire universe. Full consciousness of this more than god-like state is, as accomplished mystics have discovered, accompanied by a bliss that is inconceivable.

The Concept of No-Self

The concept of no 'God' follows inevitably from the more widely embracing one of no own-being. It is held that absence of self is the true nature of every sort of entity—abstract or material, animate or inanimate—without exception. When Buddhists speak of finding one's true self, they mean finding the no-self which is a universal possession sometimes called in English the Self. Yet this does not imply that a sentient being is a lump of flesh animated by a life-force that is snuffed out at death; it points to the profound truth that lies between the erroneous concepts of eternal existence and annihilation. Just as there is no part of a teapot, for example, which can be described as the real self of that pot, no essence of teapot independent of its substance, shape, colour, age, condition and function, so do gods, men and animals have nothing which can be divorced from the constantly shifting physical and mental characteristics of their beings. The seeming individuality of each is a bundle of transient qualities, all ephemeral and unstable, all dependent for their fleeting existence on innumerable interlocking factors to which billions of causes, prior and concurrent, have contributed. Take away all these qualities and what remains is indivisible from the own-nature (or own-non-nature) of all other entities. There can be no individual soul for, when the transient qualities are removed, what is left is the immaculate non-substance that neither exists nor is non-existent, in which there is no duality, let alone plurality. What science teaches about the constitution of matter provides some sort of a rough analogy; it is seen that 'entities' consist

53

of atoms of varied formation which are in fact no more than temporary manifestations of a single force—energy.

The Concept of Impermanence

Since nothing perceptible to the senses is static, but always at the stage of becoming, waxing, waning or ceasing to be what it was, it is reasonable to deduce that the same holds true of what is neither measurable nor perceptible. Just as the cells of the body are renewed once in seven years, so are the immaterial components of our being subject to unending renewal; indeed changes occurring in our consciousness are the swiftest and easiest to observe. There are, of course, certain propensities in each of us which are relatively constant, but all of them alter with time even though they may persist long enough to be carried over from one life to the next. The transience of everything is of course one of the primary causes of duhkha. Much of life's unsatisfactoriness results from it, and the longing for an after-life is another of its progeny. It can also be said that transience is a manifestation of lack of own-being. Without a self to persist there can be no permanence.

The Concept of 'Suffering'

As we have seen, the Buddhist term 'duhkha', of which 'suffering' is the usual translation, actually has a much wider connotation. Perhaps 'unsatisfactoriness' is closer, but it lacks the force to cover all the meanings of duhkha, which include giving rise to disappointment, disillusion, discontent, longing, desire, aversion, loss, sorrow, anxiety, shame, pain, decay, illness, death and many more. Whereas impermanence and lack of own-being are passive qualities, 'suffering' (i.e. giving rise to suffering) relates to the action of one entity upon another. To be without or to have too little of something we desire is suffering, to be forced to put up with what we dislike is suffering; the diminution or loss of our loved ones, powers and possessions is suffering; and the disenchantment which so often follows the fulfilment of desire is suffering. Of course, physical, mental and emotional satisfactions frequently give us joy, but joy can seldom balance duhkha; disillusion is commoner than ecstasy; most joys pall with frequent repetition and may give place to boredom or disgust; moreover it is our nature to be discontented with our gains and to set our targets ever higher. Want feeds on the satisfaction of want. Snatching at what we took to be nuggets of gold, we find ourselves grasping a handful of autumn leaves that turn to dust in our hands. During most of our waking hours we are plagued with a vague or explicit need for something or other, big or small, to complete the happiness of the moment. This desire can now and then be quenched, but not for long. Perhaps it could be said that duhkha is the 'sense of lacking', i.e. lacking whatever it is that is needed for our full enjoyment now or in the future.

If this analysis of the three characteristics common to all entities were the end as well as the beginning of the Buddha Dharma, then Buddhism could be properly regarded as negative, pessimistic, nihilistic; but of course so dreary a doctrine could never have succeeded, as Buddhism has done, in claiming the devotion of something like a third of the people in the world ever since it spread from its homeland more than two thousand years ago. The purpose of insisting upon life's unsatisfactoriness is twofold: by sweeping away the dross of attachment and aversion we can, in a short space of time, attain to a state of equanimity whereafter we shall live in tranquil contentment; by going further and negating the ego altogether, we can attain the divine bliss of Nirvana.

The Concept of Rebirth

Though the notion of an eternal soul free from the laws of transience and absence of own-being is rejected, it is recognized that the bundle of characteristics which constitutes a man's personality does persist—though of course in changing form— from life to life and aeon to aeon. Just as the middle-aged man has gradually developed out of the boy he has ceased to be, so has each of us developed from the being we used to be in our previous existence, bringing with us into this life many of the relatively long-term characteristics which determine our present

55

circumstances and personality. Thus the Buddhist equivalent of the Christian concept of a soul is a continuum that changes from moment to moment, life to life, until the ego is negated and Nirvana won.

This belief is too alien to the Western tradition to be easily acceptable by the heirs of a Christian or Moslem culture, but it is something that is taken for granted by about half the human race, for Hindus, Taoists and others besides Buddhists, subscribe to it. Though impossible to verify, it is not illogical. There is less logic in the theistic belief which postulates an infinite extension of life in the future for beings who had a finite origin, for it is reasonable to suppose that what had a beginning must have an end. Everything observable (matter and energy) is subject to change but never to creation out of nothing nor to total extinction, and it seems more likely than not that the same laws apply to what is not observable. Incidentally, acceptance of the doctrine of rebirth makes it easy to arrive at tentative explanations of many problems insoluble in terms of environment or heredity.

Samsara and Nirvana

Buddhists intent upon the path to Liberation are more concerned with the 'hows' of practice than with the 'whys' of existence. The Zen and Vajrayana schools, especially, have returned to the early Buddhist attitude of discouraging speculation. The human mind in its ordinary state of consciousness is probably incapable of grasping life's ultimate mysteries and time devoted to speculation would be better spent on making progress in achieving Enlightenment. In all countries, whatever the religious background, true mystics have always sought intuitive wisdom within themselves and regarded intellectual knowledge as unhelpful, just as scientists have preferred intellectual knowledge and viewed intuitive wisdom with suspicion. Pursuing opposite goals, they value opposite means.

Buddhists of whatever school believe that this unsatisfactory state of Samsara, this realm of duhkha, transience and no own-being, is the product of Avidhya—primordial ignorance or delusion. In other words, our surroundings are our own mental creations or mental distortions of reality. As to how and why Avidhya first arose, there has never been a satisfactory explanation, nor much feeling of a need for one. If snow blocks the road or hail flattens the crops, a knowledge of why snow and hail form does not help repair the damage.

Whatever caused the arising of Avidhya, which substitutes appearance for reality, its victims—sentient beings—revolve through innumerable cycles of existence, ignorant of their own exalted nature. Clinging to the notion of an ego and restlessly striving to satisfy its wants, they add momentum to the process of causation by which they are enchained; as their minds create fresh objects of desire, the mists of illusion thicken about them. Endlessly they traverse the six states of existence (gods, asuras, humans, animals, tantalized ghosts and denizens of hell) which, though some provide transient joys, are none of them free from profound unsatisfactoriness. There is no way out of this vicious circle of rising and tumbling from one state to another until, unable to bear it longer, a being decides to set about negating his ego and striving for liberating wisdom.

Buddhism's inability to offer a solution to the problem of origins is far from unique. Viewed dispassionately, none of the solutions suggested by other religions or by science is satisfactory. The Christian explanation seems to Buddhists nothing less than horrific. It is impossible to understand why an omnipotent father full of loving concern for his children should create a world in which not only are untold generations condemned to suffer for the sin of their remote ancestors, but also animals innocent of sin have to spend their lives in a welter of slaughter, devouring and being themselves devoured. Suffering is present; no one can avoid it, but suffering devised by one's own father seems especially hard to bear. If we turn to the scientists for an explanation, we are met with what amount to guesses or with silence.

Nirvana is the state that supervenes when desire, aversion and all clinging to an ego have been vanquished thus negating the last traces of a being's illusory individuality. It is a concept frequently misunderstood by non-Buddhists, who generally suppose it to be either total extinction or a variant of the theistic concept of an everlasting heaven. Nirvana is not extinction because mind (which, from the first, was the only real component of the vanished beings) persists; it is not heaven because no *being* remains to enter it. In all the hundreds of volumes of the Buddhist canon, there is no clear description of it, since by its very nature it is indescribable. However, I will venture a very crude illustration of what happens in passing from Samsara to Nirvana, which, with the reservations added at the end and with stress on its crudity, might be acceptable to most Buddhists.

Imagine an illimitable ocean in which there are innumerable vials. Each vial is filled with sea-water belonging to that very ocean and each is composed of a substance that gradually thickens or dissolves in response to circumstances. Under suitable conditions it dissolves altogether, whereupon the water it contains becomes indistinguishable from the rest of the ocean. Not one drop of water ceases to exist; all that is lost is its apparent separateness. In this analogy, the water in each vial represents a so-called individual being and the gradually thickening or dissolving vial symbolizes his mental and physical characteristics—accretions born of Avidhya and nourished by the force of karma or causality. Once the accretions have been dissolved, the being's 'separate' identity ceases. The aptness of this analogy is dependent on two reservations: (1) since the vials have only an illusory existence, the water inside and outside has never been really separate; (2) the 'ocean' is in reality mind, a non-substance free of space or time dimensions, from which it follows that the smallest part comprehends the whole; hence the water in each vial is not part of the ocean—it *is* the ocean. With these two reservations, it can be said that Nirvana is the state reached by the water in the vials at the moment of their dissolution.

Buddhists distrust such analogies, as they are liable to error and misconstruction. As I have said, Sakyamuni Buddha's own references to Nirvana consist of guarded negatives. However, the general understanding is that entering Nirvana is a return to the state of ultimate reality undistorted by Avidhya's mists. Theravadin Buddhists perhaps do not conceive of it precisely in these terms, as they speak of Samsara as a place to be left behind and of Nirvana as a place to be entered. The Mahayana doctrine is that the two are identical in all but appearance; that, since beings have never been apart from Nirvana, Liberation consists of becoming conscious of our real state. Nirvana *is* Samsara. Every sentient being has in reality always been one with the non-substance—uncreate, eternal, formless, colourless, free from attributes, of infinite extent and no extent at all. It is known that full experiential consciousness of this state is attended by the utmost bliss.

Thus, all objects, sounds, sensations and concepts, together with the three realms of desire, form and formlessness and the six states of existence—in short, all constituents of the universe—are mental creations identical with the one, undifferentiated non-substance or mind. In their multiple aspect, they are Samsara; in their uniform aspect, Nirvana. If, during meditation, this is recognized not merely with the intellect but *experientially*, then Nirvana is glimpsed in this life. When a man becomes fully Enlightened, which means that he will be liberated as soon as his present human body is cast off, then he is able to experience Nirvana continuously while still in this body—though it may be supposed that, for the sake of coping with his surroundings (eating, excreting, sleeping, talking and preaching the Dharma, for example), he is able to withdraw temporarily from Nirvana at will. However, this last point is supposition. Those who have achieved Enlightenment in this life have never been specific about such matters.

All this being so, the Zen and Vajrayana schools emphasize that we should never turn from the world in disgust or seek Liberation by shutting eyes and ears to our surroundings. Respecting everyone about us as partaking of the Buddha-nature and viewing everything as one in essence with Nirvana, we must reject nothing. The royal road to Liberation is recognition that there is no being or object in the universe from which we stand apart.

Karma and Causality

The impetus which impels a sentient being to pass from round to round of birth and death is provided by karmic force. Acts of body, speech and mind produce internal and external results which, in combination with the fruits of other acts, become the causes of further and yet further results many of which involve the doer. Thus karma (causatory energy) leads to chains of action and reaction extending from life to life and governing the circumstances of each. Belief in the action of karma must not be confused with a kismet-like fatalism. Though we are bound to reap all we sow, we are free to sow new seed that will bear good fruit. Moreover, with the gradual negation of the ego, karma's hold is loosened.

The karmic process is intricate. A criminal, for example, incurs more than legal punishment or terror of discovery; the results of his crime affect his personality either by coarsening it or by afflicting him with remorse; that coarsening or afflic- tion will in turn produce results; and those results, yet others. Thus, whether or not legal punishment follows, the conse- quences of wrongdoing are severe. Whereas a Christian may hope that his piety and good works will be accepted as atone- ment, a Buddhist, knowing that his severest judge, gaoler and executioner are himself and that sentence by this judge is mandatory, understands that virtue and evil never cancel out each other, that he will harvest and consume the fruits of each. On the other hand, in the Buddhist view, evil is not *sin* but *ignorance* (for no one able to foresee all the karmic consequences of an evil deed could bring himself to err). Hence the remedy is the wisdom which tends to diminution of the ego and to a weakening of karmic force.

This oversimplified account of karma's workings represents the level at which they are commonly understood, but the concept of karma as explained by Buddhist philosophers is very much more subtle and, perhaps, more convincing to those capable of understanding it.

Merit and its Transfer

The fruits of good thoughts, words and deeds are collectively known as merit. Merit, like the fruits of bad karma, persists for a long time; stocks of it can be built up and expended by an act of will in two ways: (1) to ameliorate our present circumstances and/or to ensure rebirth into a relatively pleasant situation; (2) to loosen Samsara's bonds and advance us towards Liberation.

Since nothing is predestined and, despite karma, there is wide scope for the play of free will, it follows that we have some degree of choice as to whether the merit will be expended frivolously on a pleasant rebirth or wisely on securing a rebirth conducive to the pursuit of Liberation. (Some Buddhists, thinking of Liberation as something immeasurably far off, prefer agreeable mundane results that will be more immediate.)

The notion that an act of will can affect the fruits of merit is carried further. It is believed that stocks of merit can be transferred to other beings. In Theravadin countries, young men often take temporary monastic vows as a means of building up merit for their parents. Vajrayana followers daily renew an act of will transferring their merit to sentient beings in general. The hoarding of merit for oneself is acceptable conduct among the Theravadins, but Mahayanists consider it ignoble. Whether or not it is really possible to transfer merit, forming an intention to do so is salutary, for all unselfish thoughts naturally lead to a corresponding diminution of the ego. Unfortunately, this reflection makes it difficult to be sincerely generous; for, at the moment of offering merit (or anything else) to others, one may be conscious of doing oneself a good turn!

The 'Elements of Being'

Divine reality is viewed as having two aspects, void and non-void. Being subtle, free from distinguishing characteristics, one and indivisible, it is void. Containing in potential form everything which ever has existed or could exist, it is non-void. Buddhists often liken it to the surface of a dust-free mirror; this, although it offers an endless procession of pictures, is uniform and colourless in itself but is not apart from the pictures it reveals. However, it must be understood that the 'mirror surface' symbolizes a uniformity which, unlike glass, is not a substance.

Divine reality in its non-void aspect is conceived of as an infinitely vast complex of universes, each of which comes into existence and, though subject to unending change, persists for an incalculable number of aeons before undergoing destruction and being manifested anew. The multitudes of beings and objects contained in this boundless flux are held to be dynamic concentrations of dharmas or 'elements of being' which are in fact tiny impulses of energy—each so brief that, in the time it takes to pronounce the sound 'phat', it is gone. Mental concepts no less than material forms are composed of these dharmas. Objects and concepts, though ultimately void, since all consist of the indivisible non-substance, really do exist in a relative sense as transient compound entities conditioned by prior and concurrent causes and devoid of own-being. In a universe thus composed, everything interpenetrates, and is interpenetrated by, everything else; as with the void, so with the non-void— the part *is* the whole.

From another point of view, the transient entities known as sentient beings (gods, humans, animals, etc.) are held to consist of five aggregates—namely forms, feelings, perceptions, impulses and consciousness—apart from which they are nothing but pure, undifferentiated non-substance. It is the conglomerations formed by these aggregates, which are in turn composed of dharmas, that give rise to the illusory individuality of beings. The 'three fires' which by stimulating karmic energy help to perpetuate the illusion are craving (and aversion), passion and ignorance. When these fires have been extinguished (the ordinary Buddhist way) or transmuted (the Tantric way), the illusion is destroyed.

The notion of reality having both void and non-void aspects accounts for some apparent contradictions in the Buddhist canon. Taught to seek Liberation from Samsara for ourselves and all beings, we are also taught that there is nowhere to be liberated from or to and no beings to cross over! Truth has to be apprehended by making a simultaneous void and non-void approach to the subtle nature of reality. What is common to both approaches is the absence of own-being. Whether we analyse something into aggregates and dharmas or view it as pure void, there is no room for the notion of its having a self or individuality of its own.

Buddhas and Bodhisattvas

The term 'Buddha' has a triple signification, of which many Westerners are not aware. Some two thousand five hundred years ago, Prince Gautama later known as Sakyamuni (Sage of the Sakya Clan) achieved Enlightenment, preached the Dharma or Sacred Doctrine and was accorded the title of Buddha (Enlightened One). The notion of a religion founded by a human being whose achievement resulted from his own effort appealed to Western rationalists and agnostics of the late nineteenth century, who seem to have ignored or failed to grasp the other significations of the word 'Buddha' and to have transmitted an incomplete account of its meaning. Ironically, this incomplete notion has since been adopted by some English-speaking Asians so as to resolve a contradiction between their traditional religion, to which they are bound by ties of affection, and their modern rationalist views in which they take great pride. Such 'modern Buddhists' stand in relation to Buddhism much as Western agnostic rationalists stand in relation to Christianity, though they might be indignant if that were pointed out to them.

Even in this first sense of a being who won divine status by his own efforts, the title 'Buddha' does not belong to Sakyamuni Buddha only; for it is held that in every age and every universe a Buddha appears; Sakyamuni is the Buddha of our age (2,500 years is a mere trifle when Buddhists speak of ages) and the names of four of his predecessors are given in the canon. While it is true that 'the Buddha' used in this particular sense does nearly always mean Sakyamuni, he is generally regarded not just as a man who became Enlightened, but as an incarnate eternal principle. Traditional Buddhism, though rational in the sense that no dogmas are imposed, does not lack a powerful supernatural element which makes it a religion in the full sense of the word.

Before considering the other principal meanings of 'Buddha', one further point needs to be explained. Sakyamuni was the fifth in a line of Buddhas held to extend backwards for as many ages and Maitreya, the Buddha-To-Be, is expected to appear in the age to come. Since Sakyamuni Buddha's time, a large number of persons are thought to have achieved full Enlightenment not fundamentally different from that of a Buddha; but for some reason they are not called Buddhas. The term for them is Arahans (or Arahants), unless they are thought to have postponed entrance into Nirvana so as to help other beings achieve it, in which case they are called Bodhisattvas.

In its second sense, the term 'Buddha' is used as a name for the spiritual principle underlying Buddhahood, of which Sakyamuni was one of the countless manifestations that occur in an infinite number of universes. The point of using the same term to mean both a principle and the human manifestations of that principle is not hard to grasp—it is that, when Nirvana is won, there is not a hair's breadth of difference between the principle and its manifestation; both pertain to the formless realm of void in which there are no distinctions. Another way of bringing out the significance of 'Buddha' in this sense is to render it 'the urge to Enlightenment'. Thus we see the Buddha in relation to ultimate reality—the stainless void—and to Avidhya or primordial delusion which distorts men's vision of their true being. In this relationship he stands as the *principle* of Enlightenment which is at the same time the *innate urge* to seek Enlightenment and the *power* by which Enlightenment is obtained. There are several ways of understanding one concept.

Midway between these human and absolute significations, namely the Buddha as a human and as a principle (or urge or power), comes the third—a manifestation that is human in outline but imbued with splendour and with the 'thirty-two superhuman marks' mentioned in the canon. It is thus that the Buddha is seen in the mind, in visions, in dreams and in statues, too; for nearly all Buddha-likenesses (including those of the

3. The Buddha of the Naga Realm

historical Sakyamuni Buddha) are intended to depict not the human but the superhuman form.

These three aspects of the Buddha are collectively called the Trikaya (Triple Body), of which: the Dharma-Body or Buddha principle, being one with immaculate reality, is of course invisible; the Body of Bliss has the splendour appropriate to a divine being: and the Body of Transformation is a temporary human (animal, angelic or daemonic) manifestation. Whether the Body of Bliss portrayed in pictures and statues is, so to speak, an individually existing divine being or a personification created by the adept's mind is left to his own understanding, for not everyone can grasp the subtleties of the Trikaya doctrine and opinions vary. Incidentally this doctrine has parallels in other religions. There are many faiths which conceive of divinity as having three aspects conjoined in one. As it seems improbable that this is the result of coincidence, it may be taken as a true reflection of mystical truth. However, the similarity must not be pushed to extremes—far from being regarded as the universe's creator, like the theist's God, the Buddha is the divine force whereby the universe is transcended.

In Mahayana texts, there are frequent references to the 'Buddhas of Ten Directions' who, in their Dharma-Body, are of course one, but each of whom has a distinctive Bliss Body and Transformation Body. They are, so to speak, personifications of abstract principles such as wisdom, compassion, healing power, stainless activity and so forth. As we shall see, the Vajrayana has a special concept of the Five Jinas each of whom embodies one aspect of Divine Wisdom.

The term 'Bodhisattva' may also mean an Enlightened Being. In its primary sense, it is however used in speaking of Sakyamuni and similar Buddhas during the lives when they were still working towards Enlightenment. For Mahayanists it has the special sense of Enlightened Beings who renounce Nirvana's bliss in order to remain in the universe and aid the liberation of their fellow beings. Pious Mahayanists often take a solemn vow to seek Bodhisattvahood, thus dedicating themselves long in advance of their Enlightenment to the service of others; Theravadins, however, deny that such a choice is possible, holding that once the karmic accretions have been burnt up with the false ego, nothing remains to be reborn as a Bodhisattva or in any other form.

There is some confusion between individual Buddhas and Bodhisattvas; the latter are generally held to be in some unspecified way inferior to Buddhas and pairs of them are often pictured in attendance on a Buddha. Yet there are some beings who are spoken of now as Buddhas, now as Bodhisattvas. For example, Avalokitesvara appears in Chinese iconography as a female (or more rarely a male) Bodhisattva, whereas in Tibet this same being under the name Chenresigs is sometimes held to be a Buddha. No Buddhist, I think, would regard this sort of confusion as at all important. Buddhas and Bodhisattvas are after all identical in that both are embodiments of the principle of Enlightenment. What is of cardinal importance is mind. Whatever is believed regarding divine beings is altogether secondary to the practice of negating the ego and attaining intuitive wisdom.

Experiential Evidence

One can readily imagine someone saying of these Buddhist doctrines: 'Admirable! The nobility of such conceptions places them in a category higher than mere legend, but what evidence is there that they are more than dreams thought up by men who love wisdom and compassion?'

No spiritual truth is amenable to logical proof or demonstration. Yet a man born colour-blind accepts that red is red and green is green although unable to perceive the difference. To suggest that something *cannot* be true because it is uncommunicable is poor reasoning; we depend on other people's accounts for most of our knowledge of places and events. Buddhism, which chooses not to be accepted on the authority of its founder, does, like other forms of mysticism, offer satisfying evidence of its validity to those prepared to master the long and difficult task of controlling the mind and opening it to the unimpeded flow of intuitive wisdom. Early intimations of the truth will presently be replaced by dazzling certainty, but that certainty will be communicable only to those who are well advanced in the same direction. This situation prevails in most branches of knowledge. Einstein's conclusions have to be accepted on trust by high-school children; it will take years before they can follow every step of his arguments with full understanding. In this day and age, however, it is not easy to find people who are prepared to spend years turning their minds inwards upon themselves in the hope of obtaining results which, during the first few years of practice, must remain hypothetical. They tend to shrug off the testimony available from accomplished mystics by ascribing it to auto-suggestion or self-hypnosis.

Such an attitude is understandable, all the more so as there have been so many religious charlatans in the world and so many people who babble of their spiritual attainments when all they have accomplished is to pile delusion upon delusion. So, in trying to arouse credence in mystical attainment, we are forced back onto the argument that states of consciousness due to sickness or fancy are recognizable by the unending variety of the thought or dream-content, whereas the accounts of genuine mystical experience reveal a striking unanimity, especially if allowance is made for formal differences imposed by circumstance. These accounts generally include such perceptions as colourless radiance, unutterable bliss (sometimes preceded by agony of spirit) and, above all, a perception of all-pervading unity in which the duality of subject and object, of worshipper and worshipped, is swallowed up.

The long-term results of repeated mystical experience are difficult to assess, because genuine attainment leads to a preference for seclusion and to disinclination to talk about it—unless from a compassionate desire to inspire others to follow the same path. Those who speak freely of making progress are generally frauds; for accomplished adepts, wary of giving leeway to their ego-consciousness, shun assertions involving the concept 'I have progressed'. On the other hand, people far advanced towards the goal are often recognizable. There is a sweetness about them and a gentle gaiety. Sometimes they give the impression of daftness; they are so unconcerned about

67

everything—one fears that, were they to meet a lion in the forest, they would stand their ground lost in admiration of its handsome whiskers and the splendour of its mane. Indifferent to personal comfort, they are content with what comes their way—much or little. All these signs apart, they can be distinguished by one special quality—an inner stillness which communicates itself to all comers, even to people who have no idea of being in the presence of someone unusual. It would seem that this stillness is apparent even to animals. There are many cases of jungle recluses who live their lives sought out but not molested by the wild creatures in their neighbourhood.

Such men are not numerous. During many years of wandering about the hills and plains of China, I now and then came across one living in some Taoist hermitage or secluded Buddhist temple and much more rarely among monks or laymen dwelling in the cities. Later I found rather more of them among Mongols and Tibetans, those dwellers in solitary regions where spiritual achievement is widely pursued. They have never, I think, been common, but their rarity does not seem to matter. Meeting any one of them would have been enough to convince me that the universe offers no activity half so precious as the pursuit of Enlightenment.

Chapter III

THE ESSENCE OF THE TANTRIC METHOD

Purpose

Most mystics, whether or not they subscribe to the Buddhist doctrines outlined in the last chapter, would probably accept the following formulation of the sacred quest without much modification:

'The world perceptible through the senses seems to us a distortion of something infinitely lovelier. We have received intimations of reality as a blissful state—formless, radiant, spotlessly pure—which we believe to be attainable in the stillness of the heart. The quest for that state is infinitely rewarding.'

To this formulation, some Buddhist mystics would add:

'Even with the greatest effort, attainment in this present life is hard. Sakyamuni's Enlightenment was the fruit of life after life of matchless endeavour. The quest, though infinitely rewarding, will be long.'

Mahayana Buddhists would declare:

'Loath to enter upon Nirvana's bliss while others remain lost in delusion, we have vowed to become Bodhisattvas and have renounced Nirvana until all sentient beings are liberated.'

Vajrayana and other Short Path aspirants would reply to the second statement:

'There are marvellous means for reaching Nirvana's brink and becoming Bodhisattvas in this very life. Everything favourable must be used and adverse circumstances bent to serve the quest.'

The marvellous means are aimed, as it were, at taking heaven by storm. Like other Buddhists, the Vajrayana followers recognize that Liberation cannot be won through divine intervention nor by faith, piety and good works. There must be strenuous effort culminating in a prodigious mental revolution—effort normally requiring many lifetimes. However, like Zen followers, they believe that an all-out attempt can result in Liberation here and now. It is this which makes the Tantric and Zen methods of greater interest to non-Buddhists unable to accept the doctrine of rebirth.

Another point of special interest is that these methods have been devised for people at widely different levels of understanding and ability. There are broadly speaking six types of Tantra, known in ascending order as the Kriya, Carya, Yoga, Mahayoga, Annuyoga and Atiyoga Tantras, which inculcate practices ranging from a form suited to simple people who at first need an object of worship external to themselves, through forms in which worshipper and worshipped are united, right up to a form in which the whole practice takes place in the mind; for the Atiyoga practice is 'devoid of distinctions of depth, extent and difficulty like a spontaneously achieved state of unity in which no rules remain to be kept'.

Reasons for Secrecy

It is sometimes claimed that esoteric doctrines of any kind are alien to the character of Buddhism. This view arises from a misinterpretation of some words spoken by Sakyamuni Buddha at the time of his Mahaparinirvana (final dissolution). Lying beneath the twin sala-tress, he declared that he had transmitted the whole Dharma, keeping nothing in his 'closed fist'. Theravadins take this to mean that the Buddha taught everything openly, whereas Mahayanists assert that he naturally communicated the highest teachings only to those fitted to apply them with understanding, skill and discretion. In that spirit, the Lamas of the Vajrayana guard much of their knowledge by transmitting it orally to selected disciples or even in silence from mind to mind. Such knowledge of delicately balanced skilful means would, if wrongly used, do irreparable harm; the powerful techniques of mind control employed without a teacher could result in madness; and the techniques for hastening Liberation by transmuting the force generated by the passions could, if misapplied, easily lead to debauchery. All sort of evils and excesses would result, producing the very antithesis of ego-negation. Therefore is it said: 'On entering the Tantric path, you are surely bound for Buddhahood—or for the Avicci Hell!'

On the other hand, these dynamic methods, properly applied, are held to be capable of magically transforming the world of here and now into a universe of unimaginable splendour. In the process, anxiety and fear are banished; the dullest object becomes a symbol of vast meaning; commonplace surroundings are transmuted into realms of enchantment; and the passions, instead of having to be painfully exterminated, are yoked like snarling tigers to the adept's carriage. The dangers of such a course are obvious. As one of my Lama teachers put it: 'While you were travelling in that cart, a tumble would have done you little harm. Now I have given you an aeroplane. Don't crash in flames!'

There are people ignorant of the reasons for discretion who seem eager to suppose that the secrecy guards some sordid mystery. The visits to the Tibetan borderlands of writers gifted with remarkable imaginations have had unfortunate results. The authorities in the Himalayan Kingdom of Bhutan, always slow to welcome foreigners, view with suspicion an interest in the Vajrayana and, if they do admit visitors, prevent their having fruitful contact with the Lamas. Worse still, the degrading notions associated with bodily functions in the West have proved infectious.[1] The President of the London Buddhist Society records that, during his visit to Peking long before the Communist regime was established, a young novice showed

[1] The prurient curiosity of some Western visitors has recently moved His Holiness the Dalai Lama to order his followers to be wary about teaching the Tantras to non-Tibetans, very few of whom have acquired proficiency in the sutra-studies which normally come first. Sincere seekers after truth will regret His Holiness's decision, but no one can deny there is good cause for it. The unhealthy attitude bred by our puritan ancestors' disgust with the body has made it difficult for many Westerners to take a balanced view of the sublime teaching of the Tantras which, since they are concerned with winning full control over body, speech and mind, provide guidance for dealing with the whole of human experience.

him sacred pictures which for centuries had elicited reverential awe, sniggering over them as if they had been filthy postcards!

There is no doubt whatever that the sexual symbolism in Tantric works constitutes a hindrance to the transplanting of the Vajrayana to a Western milieu. Among Tibetans, this aspect of the symbolism was not until recently regarded as a reason for secrecy; because, in countries where the Tantras are revered, sex is seen as a wholesome function productive of power that can be transmuted to serve lofty ends. Furthermore, as the term Yabyum (Father-Mother) implies, representations of deities embracing are treated with profound respect; they symbolize the union of the forces of wisdom and compassion by analogy to a physical union which is the source of the highest bliss next to spiritual ecstasy. Symbols are needed because spiritual ecstasy is too abstract to be movingly portrayed.

Apart from the physical, psychological and spiritual dangers inherent in the unskilful use of Tantric methods, there are other reasons for secrecy. Some of them may seem bizarre because they relate to forces belonging to the supernatural world in which it is no longer fashionable to believe. To Buddhists, the universe is alive with invisible beings, who in fact constitute four of the six orders of existence, the other two being men and animals. On the whole, devotees avoid having close relations with semi-divine or daemonic forces, all the more so as gods and demons have no power to assist them towards Enlightenment; but it is believed that the invisible powers are not slighted with impunity. Some beings of this kind have been converted and serve as Guardians of the Dharma. From their effigies in the temples of all Buddhist lands, it can be seen that their aspect is terrifying; true they have enrolled among the followers of the compassionate Buddha and threaten no one but subverters of the Dharma. Even so, they may retain enough of their former nature to make it inadvisable to try their patience. As with former commandos who have become peaceful doormen or butlers, they do not make good enemies. So, in Tibet, everything to do with them is kept secret.

Each Vajrayana sect has its special Guardians to whom new disciples are introduced at an appropriate time. Their chief function is to discourage initiates from breaking their Samaya-oath. People who keep Guardians in their houses respectfully offer them food on certain days of the month. Whether they are regarded as daemonic beings existing independently of people's minds (in the relative sense that anything in the universe can be so described), or whether they are identified with the beings lurking on the threshold of the human consciousness whom C. G. Jung calls archetypes, it is as well to enjoy their goodwill. Tibetans were not surprised when the distinguished author of *Oracles and Demons of Tibet* came to an untimely end soon after completing that monumental but dullish book. The subject of Guardians is one on which nothing detailed should be said; to write at length about demons is always held to be unwise; but his ultimate crime was to make them seem *boring*!

The Guru

In Tantric Buddhism, with its powerful techniques, finding a personal teacher or Guru is of prime importance. Besides paying the respect due to him as the giver of the most precious of all gifts, besides serving him with the devotion that Asian children accord their parents, his disciples perform Guru-Yoga during which they meditate upon their Guru's form as embodying the Three Precious Ones: Buddha, Dharma (the Sacred Doctrine) and Sangha (the Sacred Community). To speak ill of one's Guru, slight or injure him would be held a heinous crime. Perhaps with peoples less sincere than Tibetans and Mongols such extreme devotion would lead to abuse; but few Lamas genuinely accomplished in Tantric skills would dare take advantage of the sacred relationship. To be accomplished, they must *believe* in what they teach and therefore fear of appalling karmic consequences would deter them. Lamas may err, as fathers sometimes err towards their children, but seldom with intent.

Various Types of Adept

An important reason for attempting the arduous Short Path is that a more leisurely quest, since it involves a whole sequence

73

of lifetimes, increases the opportunities for relapsing and negating previous achievements. The requirements for Short Path adepts are not rigid; they may be monks, nuns, yogis, hermits, married clergy or laymen, but few ordinary laymen are in a position to give themselves single-mindedly to the rigorous training that is essential to success in so gigantic a task.

There are many Tibetans who do not aspire to the Short Path, because they are too busy or feel otherwise incapable; even monks may sometimes be too much involved in the duties of administering a monastery. For them the Vajrayana provides other practices suited to their circumstances. There are also some people who employ Tantric techniques to achieve goals other than Liberation. Buddhists may choose to devote their efforts to making their lot in Samsara more pleasant, though this is not considered a wise choice. There are special techniques for gaining or enhancing health, wealth, power or fame; and, though it is thought appalling to wish to harm others, there have been cases of backsliding adepts who have misused their knowledge, heedless of the consequences to themselves in this or future lives. Indeed, Tibet's poet-saint and Tantric adept, Milarepa, wreaked fearful havoc on his enemies before he was taken in hand by Lama Marpa. Besides, however well the secrets are guarded, some leak out. In themselves, Tantric methods are like swords—good or bad according to what use is made of them.

The Short Path

My knowledge of the Short Path is that of an initiated but insufficiently instructed layman; that is to say I cannot write with much authority and, even if I could, I should not be authorized to say much more than I have done.

Devotees entering upon the Short Path are taught that henceforth they must do more than practise virtue and eschew evil. They must strenuously cultivate a revolutionary and, as it were, magical attitude to life that will transform their responses to their surroundings. Regarding conduct, whatever karmic defilements, desires and appetites cannot be quickly discarded must be skilfully utilized. What cannot be vanquished must be ennobled or, failing that, yielded to in special ways. Vanquishing is best, but not if it entails mental confusion and dangerous frustration. Ennobling means transferring the force of the desire to an object identified with the goal of Liberation. Yielding means either observing the act, its causes and results in such a way that lessons can be drawn that will henceforth diminish the desire's appeal, or else employing a technique that will render it harmless. Neophytes lacking sufficient strength of character and skill should not attempt the Short Path but adhere to the ordinary Mahayana code of conduct which requires three virtues of body, four of speech and three of mind: namely, mercy, generosity and restraint; speech that is truthful, kindly, gentle and profitable; eagerness to be generous and helpful and, above all, faith in spiritual values. These rules may not be set aside unless for lofty reasons.

The Short Path practice is divided into physical, mental and combined categories, most of them conjoined with the peculiarly Tantric form of meditation known as visualization, which involves body, speech and mind simultaneously. By the manipulation of forces conjured up by means of mental power, mudras, mantras and dharanis, samadhi (a blissful, void state of mind) is rapidly attained, and the influx of intuitive wisdom accompanied by advanced mystical states follows.

A proper orientation of the adept's mind converts all virtues and vices into stepping-stones to spiritual achievement. Nothing can frighten or disgust him, for the vilest dross is transmuted into pure spiritual essence; the 'animal' processes—excretion, eating, drinking, sexual intercourse, breathing and the pulsing of the blood—are transformed into divine functions. All sounds —the clatter of trams beneath a bedroom window, the thunder and scream of bombardment, the whine of a dentist's drill, or the howling of demons—become sweeter than the music of wind in the pines or the thrilling voices of Dakini. Whatever meets the eye—the glow of massed chrysanthemums, factory chimneys or brick walls seen across a prison courtyard—all these take on a mysterious meaning. The ordinary recluse needs the support of tranquil surroundings, perhaps a hillside hermitage where he can delight in the blooming of alpine flowers and pass his nights in contemplation of the moon; whereas those who tread the Adamantine Way distil peace and beauty from within; withdrawing from nothing, irked by nothing, they are gradually immersed in a plenitude of bliss.

The combination of swift, dynamic techniques involving attitude, conduct and practice, has nothing to do with the relative wisdom needed for dealing with mundane affairs, nor with scholarly knowledge. The adept's intention is to construct for himself a 'diamond-body' that can sustain repeated entry into exalted states of consciousness and not be burnt up by the influx of extraordinary forces. With such a body and with his new powers of intuition, he can mystically experience reality and thereby attain immediate Liberation.

Attitude

One of my Lama teachers summed up the general requirement for developing a Tantric attitude in three injunctions: 'Recognize everything around you as Nirvana; hear all sounds as mantra; see all beings as Buddhas.'

Recognizing everything as Nirvana means becoming aware of the void and non-void nature of objects experientially. Everything must first be regarded and then experienced in two novel ways: as intrinsically void, since Nirvana is void; as intrinsically perfect, since reality even in its non-void aspect can be recognized as a realm of unimaginable perfection if the consciousness is, so to speak, transposed to another key. An absolute conviction that everything is void, reinforced by the experience of its voidness during meditation, obliterates fear, anxiety and disgust. The adept learns to disengage himself from terrifying or revolting circumstances as easily as a theatregoer can cease to be involved in the action of the play. His tranquillity becomes unshakeable.

By an inner transformation of his way of perceiving things, the adept comes to see everything as pregnant with beauty, as though the world had been magically transformed. This is not just a matter of piously telling oneself that it is beautiful

76

but of experiencing this as a fact. That it can be done is illustrated by an unsought experience of my own. Once I happened to be driving towards a long low walk backed by trees, at the sight of which my heart leapt, for since my last visit they had burst into a mass of scarlet blossom; but on coming nearer I discovered that there was no blossom; a corrugated zinc fence treated with a coating of red lead had been erected to heighten the wall. Few things could be uglier, yet the sight had entranced me for as long as my mind mistook the hideous painted metal for massed flowers. By a revolution of mind, beauty can be perceived even in formerly repellent objects such as dung, intestines or decaying corpses—all of them manifestations of the immaculately pure non-substance.

Recently, users of mescaline and LSD have reported seeing everything without exception as exquisitely beautiful as a result of a temporary mind-change. This is further evidence of the possibility of bringing about a permanent mind-change of that sort. One of several reasons for the prevalence in Tibetan iconography of such objects as corpses, skulls and blood relates to the technique of perceiving everything in the universe as holy.

Hearing all sounds as mantra requires the same technique. Mantras are sacred invocations recited in a special tone of voice; here, however, the word signifies divine melody. Again from my own experience comes an example. At one time my meditations in the early hours of the morning used to be interrupted time after time by learners driving motor-tricycle-taxis in low gear round a square near my window. By mentally converting the horrid din into the rattle of the Lamas' hand-drums heard above the noise of a cataract, I made it most helpful to my meditation.

In the Vajrayana practice, sound plays a very great part. The thunder of the eighteen-foot trumpets of the Lamas, the liturgical use of drums, gongs and cymbals, the deep-throated chanting and the sonorous recitation of mantras—all are potent in producing valuable psychic effects of a different order from the effects of music as ordinarily understood.

Seeing all beings as Buddhas is an injunction familiar to Zen followers. It is based on the understanding that every being has within him the Buddha-nature, the meaning of which is: (1) that all beings including Buddhas are ultimately manifestations of the undifferentiated non-substance, and (2) that each being is endowed with the urge to and capability of Enlightenment. In practice, the injunction means that we must treat everyone with the consideration and respect due to a potential Buddha, be eager to serve him and loath to do him harm. A subsidiary result is that we shall seldom incur enmity, but the main purpose is to develop the Tantric attitude of mind which leads to actual perception of the holiness of beings and to the negation of the ego.

In the carrying out of these injunctions, a dual process is at work. Intent on causing his mind to leap into another dimension wherein he perceives things not as potentially but actually perfect, the devotee first imagines them so; and thereby promotes the influx of intuitive wisdom which causes him to see them so. The first process involves an element of make-believe; the second is intensely real. As time goes on, he reaches a point at which he sees each grain of sand as containing the entire universe. This blissful vision, normally attainable only under the influence of yogic trance or drugs or at moments of intense romantic feeling, becomes a permanent possession—the adept's *only* mode of vision.

Conduct

The conduct proposed for Tantric adepts is, since it pertains to the principle of non-duality, beyond the dualism of good and evil; but the object of relaxing the ordinary rules is to attain to perfection as rapidly as possible. Descent into the libertinism practised by certain Hindu Tantrists in Bengal or by the medi-eval Christian antinomianists is fraught with peril and in any case unthinkable, for it would involve a breach of the Samaya-pledge; it is taught that the Tantric adept, having set powerful forces in motion, would be destroyed by their misuse as surely as an electrician is burnt up when the current from the mains is accidentally diverted through his body.

However, before proceeding to discuss Tantric conduct, it is necessary to understand the ordinary Buddhist attitude to wrongdoing. Buddhists of all sects are enjoined to refrain from killing, stealing and improper sexual intercourse; from lying, slander and harsh or idle talk; and from covetousness, malice and doubts of the Dharma's excellence. If they are monks or strict laymen, they must also abstain from intoxicants and, in China, they eat no flesh. This conception of good conduct differs from Christian morality in two ways: (1) it is not God who is offended by, but man who has to pay the price of, wrongdoing; (2) there is no idea of sin, but only of grievous folly—ignorance, in fact. This difference is significant. A Buddhist is not weighed down and frightened by a burden of sin. If he has erred, he must pay, but the debt can be paid in full; he does not face eternal damnation and his redemption lies firmly in his own hands. In practice, this absence of the sin-concept means that each action will be regarded not as good or bad *per se*, but in relation to its whole context. Thus for example 'improper sexual intercourse' signifies intercourse that has harmful results for those concerned or for others indirectly involved.

Buddhist morality hinges on two separate concepts, the duty of compassion and the need for self-control. Whatever harms others is wrong; whatever harms the doer is wrong. If no one is harmed, there is no wrong. The special Tantric practices with regard to conduct are principally concerned with avoiding harm to the adept himself. As regards harm to others, all Buddhists, Tantric or otherwise, abhor it equally. The purpose of conventional Buddhist self-control is to conserve one's mental and physical energies for attaining Enlightenment and to decrease tanha (inordinate desire) as a means of diminishing duhkha (suffering). For Short Path adepts, so much energy is needed that conserving it and acquiring more become a prime concern.

Owing to karmic accretions from past lives, most beings have passions and desires which are stronger than their power of control; eliminating them is the work of many lifetimes and their persistence a grave obstacle to Liberation. Merely willing

79

oneself to be passion-free does not help. Therefore the Tantric adept is instructed to make use of three methods—vanquishing, ennobling and yielding in a special way.

Vanquishing is ideal, if it can be done safely. Merely refusing to yield to a desire without uprooting it may bring about severe psychic disturbances. A cobra swept out of sight under the bed troubles the rest of the man who sleeps there. Desires can sometimes be uprooted through clear recognition of their consequences. Some drug addicts manage to cure themselves for fear of prison and disgrace or because they resent their state of dependency. Then the cobra is secured and can do no more harm; but it is not often that the victim of powerful desires can banish them abruptly without danger to health and mental equilibrium. There have been priests ready to die rather than break their vows of celibacy who have developed grave nervous maladies. Such people can abstain from 'sin' but not vanquish desire.

Ennobling connotes something wider than sublimation, for it includes transference of the force of passion to objects mentally created. From the assumption that Nirvana and Samsara are one, it follows that desires and their objects also partake of the holiness of reality's manifestations. There are two methods of employing them as instruments for good, of which the first is ordinary sublimation like that which enables a school teacher to derive from his concealed love for one or more pupils of the opposite sex an eloquence and inspiration that are of very great advantage to all his pupils. This kind of sublimation has often inspired heroism and self-sacrifice on the field of battle. It is well understood in the West.

The second method is of a somewhat different order. Essentially what has to be done is to create mental symbols related to the spiritual goal, transfer the force of desire to the symbol, and then banish the symbol so that the desire is concentrated directly on the goal. If the adept is accomplished in the art of visualization, there will not be much element of make-believe, for he will have learnt to produce mental creations which are more real to him than the ordinary objects of his environment. It is possible to create a lovely female form for

80

which the adept feels all the ardour and chaste devotion which medieval knights reputedly felt for their ladies. Mental creations can also call forth the blazing emotion of a blood-stained warrior for the objects of his hate. The emotion of love is skilfully transferred to the immaculate goal and that of hate to whichever of the monsters of greed, hatred and envy is to be overcome. That mental creations can become so real for the adept is because the very nature of reality is void and all phenomena are the creations of mind; it follows that visions, dreams and imaginings are not less but 'more real' than the objects against which we may stub our toes, for their non-void forms are more akin to the real state of void. (Naturally such comparisons have only a relative significance, since ultimately there cannot be more or less of any quality or thing.)

The Vajrayana symbolism and iconography contain many indications of the importance attached to ennobling. Both sex and the dark, bloody passions are represented in stylized or symbolical form. We have seen that the union of the mighty forces of wisdom and compassion is often depicted by direct stylized analogy to the Yabyum (Father-Mother) figures of deities locked in ecstatic embrace.[1] A symbolical representation of the same concept is the ritual vajra-sceptre[2] and vajra-bell of which the significance is much less obvious. In both cases, the innate holiness of energy is implied. For non-dualists, there can be no distinction between energy that is holy and unholy. All that proceeds from the immaculate void is sacred. The harnessing of every force to serve a high spiritual end is fundamental to Tantric practice.

Yielding is of two kinds: (1) yielding accompanied by sustained attention to the act, its causes and its consequences; (2) yielding accompanied by mental transference of the object of desire into something else—a process related to, but not the

---

[1] Confusion has arisen between Hindu and Buddhist Yabyum figures. The Hindu concept is that of a passive male deity embracing (or even being danced upon by) his spouse, who represents his activity or *power* and is therefore called his shakti. With Buddhist figures, the term shakti should never be used; the male figure is active, representing compassion and also skilful means; the female figure is passive and represents wisdom.

[2] See the chapter on Tantric Symbols.

same as, ennobling. The former is relatively easy. The goals of desire, once attained, seldom come up to expectation; they prove to be a poor reward for the wealth, time and energy expended. Repeated attainment diminishes satisfaction until a point is reached where none remains. What is worse, the pursuit may set in train unfortunate results that persist long after desire has turned to ashes. The lessons drawn help to dissipate the desire.

The second and more difficult way of turning yielding to profit requires special techniques taken from the Upaya-Margha or Way of Skilful Means. No general description will suffice, but I am not in a position to give details. At the superficial level, the practice is that of keeping the high goal in mind at all times night and day. For example, while eating, the adept equates his own body with the ultimate goal by visualizing it as a deity and mentally converts each mouthful of food into an offering that must be made with reverence, the resulting pleasure being a reflection of 'Bliss-Voidness'. During sexual intercourse, he withdraws his mind from his immediate environment, equates his urge with the urge for Liberation and directs the force of it to his longing for the goal. At a profounder level, by the use of symbols, he transmutes his perceptions so that, while his physical action proceeds in the normal way, his mind functions in a different dimension: doer, act and object are all visualized in abstract forms not closely related to their physical counterparts; the only links between them are the *force* of desire and the bliss of enjoyment.

On this subject, a great Nyingmapa Lama said: 'When desire arises, it must be seen as the companion to "Bliss-Voidness" and regarded accordingly. If the adept is skilled in utilizing the expression of his desires as part of the Path of Enlightenment, then this expression is to the benefit of himself and all beings. If not, the desire must be relinquished. As soon as desire arises, the attractiveness and the perception of its attractiveness must be seen as void in reality—voidness arising in the form of bliss. Next voidness and bliss must be combined by thinking back and forth from one to the other until their identity is fully apparent. (The attraction is liberated into voidness and the voidness arises as bliss, of which the attraction is the basis. With this realization, one should enter samadhi. The deity visualized, i.e. the transmuted object of desire, being of the Bliss-Void Nature is of the nature of one's own mind. By this meditation, desire is rendered harmless.)'

Scholars with access to Tibetan and Sanskrit texts have mentioned another technique—the *creation of opportunities* for yielding. This is a very different matter from making the best of necessity. Deliberate stimulation of strong attraction or repugnance would be justified by the belief that immorality is a necessary stage in reaching the amoral conduct that is consonant with the principle of non-duality. That this technique was used at some time in the past is clear from ancient texts and from the vestiges that remain: the offerings used in some rites, though now composed of wholesome substances, are described in the liturgy as being made of various repulsive materials. Such offerings are subsequently consumed by the participants; that people should have been willing to offer revolting foods to deities and eat them points to the notion of destroying aversion as well as desire so as to achieve a mental state of non-duality. However, I have never heard a Lama speak of this technique and I am inclined to think it rare now, though, to be sure, not hearing of something is no sure guide to its absence when we are dealing with esoteric matters.

Visualization

For mental practice, the Vajrayana utilizes all the traditional Buddhist meditational methods—thought-control, achieving one-pointedness of mind and cultivating awareness; but these are chiefly for beginners. The characteristic Tantric method of meditation is visualization, which involves the three faculties of body, speech and mind. There are besides some difficult Hathyoga-type physical practices of which visualization forms a part; the results they produce fall not far short of miraculous, for example the melting of thick ice by contact with the body of a naked man, though the air temperature be sub-zero. Some of these yogas are briefly mentioned in the second part of this book.

Visualization is normally performed in a meditation cell or in the shrineroom of a monastery or private house. However, some adepts, especially those of the Kargyupa sect, prefer solitude while they are mastering it. Walled up in a room or cave for a specified time—say, three or seven years—the adept hears no human voice but his own. Food is passed in and slops removed through a hole in the wall and his days are devoted to a chosen sadhana (visualization practice). By the time he emerges, he has become so skilled in creating mental constructions that he clearly perceives the exterior world in its real character as a manifestation of mind. After some twenty years of concentrated study followed by perhaps seven years practising in solitude, a Guru knows what he is talking about; he does not need to rely on books and hearsay.

The purpose of visualization is to gain control of the mind, become skilled in creating mental constructions, make contact with powerful forces (themselves the products of mind) and achieve higher states of consciousness in which the non-existence of own-being and the non-dual nature of reality are transformed from intellectual concepts into experiential consciousness—non-duality is no longer just believed but felt. In short, visualization is a yoga of the mind. It produces quick results by utilizing forces familiar to man only at the deeper levels of consciousness, of which ordinary people rarely become aware except in dreams. These are the forces wherewith mind creates and animates the whole universe; ordinarily they are not ours to command for, until the false ego is negated or unless we employ yogic means to transcend its bounds, our individual minds function, as it were, like small puddles isolated from the great ocean.

How visualization achieves its results is hard to convey because it is based on assumptions foreign to Western thought (although not quite unfamiliar to the Jungian school of psychology). The methods bear a more than superficial resemblance to magic arts generally dismissed as hocus-pocus. By Vajrayana adepts, however, the fundamental identity and interpenetration of all things in the universe is accepted as self-evident and the mandala (great circle of peaceful and wrathful deities) on which visualization is often based is recognized as a valid diagram of the interlocking forces which in their extended form comprise the entire universe and in their contracted form fill the mind and body of every individual being. Each of the deities with whom union is achieved has a vital correspondence with one of those forces; therefore the mind-created beings can be used to overcome all obstacles to our progress. Dr Edward Conze, in his concise work *Buddhism*, has lucidly expressed the essence of the method in these words:

'It is the emptiness of everything which allows the identification to take place—the emptiness which is in us coming together with the emptiness which is the deity.' By visualizing that identification 'we actually do become the deity. The subject is identified with the object of faith. "The worship, the worshipper and the worshipped, those three are not separate." '

The sadhanas or specific visualization-rites are taught individually so as to suit the disciple's personal characteristics, strengths and weaknesses, degree of intelligence and level of attainment. (In certain cases, particular sadhanas are used to achieve more limited objectives than Nirvana, but with these we are not concerned.) After initiation and instruction, the adept performs his sadhana as often as possible. Ranging from about one to several hours in length, they are performed several times a day until a point is reached at which a more advanced sadhana can be undertaken. Each of them has a set pattern designed to bring body, speech and mind into play. They begin with some preliminary rites and meditations—worship, offerings, breathing exercises, generating Bodhicitta (Enlightened Mind) and meditating discursively on: the voidness of being and of oneself, the brevity of life and need to attain Enlightenment while the opportunity offers, the harm caused by our ill-considered actions and our debt of gratitude to the Buddha and our Guru. Reviewing our shortcomings we vow to transcend them and to work unceasingly for the Liberation of ourselves and all beings.

Like the visualization which follows, these preliminaries involve the use of mudras (sacred gestures), mantras (invocations), bija-mantras (the seed-syllables from which the visualizations spring) and whirling dharanis (revolving strings of syllables). The mudras, mantras and visualizations correspond to body, speech and mind.

The deity or personified mind-force invoked varies with the sadhana. As the rite progresses, this deity enters the adept's body and sits upon a solar-disc supported by a lunar-disc above a lotus in his heart; presently the adept shrinks in size until he and the deity are coextensive; then, merging indistinguishably, they are absorbed by the seed-syllable from which the deity originally sprang; this syllable contracts to a single point; the point vanishes and deity and adept in perfect union remain sunk in the samadhi of voidness, sometimes for hours and occasionally for days.[1]

The 'reality' of the deities mentally created become apparent as the adept progresses. Without experience, visualization is difficult. A minute description has to be memorized: posture, clothes, ornaments, hair, body-colour, eyes, expression, arms, hands, fingers, legs, feet and sometimes environment. Beginners have to create the parts separately and, as more and more are envisioned, those created first vanish. It is as though a sculptor's statue were to begin melting while he was still at work on it. With practice, however, the adept learns to evoke instantaneously a figure complete in all its parts. This is easier if the figure is, like a Buddha-statue, symmetrical; but there are some like Arya Tara's which have arms, legs and fingers all in different positions. Some visualizations require the conjuring up of a whole panorama of brilliantly coloured figures which undergo transformations as the rite progresses, before merging into the deity that enters the adept's skull and alights in his heart. Mastering the art of visualizing a coloured figure that is perfect in every detail is only the first step, for the figure

[1] A disciple of my first Lama relates that, once while travelling, the old gentleman and his followers sat down by the wayside to breakfast off some mo-mos (dumplings) they had bought the day before. Deciding to meditate first, the Lama plunged into samadhi. As soon as he regained his normal state of consciousness, he asked for some mo-mos, only to discover that they were stale and that the stuffing was rancid. Glancing at the awestruck faces around him, he asked how long his samadhi had lasted and was embarrassed when they told him he had sat motionless for three whole days, during which they had not broken their fast.

will be static—a mere picture.[1] With further practice, it comes alive like a being seen in a dream. Even that is not enough. As higher states of consciousness supervene, it will be seen to exist in a much more real sense than a person, let alone a dream; moreover, persons like other external objects of perception are of little consequence to the practice, whereas this shining being has power to confer unspeakable bliss and, after union, to remain one with the adept and purify his thoughts and actions. In time the sense of its reality may become *too* strong and endanger the adept's concept of everything (the mind-created deity included) as being intrinsically void. The Lama will now order him to banish the deity—a task more difficult than its creation.

The Interplay of Body, Speech and Mind

Some of the means whereby body and speech are conjoined with the mental activity taking place during the sadhana have no close counterparts in religious practice in the West and have therefore been ignorantly classed with magic.

The body takes part through prostrations, offerings and mudras. Offerings are made by holding or touching with the fingers symbolical objects such as flowers, incense, lights, water and grain while mentally creating what they symbolize. Mudras are symbolical gestures made with hands and fingers not unlike the gestures of an Indian dancer. They must be

---

[1] The venerable Khantipalo, a learned English Bhikkhu resident in Siam, has supplied me with the following note on Theravadin practices from which the Vajrayana techniques may have been derived. However, it will be seen that the Kasina technique stops short of creating or evoking figures with a view to utilizing the forces they symbolize.

'Kasina practices (ten are listed in the "Path of Purification" based on colours and elements) seldom rely upon outward supports as taught in Siam. They are practices to be done with the guidance of a good Teacher by those who see *nimitta* (or visions). These may be simply colours or may be pictures—perhaps of one's "own" body as a festering corpse, etc. Beautiful visions are also common. Vajrayana techniques appear to utilize the nimitta (as many Theravada Teachers do) for visualization of both the gruesome and frightening—such as the krodha forms, and the beautiful Bodhisattvas and Sublime Buddhas. Mantras in a simple form called "Borikam" in Thai (parikamma) such as the repeating of "Buddha", "Arahant", etc., are widely used in Theravada.'

conjoined with their mental equivalents, for their power is derived from the adept's own mind which alone can evoke the mystical forces to which they correspond. Their chief function is to help in the achievement of higher states of consciousness.[1]

Speech in this connection means mantric sound. Mantras help to call into being the mental creations and to bring about their transformation. There are others for converting material offerings into their subtle equivalents and special ones for focusing the mind upon difficult conceptions, such as the mantra which runs: 'Spotlessly pure (void) is the nature of all dharmas (components of being); spotlessly pure am I.' The majority, however, are strings of sound which have no verbal meaning or at least no meaning detectable from the arrangement of the syllables. They range from three to a hundred and three syllables and are generally recited in multiples of 3, 7 or 108.

The principle underlying the use of mantras is not easy to grasp, but it is not totally unknown in the West. The word 'amen' has a mantric significance; and striking evidence that the creative quality of sound was once understood is furnished by the first sentence of the gospel of St John: 'In the beginning was the Word and the Word was made flesh.' Most sensitive people recognize that certain arrangements of sound induce an exaltation out of all proportion to their verbal meaning; the strange effect of certain lines of poetry composed of simple, familiar words cannot be wholly explained in terms of meaning.

To use a mantra, the adept dissolves his mind into emptiness and, with the mantra's aid, conjures from the shining void the force with which he intends to unite. Its exact sound will have

[1] A knowledge of the principal mudras assists in the study of Buddhist iconography, in which they are used to distinguish deities from one another or to show the correspondence between different forms of the same deity. For example both Amitabha and Amitayus, respectively the Transformation and Bliss Bodies of the same Buddha, are depicted with upturned hands resting upon each other in the mudra of meditation. Often the mudra identifies a deity's function or significance: Arya Tara, personification of the saving power of Wisdom and Compassion, has her right palm extended outwards and pointing down with thumb and finger forming a circle to symbolize protecting power; her left hand is held palm outwards and pointing upwards with thumb and middle fingers joined so that three fingers are erect, symbolizing the Three Precious Ones of which she is an emanation.

4. Amitayus Buddha, an aspect of Amida Buddha

been communicated to him by his teacher, for its written form gives no indication of such matters as stress or tone of voice. The idea of people solemnly reciting a string of apparently meaningless syllables perhaps a thousand and eighty times at each sitting may seem ludicrous; but it is not difficult to discover that mantric sound is a more efficient means of communication than prayer. The *meaning* of a prayer distracts the mind and limits its thought content to whatever is said; whereas if, say, the sacred sound *Om* is repeated over and over again in a deep (but not loud) voice, concentration on what lies beyond the limitations of thought and speech is marvellously promoted.

Mantras skilfully used produce results ranging from minor changes in the state of consciousness to changes of startling magnitude. Used by advanced adepts, they can effect temporary material changes in objects. These are not miracles but extensions of the principle which causes certain thin, high sounds to shatter glass. Mantras have no magic of their own; divorced from related mind processes, they become mere abracadabra. Their maximum effect is achieved by the co-ordination of body, speech and mind in mudra, mantra and dhyana (meditation).

Besides reciting mantras or combining their recitation with yogic breathing exercises, it is usual to visualize their component syllables in colour. For use in this way there are bija-mantras and dharanis. A bija or seed-syllable is visualized as springing from a void 'spotless as a turquoise autumn sky' and magically transforming itself into a lotus. This unfolds to disclose a second bija-syllable which instantly assumes the form of a deity. In the deity's heart shines yet another bija and within the tiny circle at its top (representing the nasal 'm' or 'ng' with which the syllable ends) is one so small that only the mind can perceive it. This is the essence within essence that connects the manifestation with the void.

Dharanis or written mantras are often visualized in the form of a circle. At times, one of them is seen whirling round in the deity's heart; or, if adept and deity have merged, in the heart of both of them. Their whirling produces the perfect, limitless stillness of the void. Like bijas, dharanis glow with colour—

whether white, blue, yellow, red or green will depend on the part of the mandala to which the deities belong.

The Significance of Rites

Ritual *for its own sake* was held by the Buddha to be one of the four great hindrances to Enlightenment. In his day, there were Brahmins who believed in the magical efficacy of rites, supposing that a Vedic ritual perfectly performed would have the desired material effect whether or not the minds of the officiants were properly concentrated. The current Western distaste for empty religious forms reflects the Buddha's attitude. The Tantric view is that rites are a hindrance to progress when looked to for mechanical results, whereas those employed to help in evoking desired states of consciousness are of inestimable value, especially to adepts still in need of symbolic aids. Such traditional aids as the use of ritual implements or offerings of incense, flowers and lights are never deemed essential. The sadhanas can be well performed in a bare cave and, if some sort of support is still required, mudras and mantras can be used to create in the mind whatever is necessary.

In the early stage of most sadhanas, the adept mentally creates an offering in the form of 'Mount Sumeru, the four continents, the sun and moon as ornaments'. Throwing rice-grain into the air, he envisions a miniature of the entire universe glittering with coloured rays which leaps from his hands, scatters in a million beads of light and returns to the void. This is no worthless offering, for it symbolizes the adept's willingness to make sacrifices vast as the universe itself for sentient beings, and it reminds him that the entire universe is the void creation of his own mind. In the two-hour sadhana I was first given to perform, there were rites serving as symbolic reminders of almost every vital aspect of the Buddha Dharma which, set out in full, occupies several hundred volumes.

In the West, there are people who suppose that 'pure Buddhism' involves no rites. If that is so, there is no pure Buddhism anywhere. Even the Theravadins and Zen followers, who are the most austere Buddhists, perform quite elaborate rites morning and evening. In the eyes of Buddhists of all sects, rites with the proper mental accompaniment are an absolute necessity; deprived of its supernatural content, Buddhism would be no more than a system of ethics and psychology. With meditation but no rites, it would fortify the ego-consciousness it sets out to negate; its followers would be likely to herald each trivial success in meditation with such thoughts as '*I* have achieved this; *I* have reached such-and-such a stage.' Spiritual power has to be recognized and worshipped—though certainly not thought of as a creator-god. What is worshipped is the Buddha as the principle of Enlightenment, the urge thereto and the power by which it is won. Between the Buddhist sects which emphasize self-power and those which stress other-power there is no difference. Man as his own saviour depends on self-power, that is to say his power of mind; but mind is not his exclusive possession, it is everywhere—the container of the universe— and therefore other-power. What is inside is also outside; what is self is also other.

To maintain a proper balance, Buddhists worship the Buddha as symbolized by statues and sacred pictures; but in meditation they look to the Buddha in their own minds. Reverence paid to sacred symbols teaches awe and humility; reverence accorded to mind—the Buddha within—teaches reliance on one's own effort to achieve Liberation. Most Buddhists perform rites in a temple or household shrine, whereas meditation is done in some secular place—a balcony or bedroom. Tantrists combine worship and meditation in one by means of the sadhanas.

Fruits of the Path

It is taught that the ultimate fruit is Enlightenment. Earlier fruits are increasing control over body, speech and mind, the progressive negation of the ego and the development of ever higher states of consciousness—all of them accompanied by an increasing influx of intuitive wisdom. The degree of progress is obvious to the adept himself. The extent to which the deities visualized are purely imaginary or correspond to real universal forces is a matter of opinion; that their visualization produces results is a matter of fact. When a small degree of progress has been made, as soon as the visualization begins the adept is transported into a magical world which defies description. It is as though every object were imbued with the very quality which characterizes whatever it is that gives him the keenest possible aesthetic pleasure combined with the quality of whatever it was that aroused his emotion to the highest pitch in his experience. While he is in that magical state, the most ordinary object—say, a door-knob—gives him as much joy as the loveliest form imaginable. This is another of the phenomena to which users of mescaline have testified.

Fake progress may deceive and impress others, but never an accomplished Lama. The adept's Guru has merely to ask him a few questions framed in the light of his own spiritual experience to discover the precise extent of his attainment. He will grade his future teaching accordingly.

Marked progress in spiritual communion brings with it what are generally termed psychic powers, of which telepathy is the most common. Adepts are warned against cultivating such powers for their own sake or deliberately using them except in case of dire emergency. Telepathy, which does not depend on deliberate use and is therefore regularly employed, is valuable to a Lama in gauging his disciples' achievement.

Unconventional Morality

Tantric followers have to face the fact that their attitude to life offers unusually wide scope for abuse and calumny. In judging its spiritual value, it must be borne in mind that the Tantric path is not for sinners but for saints. Short Path adepts generally find it easier to become monks or recluses. A Nying-mapa Lama who marries chooses a wife who is willing to give most of her time to spiritual tasks, not one who will delay his quest by frivolity. Devotees are forbidden to depart from Buddhist conventional morality unless their conduct truly proceeds from the desire to attain experientially to the voidness of opposites. They must never lose sight of their prime objective. Subject to these conditions, advanced adepts are permitted to do what seems good to them, regardless of the normal rules of conduct. To consider abiding by the rules as necessarily good or transgressing them as necessarily evil would be to tie themselves down with the dualism they have set out to transcend. On the other hand, the injunction to go beyond rules does not mean that there is merit in breaking them; rather it is an injunction to recognize their emptiness. The hair-raising allegories about Guru Rimpoché are intended to shock people into this recognition.

A libertine is one who responds eagerly to the promptings of his desires for the sake of immediate pleasure. It is quite another matter to respond soberly in order to profit from the subsequent disillusion and gradually lay desire to rest, especially if the alternative is to stifle them and suffer the severe consequences of a too rigid suppression. Ceasing to think in dualistic terms, the adept must bring awareness and understanding to bear on every one of his actions, judging each on its own merits and in terms of the causative and concurrent circumstances, so that valuable experience can be gained from each. He should care not at all for convention, let others judge him as they will. For an act in itself cannot properly be considered good or bad (unless another being is made to suffer). Its quality will depend on the intention and on the use made of it. These are matters which only the adept himself can judge—save perhaps for his Lama who has through the years gained an intimate knowledge of his mind.

Inevitably such conduct is open to condemnation from some quarters. Sordid people judge others by their own standards, reading crude motives into every sort of action. Hypocrites will be likely to see their own vice in every unconventional act of a man sincerely seeking spiritual advancement. It is hard to convince them that others may act from lofty motives. A true adept, however, will not be put out by misguided criticism. So long as he can conscientiously approve of his own behaviour and be in no doubt of his Lama's approval, all will be well. The Tibetans have a fund of humorous stories that make this point—some of them refreshingly earthy.

Chapter IV

PSYCHIC AND MATERIAL SYMBOLS

A Question of Reality

The Tantric use of symbols involves a mystery—one that is rare and curious, though possibly not without parallels in other forms of mysticism. There are symbols and symbols, those employed to convey knowledge to others and those required for penetrating to the utmost depths of one's own consciousness. The Vajrayana symbols range from straightforward diagrams, shapes and objects devised for teaching purposes to something altogether different—symbols seemingly endowed with life which hover on the frontier between symbolic entities and actual beings that are scarcely distinguishable from gods and goddesses. These are the hundred deities of the mandala who are held to exist simultaneously in the mind and body of every individual. That these lively deities belong to a chapter on symbols and form no part of the pantheon of 'real deities' such as the gods of the mountains and streams will presently become, not altogether clear, perhaps, but more or less comprehensible.

The whole range of Tantric symbols can be arbitrarily divided into three broad categories: the straightforward teaching aids which, because relatively less important, have been left to the end of the chapter, the extraordinary living symbols which defy really satisfactory explanation, and a middle category which resemble diagrams designed for teaching purposes but are less straightforward than they seem because there are grounds for supposing them to be spontaneous productions of the human consciousness and not deliberate inventions. As the different categories are closely interconnected and have undoubtedly influenced one another's development, I have not been able to arrange my examples so that each category is dealt with in turn, but it may be well to introduce the subject by defining them.

What may be classified as symbolic objects purposely devised or else borrowed from other faiths for use in instruction or as reminders include the Adamantine Sceptre (vajra-sceptre) and the chorten or reliquary tower, the appearance of which can be seen from the photographic illustrations. They have many counterparts throughout the world such as royal sceptres with symbolic eagles or crosses at the head, churches built in cruciform shape and those rocket-shaped monuments which testify to man's determination to voyage among the planets. Of the symbolic diagrams, there are some like the Wheel of Life which are analogous to diagrams used in the classroom to illustrate, say, semantic or mathematical problems; and others like the mandala designs which seem to be not deliberate inventions but to have sprung spontaneously from the mind; it is these which form the middle category because, while the details show signs of having been consciously worked out, the general patterns can be recognized as having been arrived at instinctively.

The truly extraordinary category, namely the deities of the mandala, do have some (generally unrecognized) counterparts outside the Vajrayana, but opinions may vary as to whether they ought to be classified as symbols. They have all the appearance of living immortal beings and questions as to whether these beings are real or mere symbolical entities are difficult to answer. In a mystical context, however, the distinction between 'real' and 'unreal' is never sharp and perhaps not meaningful for, if everything is held to be a creation of mind, then imaginings, dreams and material objects are seen to be much more alike than would otherwise be the case: indeed it follows logically from the premise that their natures are identical. Once we accept the doctrine that the entire universe is mentally created, we are bound to recognize all sentient beings, including ourselves, as partakers in the act of creation; viewed one way, our minds are to all intents and purposes individual entities; viewed another, they are indivisible from universal mind. It follows that distinctions between the products of a man's private thought and the objects in his environment—themselves products of creative mind—have only relative validity. From the first point of view, which is that of a man in what most of us have come to regard as his *ordinary* or *natural* state of consciousness, horses are animals existing independently of whether we choose to think of them or not, whereas dragons and unicorns exist while they are in our thoughts and vanish as soon as we turn our minds to something else. From the alternative point of view, which is held by mystics, the horses at the nearest stable are precisely as real or unreal as the dragons and unicorns in our minds—intrinsically all of them are void.

Now the mandala deities, who will often appear in this book, are from the 'everyday' point of view on a par with ogres, fairies, dragons and unicorns—mere figments of imagination. Nevertheless, whether empowered solely by the devotee's mind or not, they make a powerful impression of having a life of their own. Vajrayana adepts are by no means unanimous as to how far the divine beings invoked during the sadhana practice derive from their own minds and how far they have, relatively speaking, a separate existence like the people and animals in their environment. Probably this uncertainty arises from the instinctive tendency, even among Vajrayana devotees, to make a distinction between their own minds and universal mind as though there could be any real difference between, say, the waves and the sea.

Before going further into this question, it is necessary to explain why these beings (whether real or not) who resemble gods and goddesses, and are to some extent treated as divine personages by their devotees, should be discussed in a chapter on symbols. After all, Christians and polytheists do not normally think of God, Jesus or the gods as *symbols*. To them, the objects of their adoration are entirely real and as separate from themselves as parents from their children. However, the concept of the mandala deities is more subtle. The higher-level explanation given by the Lamas and set forth in the sacred books is that these deities are truly products of the devotees' minds, even though there are occasions when they spring forth uninvoked and behave autonomously. They are purely conceptual entities, though with colour, form and movement like living beings. The reason for their existence is that there are certain levels of consciousness which cannot be reached by the ordinary processes of logical thought. The deities of the mandala are, so to speak, instruments for communication between those levels and the 'normal' or everyday state of consciousness.

This explanation, taken by itself, would suggest that long ago some Lama (or, more probably, some learned Acharya at Nalanda) deliberately devised beings of certain shapes, colours, etc., for people to meditate upon as a means for arriving at levels of consciousness otherwise difficult to reach. If that were so, there could be no argument about it; those deities would be symbols in exactly the same way that abstract geometric figures are symbols used to help students arrive at certain mathematical conceptions. Since the sacred books state repeatedly that the deities of the mandala exist only in the percipient's mind (which deliberately pictures them as divinities), it is proper to call them symbols. In other contexts, however, there are disconcerting statements such as that, when a man comes to die, the deities of the mandala arise from his mind and appear before him. This disposes of the idea that the deities are deliberate creations of the sages of Nalanda; for, if that were so, they would be no more likely that Euclid's geometric figures to arise in the mind during the period that intervenes between death and incarnation. One therefore tends to try bridging the gap between the concept of symbols created for meditation purposes and that of actual gods and goddesses by ascribing the deities of the mandala to the category of what Jung calls archetypes, figures existing in the minds of all men as part of humanity's common heritage. On the other hand, Jung never spoke of archetypes as sometimes taking over control in the way that the mandala deities are apt to do.[1] Altogether, the

---

[1] Madam David-Neel, a French lady who spent many years in Tibet, describes how she was taught to create the figure of a Lama by sheer power of mind. The figure was apparent not only to herself but to whoever was in her company at the times when he chose to appear. In course of time, this 'Lama' became unfriendly and caused her a good deal of apprehension. It took about six months of struggling with this mental creation before she succeeded in dissipating it. See *With Mystics and Magicians in Tibet*.

precise nature of these deities is not clear; what can be said is that they exist in a very real sense for the adept skilled in evoking them.

To put the matter in a nutshell, it might be thought that a problem likely to vex many an initiate as the mandala deities become increasingly real to him is to decide whether: they are created by his own mind and cease to be as soon as he stops thinking of them; they were created long ago and have since been sustained and endowed with life by the collective mind-force of innumerable adepts; they are creations of universal mind and exist independently of their devotees to the extent that anything in the world can be said to have a personal existence.

Among Tantric Buddhists, however, such conundrums have small importance; questions about degrees of reality or modes of existence are meaningless to people who are convinced that nothing in the world exists individually except as the object of wrong perception. In that context, all that matters is how far something *appears* to be real; and it can be confidently affirmed that, to the skilful adept, the deity he regularly invokes becomes more real than his parents, wife or children.

The Purpose of the Symbols and Deities

The negation of the ego and attainment of intuitive wisdom *here and now* is an almost superhuman task. Tantric Buddhism is a science of dynamic mind control which produces levels of consciousness deeper than conceptual thought. In describing those levels, words fail; in experiencing them, logical thought is transcended—hence the need for symbols. Some of them, such as the symbolic ritual instruments, are mere 'props' to assist in turning thought in a particular direction. Others, including the mandala deities, prepare minds still at the ordinary level of consciousness for what will be perceived at deeper levels, thus helping to accelerate the process; much more than that, they seem to be related to powerful forces which function not only in the minds of adepts but everywhere throughout this mentally created universe. Though the source of their power may be inexplicable, pictures of them seen for the first time may strike even a Westerner as somehow familiar; he may recollect having encountered them before in visions, dreams and legends. That many of these symbols and/or divine beings are not the arbitrary creations of the Lamas has been borne out in recent years by evidence from at least two sources. Jungian psychologists know their habitat to be what they call the collective unconscious: Jung's patients, though ignorant of oriental mysticism, drew from their own minds patterns essentially the same as those of the yinyang circle and of the mandalas. Still more recently, users of LSD and mescaline have encountered in the recesses of their own consciousness not only elaborate abstract symbols closely according with the Tibetan mandalas but also beings that are recognizable counterparts of the mandala deities.

Whatever the explanation,[1] the evocation of the mandala and its deities is the means whereby the Tantric adept conjures up and unites himself with the forces needed for the rapid destruction of his ego. Therein lies their inestimable value. Whether their power is divine, magical or purely psychological does not affect the practical results achieved.

A Pre-Tantric Parallel

The ancient yinyang symbol of the Chinese Taoists makes a useful introduction to what will be said about the Tantric symbols, because it illustrates how conclusions arrived at by experimental science have sometimes been anticipated by ancient sages who reached them intuitively by delving deep within their consciousness; moreover it leads up to the principle underlying the Tibetan mandala. Indeed, for that reason, it is widely known in Tibet as well as China. Though antedating Buddhism it is in perfect harmony with the Tantric conception of the universe and, as what it symbolizes has been largely corroborated by modern physicists, it is germane to our thesis, which is that such symbols are not arbitrary creations but arise spontaneously from the depths of consciousness.

[1] An attempt to explain the nature of the mandala deities will be found in Part II, chapter III.

More than three thousand years ago, the Chinese used the yinyang diagram to illustrate the emergence of 'the myriad objects' of the universe from a pure, undifferentiated and therefore formless matrix.

Diagram 1
The Chinese yinyang symbol

The circle symbolizes T'ai Chi (the Matrix) which is formless and above duality. Here, however, it is manifesting itself as the progenitor of the universe; hence it is divided into yin (the dark) and yang (the light) which signify the negative and positive poles exemplified by all conceivable pairs of opposites—passive and active, female and male, moon and sun, etc. Each contains within itself the seed of its own opposite (a tiny circle of the other's colour). If an infinite number of parallel lines were drawn across the circle, the spaces between them would each consist of yin and yang in different proportions; the meaning is that the differences between the structures of all the substances in the universe are determined by the proportion and arrangement of negative and positive in each. This concept of structure (both physical and psychological) has many parallels in modern thought. The psychologists assert, as did the ancient Chinese sages, that all people, male or female, have within them in a certain degree characteristics properly belonging to the opposite sex, i.e. that no man is wholly male and no woman wholly female. Then again, both Hegel and Marx based their philosophies on the principle that everything contains within itself the seed of its own opposite, as illustrated in the diagram. Most interesting of all, because to some extent amenable to laboratory demonstration, is the parallel with the views of modern physicists. Besides having discovered that differences between substances are due to differences in the atoms of which they are composed, which in turn depend upon the proportion and arrangement of positive and negative components, physicists now assert that matter is non-material in origin being in fact a product of energy, which some of them are inclined to equate, Mahayana Buddhist fashion, with mind. It is fascinating to ponder on this testimony to the correct intuition of Chinese sages living some three or four thousand years ago. This, coupled with the fact that people unacquainted with the yinyang symbol sometimes come across it in their own minds by introspection, makes it virtually certain that Jung was right in inferring that such symbols are man's common possession, a part of his collective (un-)consciousness.

The eight figures round the circle are of less immediate interest in this context. Their purpose is to point to the infinite number of combinations and arrangements of negative and positive which produce the endless variety of entities in the universe. – – stands for negative; ⸺ for positive. Thus we get:

The circle = one = void, infinity, the matrix.
– – and ⸺ = negative and positive

{ ⸺⸺, – –⸺, ⸺⸺, – – – – = four emanative combinations

{ ⸺⸺⸺, – – – –, – – – –, ⸺⸺⸺, – – – –, ⸺⸺⸺, – – – –, ⸺⸺⸺ = eight

and sixty-three
other combinations of six lines = sixty four

And so on, by redoubling to infinity.

The Mandala

Before coming to the exceedingly important subject of the mandala, it will be well to examine the Tantric equivalent of this Chinese yinyang concept, because it forms the mandala's basis.

The main symbol of Buddhism and one often seen on the foreheads of Buddha-statues is a swastika drawn like this, which is in fact an abbreviated form of in which there are four dots. These dots represent emanations from the central point at which the arms of the mandala intersect. The arms themselves indicate that the one (matrix or void) from which the emanations have sprung embraces them, i.e. is in reality never apart from them. Simplified in another way, the figure becomes and thus or , which is the design of the mandala's core. This design is built up thus:

o   ONE

o-O-o   passivity-ONE-activity

ONE
from which emanate four main
streams of energy-wisdom

ONE
with further emanations of
energy-wisdom

And so on   ONE
to infinity   with emanations subdividing
to infinity

5. A Grand Initiation Mandala

This series of diagrams constitutes a greatly simplified illustration of the structure of the universe which closely accords with the more widely known Chinese Taoist concept. The mandalas embodying this core are very elaborate designs based on a number of concentric squares and circles studded with 'gates' and, generally, with numerous figures of Buddhas, Bodhisattvas, Vajra-Goddesses, Guardian Deities and so forth— all contained within a circle inscribed in the form of a stylized lotus. Almost the entire surface is covered with intricate designs, all with precise symbolic meanings. (Less complicated mandalas are either simplifications of that design or else detached sections of the grand mandala of peaceful and wrathful deities, which is a symbolic representation of the entire universe and equally of the human body. That it can be both of these is explained by the Vajrayana doctrine that the microcosm and macrocosm are of identical construction. The mandala given in the photographic illustration is an abstract one with the deities represented by symbols.

Mandalas are sometimes drawn in colour on the ground; but in these days scroll paintings are more widely used as they can be rolled up and kept for future initiations. The diagram on page 104 shows the design of a fairly (but not very) intricate mandala reduced to its barest essentials.

The outermost circle, painted in lotus form, represents the universe's periphery. In his meditation, the adept envisions a lotus unfolding in his heart which then magically expands to become the universe. The centre or core is in the ⊙ form already described. The middle circle contains five Buddha-figures called Jinas (Conquerors, *not* 'Dhyani Buddhas' as some Western writers would have it, for that is a term used only in Nepal). They are arranged thus ⋅⋮⋅ with one in the centre and one at each compass point. (In some mandalas, each of them would be attended by two Bodhisattvas, thus forming the pattern ⋰⋮⋱). This part of the mandala signifies the core of the universe, i.e. the fivefold emanation of energy-wisdom from the void (equated with pure mind). It will be noted that the ⊙ form is repeated in all the other circles, thus making each of them a

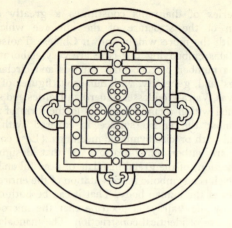

Diagram 2
Outline of a mandala

replica of the larger pattern to which it belongs; this is to
signify the interpenetration of all things, the identity of
microcosm and macrocosm. Each of the little circles drawn in one
of the concentric squares is, in the original from which the
diagram was taken, a Bodhisattva-figure and the four in the
gateways are Guardian Divinities. If the mandala were more
elaborate, there might be hundreds of other divinities placed in
appropriate positions.

Such mandalas are intended to reveal the pattern of secret
forces that operate in sentient beings and in the universe at
large; they express the emanative nature of existence. Nirvana
and Samsara being one, in their non-void form both are permeated by those forces; in their void form there cannot of course
be a multiplicity. To deal with the mandala in detail would
require a whole book;[1] what is essential is its core and this is
reproduced in diagrams 3 A to D. Each of the Buddha-figures
or Jinas in the four circles grouped around the fifth symbolizes

[1] See Professor G. Tucci's *The Theory and Practice of the Mandala*, Rider.

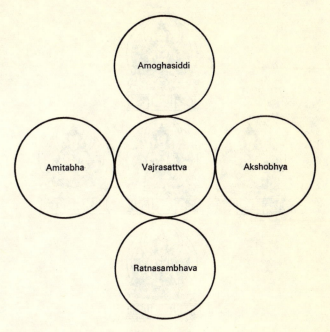

Diagram 3A

a particular type of energy-wisdom emanating from the undifferentiated energy-wisdom of the central Jina, which is called Pure Absolute Wisdom.

Diagram 3A gives the Sanskrit names of the five Jinas or wisdom-energy-aspects of the Buddha principle. These names vary, however, according to the sect for which the mandala was constructed. The one in the centre is sometimes interchanged with the one to the east, or another name substituted, in which case the two Buddha-forms are suitably altered. Those to the south, west and north seldom vary.

Diagram 3B shows that the five Jinas are easily distinguishable from one another, even if reproduced separately from the

Diagram 3B

mandala, for their colours, symbols and the positions of arms, hands and fingers are different for each one.

Diagram 3C indicates the kind of wisdom inherent in each emanation; this is of special importance as these five wisdoms are no other than the five aggregates of being and the five kinds of sense-perception transmuted into liberating wisdom as a result of progress along the path.

Diagram 3D gives a few more details by which each of the five Jinas can be distinguished whether depicted in a mandala or separately. The Jinas are equated with many sets of concepts besides those mentioned, e.g. bijas (seed-syllables), realms of existence, types of evil to be remedied, elements, seasons,

106

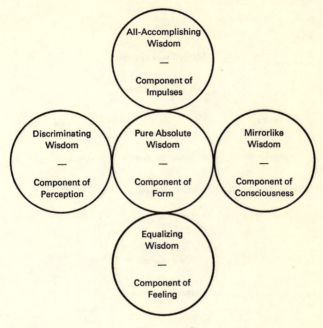

Diagram 3C

times of day, tastes, bodily functions, kinds of symbolical offering—there is no end to the list, for the Tibetans love to fit as many concepts as possible into the mandala.

It will be recalled that many of the Tantric symbols are held to be universal symbols proceeding from the depths of consciousness and not created for convenience like the diagrams with which, say, a biologist illustrates his lectures. As Professor Tucci puts it: 'Such visions and flashing apparitions occur through some intrinsi cnecessity of the human spirit [and mandalas] assume definite forms with rays, flowers, round and square patterns about a luminous central fountain. Men by introspection discovered these things by reflecting on them,

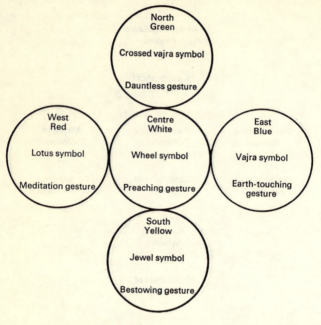

Diagram 3D

and then, combining them with cosmological conceptions, fixed their pattern in regular paradigms.'

This opinion can be substantiated. Though the details (Jinas, etc.) are of course of purely Buddhist significance, it is easily seen that the essentials of the design are universally present in the human consciousness. The cross (a religious symbol much older than Christianity) and the ancient Hindu swastika are both representations of the mandala's core; and those familiar with that fivefold design will recognize it in varied contexts all over the world.

When a neophyte is initiated into a great mandala drawn upon the ground, he is led step by step towards the centre and instructed more deeply in its mysteries as he goes. Perhaps at intervals of a few years he will be reintroduced to the mandala so that the whole mystery can be revealed to him at a higher level of understanding. Gradually he becomes more fully aware of the forces governing existence and learns to master them; thereafter the world-creating urge wihch has been driving him deeper and deeper into delusion is reversed and the same energy is utilized for the attainment of Liberation. The first step is to project the forces into a form which can be visualized in the adept's mind. The next is to discover how he can conform with them and make them serve him. Thus his primeval consciousness is reintegrated and recovers its integrity.

In considering the mandala, it should be remembered that, though symbolism requires name and form, what is symbolized here is formless. Hence there are no hard and fast rules. We have seen that the names given to some of the all-important central figures vary from sect to sect. On the other hand, the essentials of the general pattern remain unchanged, for it proceeds from a level of consciousness deeper than that of controlled imagination. As to the names and pictures of the central figures, these could be changed to suit the meditational needs of people of other faiths. However, if that were to be done, some problems would arise. Christians, for example, share the Buddhist and Hindu belief in the threefold aspect of divinity which in Buddhism accounts for the Trikaya or Three Body concept, but the essential fivefold basis of the mandala might be more difficult to fit into a Christian framework, even though the cross itself is a symbol that exactly conforms with the mandala's core. A great deal of information on mandalas will be found in Professor Tucci's book and also in the Lama Govinda's *Foundations of Tibetan Mysticism*. The latter, as its name implies, is written from the point of view of a Buddhist mystic, whereas Professor Tucci's work would perhaps be of greater interest to people not specifically concerned with a purely Buddhist interpretation.

The Peaceful and Wrathful Deities of the Mandala

The energy-wisdom symbols at the mandala's centre are depicted in a number of forms; that is to say there are several different sets of Jinas. The most widely used is the group of Jinas in their peaceful Body of Transformation aspect. Except for their gestures and colours, they all look very much like ordinary Buddha paintings. If the Body of Bliss aspects are shown instead, they are easily recognizable by elaborate head-gear and a profusion of ornaments, but the colours and gestures remain as in the first set. The Dharma-Body aspect is rarely depicted at all. Being formless, the Dharma-Body is impossible to portray satisfactorily and it could not have five aspects. Occasionally, however, it is symbolized by a shadowy blue naked figure seated above the central Jina to represent the Dharma-Body of all the Jinas together.

In some mandalas, the Jinas are shown in Yabyum form to represent the five kinds of energy (Jinas) interacting with the five kinds of wisdom (their partners). The female forms have the following names: the Sovereign Lady of the Void (centre), the All-Seeing (east), the No-Otherness (south), She of the White Raiment (west) and the Saviouress (north). The first and third names are self-explanatory; the second is a synonym for Buddha-Wisdom; the fourth suggests the void, white being the nearest approach to no colour; and the fifth means, of course, Liberation.

The Bodhisattvas, Vajra-Goddesses and other deities which sometimes surround the central figures are all symbols of abstract qualities and a Lama learned in such matters could explain the psychic significance of every one of them.

Sometimes all the figures in the mandala are depicted in wrathful aspect; with haloes of flame, gruesome ornaments and hideous mien, they dance upon corpses. In this form, the mandala portrays the universe with the five wisdoms clouded by the passions and delusions of sentient beings which result from the operation of Advidhya. The terrifying figures no doubt closely resemble the fierce gods and demons of pre-Buddhist Tibet; but it would be wrong to suppose that they typify divine wrath, for their functions are quite unlike those of medieval Christian demons. Their purpose is not to torture sinners but to overcome evil. Their clenched teeth and ferocious expressions are those of beings exerting all their strength in the battle against passion and delusion; their weapons are for cutting off defilements (klesa or karmic accretions) and the corpses beneath their feet are the passions they have slain. Furthermore, these wrathful forms are essential to the Tantric concept of non-duality; beauty and ugliness are two aspects of every object of perception. Yet another reason for them is the belief that, when a man dies, he spends forty-nine days in the bardo or intermediate state which precedes rebirth; during that time he will encounter thought-forms emanating from his own consciousness which will have the appearance of the wrathful deities. Familiarity with the mandala will help disperse his fear of them.

During a sadhana, the deity visualized is one of those who appear in the grand circle of peaceful and wrathful deities, each of whom corresponds to some aspect of consciousness and is the antidote for one of the karmic accretions such as passions, desires and evil tendencies. All proceed from mind, though we have seen that it is not always clear whether they are thought of as creations of the adept's own mind which arise only in response to his invocation or whether they are held to emanate like external beings and objects from mind itself and to that extent have an independent existence. This is a question it is not easy to discuss with the Lamas because they make no distinction between individual minds and mind. They would be likely to reply that, since only mind is real, there can be no such distinction. Yet to my cruder way of thinking, there is, relatively speaking, a genuine difference. I sincerely believe that my individuality is illusory, but I cannot help *feeling* like a person and it seems to me that I act like one. Therefore I tend to make a distinction between an imagined object created by, so to speak, my own mind, and an object, albeit created by mind, which would be there for other people whether I were awake or asleep, alive or dead. However, this distinction obviously results from my imperfect comprehension of the doctrine of the illusory nature of all objects. What is of great practical importance to the adept is that the beings evoked during a sadhana —whatever their origin and nature—do in fact function in the way expected of them. Whether Jove existed in the same way that Pythagoras did can have been of small importance to a Greek who received a cup of nectar or a fiery thunderbolt from that deity's hands. Now, though deities evoked during a sadhana do not actually conjure cups of nectar from the air or hurl real thunderbolts at breakers of the Samaya-pledge, they do alleviate spiritual thirst, help in the achievement of special states of consciousness and impose psychological punishment on those who break the pledge. In other words, regardless of the extent of their reality, invoking them is effective.

Another problem concerns the five Jinas. The five wisdom-aspects of the Buddha principle or urge to Enlightenment are naturally represented by Buddha-forms; but when the word energy is introduced, there is a danger that the symbolism will be misunderstood. It is a fundamental tenet of Buddhism that the Buddha principle did not create but is the Conqueror (Jina) of Samsara; now if the Jinas are regarded as symbols of five forms of energy proceeding from the centre and sub-dividing to produce all the mental creations that constitute the abstract and concrete contents of the universe, there is on the face of it a contradiction of that tenet.

This is a problem I did not raise with my Lamas, so I am bound to rely on my own interpretation, whatever that is worth. It is as follows. Mind, which manifests itself as wisdom, is intrinsically void; yet everything proceeds from it and is therefore mind's creation, and the same applies to the energy which makes creation possible. The Buddha principle can rightly be equated with mind = wisdom = energy. So it could be said that everything real is Buddha-created. However there would have to be a very important proviso to that statement, namely that what is created is, like its progenitor, void. That we *perceive* it as non-void and imperfect is due not at all to the Buddha principle but to the (admittedly unaccountable) action of Avidhya. Thus the wisdom-energy creation is void (Nirvanic in nature); it is our *perception* of it that is non-void (Samsaric).

Therefore, though the existence of Nirvana-Samsara is due to the play of wisdom-energy, the Samsaric aspect results from delusion which is certainly not a creation of the Buddha principle. To put it very simply: the void universe is a Buddha-creation; the plenum is a creation of *our minds*. In practice this means that when beings err, they are utilizing a void-created energy, but that energy has been clouded by Avidhya and is therefore used improperly. It will be remembered that each of the Jinas stands not only for a kind of wisdom-energy but also for one kind of faulty sense perception to be remedied. It follows that these two are in essence the same, the first free of Avidhya, the second distorted by Avidhya. The purpose of the mandala is to set men face to face with this fact prior to teaching them how to convert their five energies from their present clouded form to the pure wisdom-form which brings Enlightenment.

However, by and large, the Lamas are not concerned with such metaphysical arguments but with *practice* leading to Enlightenment. They employ the mandala to illustrate existence at whichever level is best suited to the intelligence of the disciples they are instructing. In considering Buddhism in general, but especially Tantric Buddhism, it should be remembered that the prime concern is practice. If something is conducive to spiritual advancement, it is good; whether the theory behind it is properly understood or not matters much or little according to the extent to which that understanding affects the quality and direction of the practice. True, Buddhism is a religion that vaunts reason, but it *is* reasonable for a man to use the electric light in his dwelling whether he understands how the current is produced or not. In my view, this analogy is very pertinent to the evocation of Tantric deities. Their power is there to use whether we understand their nature or not.

Of the deities other than the Jinas and their attendant Bodhisattvas who represent respectively the primary and secondary emanations of wisdom-energy, there are two especially important orders of being, the Dakinis (or Khadomas) and the Yidams —though, strictly speaking, the Yidams do not form an order of their own, since any of the peaceful and wrathful deities can be adopted as a Yidam.

The Dakinis, who are always portrayed in female form, play a great part in an individual's attainment of Enlightenment, for they are in fact the forces welling from within himself by which he is driven to master the hostile array of cravings, passions and delusions and transform them into the winged steeds that will carry him forward to Enlightenment. In metaphysical terms it might be said that a man's Dakini is the universal urge to Enlightenment as it acts in him. The Dakinis are often ferocious in appearance; with their terrifying expressions and gruesome ornaments, they are reminiscent of the dread Hindu goddess, Durga. Often their terrible bodies are unclothed and some have such unusual characteristics as a single leg and eye. Possibly the iconographers are, as Dr Snellgrove suggests, following a tradition that goes back to the primitive beliefs current in pre-Buddhist days in the part of the Himalayas lying to the west of Tibet. If so, when someone from another part of the world beholds a Dakini during his meditations, she may appear in some very different guise, perhaps that of La Belle Dame Sans Merci; whereas Tibetans, expecting to see them in the forms portrayed by the iconographers, behold them so. In any case, it is usual for an adept to take to himself one of the Dakinis as his personal symbol of communication with divine wisdom; by uniting with her, he penetrates to the true meaning of doctrines too profound to yield their secrets at the everyday level of consciousness. I have received no first-hand instruction about the Dakinis, because, like most of the devotees whose Yidams (guardians) are female, I was taught to treat my Yidam also as my Dakini. The female Yidams generally have a lovely beneficent appearance sharply at variance with traditional conceptions of the Dakinis. What can be said in general is that the Dakinis are the symbolic forms in which the yearning for Enlightenment and the means to it are pictured for certain meditational purposes.

The Yidams are deities adopted by individuals as their mentors and guardians. When an initiate enters upon the path, his Lama will select for him a Yidam well suited to his special requirements. If he has fierce passions to subdue, his Yidam will be one of the wrathful deities. If he is easily enslaved by the lovely forms of women or, alternatively, someone in emotional distress who needs a comforter, a female Yidam will be chosen. As a comforter, her role is obvious; in the other case, she is to be visualized as very young and very beautiful but adored with the chaste devotion which, say, a member of the royal household might lavish upon a lovely princess whom he serves. The adept may in his imagination be warmly intimate with his Yidam, but his love must be idealized so that, however much he is moved by her beauty, his thoughts are free from lust. The most frequently encountered Yidams of this kind are the twenty-one Taras, each of whom has subtly different correspondences with psychic realities; it is the Green, White and Red Taras who are usually selected. In certain types of sadhana, the Yidam is equated with the Dakini and even with the Guru, so that devotees of the green Tara, for example, invoke her with the words: 'Guru, Yidam, Dakini, Maha Arya Tara-yeh!' A Yidam who is also taken as a Dakini performs a dual function during meditation; primarily she is the urge to Enlightenment viewed as an essential part or partner of the adept's own self and visualized under the aspect best suited to his stage of spiritual, intellectual and emotional development.

All the deities considered so far are to a greater or lesser extent symbols either of prime universal forces proceeding directly from the void or else of forces intimately connected with the mind of the individual adept. There is a third category which have no proper place in the mandala but may sometimes be depicted in its outer parts—namely actual gods and demons belonging to the six orders of sentient beings who are therefore held to exist in just the same way as men, animals and so forth. As used to be the case in medieval Europe, in Asian countries it is taken for granted that there are all kinds of supernatural beings, the highest of which are called gods in some countries and go by less high-sounding names in others; but whether we speak of gods and demons or angels and devils, the concept is much the same: such beings are empowered to help or afflict only to a limited extent. Tibetans are no exception; they too pay court to supernatural beings but only with a view to obtaining their protection or mundane favours. The gods have nothing to do with the search for Enlightenment. Buddhism, with its usual tolerance, enjoins that they should be respected and, if they are hungry, fed; it has enrolled some of the most ferocious as Guardians of the Dharma.

This attitude towards supernatural beings was delightfully illustrated by a Lama who was soon to become Abbot of Samyé Ling in Scotland. Told of a druidic circle of stones in the neighbourhood of his future gompa (monastery), he said thoughtfully: 'One of these nights, I must go to that circle to meditate. If the local deity appears and seems well disposed, I shall perhaps invite him to become one of the Guardians of our gompa.'

The resemblance between the wrathful forms of the mandala deities and local Tibetan or Hindu deities has led to the misconception that Tibetan Buddhism is so mixed with pre-Buddhist and Hindu beliefs and practices as to merit the epithets 'debased' and 'polytheistic'. Dr Snellgrove has dealt with this criticism very ably in his *Buddhist Himalaya*. He says:

'It is interesting to observe that however great may be the divergence between the Buddhism of the early schools and the stage we have now reached, nothing new has been adopted without first ensuring that it should accord with the doctrinal position. The doctrine itself still remained consciously Buddhist and what is more remarkable still continued to do so, even when feminine partners were introduced into the system.'

Nor do the forms of the mandala deities indicate, as is sometimes alleged, the emergence within Buddhism of theism. No deity is held responsible for the creation of Samsara with its billions of worlds; none can by grace alleviate the effects of man's own ignorance and want of effort; every being must win Enlightenment for himself. The forces at work in the universe are visualized in plural form because, in its non-void aspect, the universe is in fact plural. Buddhism has always advocated the use of expedient means to lead people to make the effort that is so vital to their well-being. The mandala and all its deities are precisely that—expedient means for guiding sentient beings from the particular to the universal. As for supernatural beings such as the gods associated with certain mountains or localities, these have nothing to do with Buddhism. Buddhists are free to worship them or not, just as Christians are free to practise spiritualism.

In the following paragraphs something will be said about a quite different type of symbol—solid objects which have nothing to do with visualization and are used merely to focus the thoughts on certain principles.

The Vajra or Adamantine Sceptre

The Vajrayana takes its name from Vajra (adamantine) and Yana (vehicle). Vajra stands for a substance so hard that nothing in the universe can dent or cut it. Irresistible, invincible, shining and clear, it is in fact the non-substance of the void, the 'substance' of the Dharma-Body of the Buddhas; and, when an adept is so close to Liberation that nothing can affect his resolution or deflect his course, it is said that he has attained a Vajra-body and become a Vajra-being. Henceforth he can bear the strength of any psychic force as easily as the Vajra-substance, if it existed in physical form, could bear the strongest heat or the most powerful strokes of lightning. In the hope of achieving the revolution of his whole being whereby a Vajra-body is attained, many a Tibetan adept uses 'Dordje' (the Tibetan equivalent of the Sanskrit Vajra) as part of his name. The Buddha principle in its purest form is called Vajrasattva or Vajra-Being and this is the name often given to the Buddha-form in the centre or to the east of the mandala.

In its philosophical sense, Vajra means wisdom hard and sharp as a diamond which cuts through erroneous conceptions and leads to Buddhahood. Hence Buddhas and Bodhisattvas are called Vajra-Dharas, Wielders of the Vajra.

The ritual implement called vajra or, rather, dordje is a sceptre-like object some two or three inches long made of bronze, silver or gold. Originally the symbol of the Hindu deity Indra, it once

117

signified a thunderbolt, but Buddhists no longer think of it as having this meaning. It is used in conjunction with a vajra-bell or dordje-bell of which the handle is shaped like half a vajra-sceptre, as can be seen in the photograph of ritual implements. Together they symbolize skilful means (which is equated with compassion) and the wisdom wherewith Enlightenment is won. Like the yin and yang, they also stand for the passive and active qualities which reach perfection only when united. The Lama holds one in each hand while performing the various mudras which form a part of most rites.

The shape of the Vajra-sceptre conveys the same concept as diagram ∘O∘, that of the One becoming two, of the non-dual revealed in countless pairs of opposites. Most of the sceptres have some sort of round or cylindrical design in the centre with stylized lotus blossoms facing away from it on either side. From each lotus rise five prongs which spread out and then curve round so that the tips meet. These prongs are another way of symbolizing the five energy-wisdoms of the mandala.

When we come to discuss the mantra *Om Mani Padme Hum*, we shall see that the two middle words mean 'jewel' and 'lotus' respectively. The jewel in the lotus may be taken as the truth to be found in the heart of the doctrine and the two words have many similar pairs of meanings. The vajra-sceptre can be held to represent the jewel, and the vajra-bell the lotus. Thus, besides having their own significations, they relate to the core of the mandala and also to the famous mantra. Tantric symbols invariably interpenetrate; again and again one comes across symbols which hint at the meanings of other symbols and yet others, thereby symbolizing the interpenetration of every aspect of the universe. The effect of Tantric studies is like that of breaking open a ball in which is discovered a second and in that a third and so on until one comes to what seems to be a solid centre; but it breaks at a touch and inside it is found precisely that ball which had originally enclosed them all; then the whole sequence is repeated again and again until Enlighten-ment dawns. One gets an impression of meanings within meaning and, above all, of the presence of the whole in each of its parts. This result deserves consideration by those who are at first repelled by the intricacy of Tantric symbolism. The presentation of the central truths in all sorts of interconnected ways produces a powerful impact that drives them home at various levels of consciousness.

The Wheel of Life

At the entrance to most Tibetan gompas, there is a large fresco of the Wheel of Life, which is a superb painting signifying Samsara as the plaything of delusion. In the centre of the wheel are three creatures: (a) a cock signifying craving and greed; (b) a snake signifying wrath and passion; and (c) a pig signifying ignorance and delusion. Around them is (d) a narrow circle half of which is filled with happy-looking but rather worldly people going up, and half with naked wretches falling down. Then come (e) six segments of the circle representing the six states of existence separately (gods, asuras, humans, animals, hungry ghosts and denizens of hell) or five segments with the first two orders in the upper and lower parts of the same one. The rim (f) is divided into twelve sections each with a picture signifying one of the links in the twelvefold chain of causality whereby beings are ensnared life after life. The whole wheel is in the grasp of (g) a huge and hideous demon who resembles Yama the Lord of Death and wears upon his head-dress five skulls. Near the top of the picture stands (h) the Buddha pointing not at the Wheel of Life, but at (i) another more simple and very beautiful wheel with eight spokes—'Asoka's wheel' which for more than two thousand years has been a symbol of the Dharma, i.e. the Doctrine of the Buddha, and in another sense, Universal Law.

The significance of the picture is as follows:

(a, b and c) Three creatures: craving, wrath and ignorance are the three fires of evil which make sentient beings the victims of Avidhya—primordial delusion.

(d) As a result of relative victories or defeats in their contest with the ego, sentient beings rise or fall within Samsara's round,

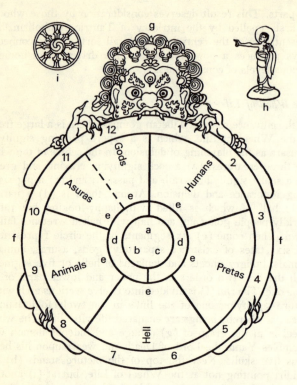

Diagram 4
Key to the symbolism of the Wheel of Life

each rise being succeeded by a fall if evil karma is acquired in the new existence; and each fall being succeeded by a rise when the evil karma is worked off or if the being acquires merit. All these beings endlessly revolve among the six states.

(e) Conditions in each state of existence are depicted graphically.

(f) The twelve links in the chain of causation are illustrated

6. The Wheel of Life

in slightly different ways by different artists, but generally they are as follows:

1. A blind man	Primordial ignorance
2. A potter	Fashioning: ignorance giving rise to elemental impulses
3. A monkey playing with a peach	Tasting good and evil: impulses giving rise to consciousness
4. Two men in a boat	Personality: consciousness giving rise to name and form
5. Six empty houses	Six senses (including mind): personality giving rise to sense perception
6. Love-making	Contact: the senses giving rise to desire for contact with their objects
7. Blinded by arrows in both eyes	Feelings of pleasure and pain: contact giving rise to blind feeling
8. Drinking	Thirst: feeling giving rise to thirst for more
9. A monkey snatching fruit	Appropriation: thirst giving rise to grasping
10. A pregnant woman	Becoming: grasping giving rise to continuity of existence
11. Childbirth	Birth: birth giving rise to rebirth
12. A corpse	Decay: rebirth giving rise to renewed death and further rounds of birth and death for ever and ever

(g) Yama, Lord of Death, represents Avidhya with the entire universe in its clutch. Merely rising from one state to another, even though it be to the heavenly bliss of the gods (devas), brings no release from delusion's grasp; sooner or later the gods will tumble back into the more unsatisfactory states—no permanent gain accrues from utilizing merit to procure a pleasant rebirth. The five skulls in Yama's head-dress represent the five senses, the five illusory perceptions, the five kinds of wrongdoing, the five aggregates of being—the very opposites of all that is personified by the five Jinas at the core of the mandala.

(h and i) The Buddha points to a proper understanding of the Doctrine and conformance with Universal Law as the only way to Liberation. Sentient beings have a choice between aeons of suffering and Nirvana's bliss, the fruit of Enlightenment.

Among the many lessons to be learnt from contemplating this symbol is the futility of piling up good works without making a genuine spiritual advance. Good works at best qualify people for transient joys in the highest of the six states of existence, where they are still subject to duhkha even if it is in the form of general dissatisfaction rather than acute suffering. Heaven offers no permanent way out of duhkha in its severest forms. Moral action is admirable in itself; it benefits both doer and recipient, but it does not lead to the conquest of delusion. If the benefits of a virtuous life are to be lasting, there must be a revolution of the consciousness that goes far beyond morality and piety.

The Chorten

Chortens are reliquary towers. The smallest, which are about one foot high, are used on private altars together with a statue and a sacred text to represent the Buddha's three faculties of Body, Speech and Mind, with the chorten signifying Buddha-Mind. The largest are huge bottle-shaped towers which may be more than a hundred feet high and contain relics of Sakyamuni Buddha or of some great sage. Between these two extremes are chortens from 10 to 30 feet high which are sometimes used to mark sacred spots and sometimes to house the ashes of departed Lamas. It is the custom to walk round chortens in a clockwise direction, thus keeping the right shoulder always towards them, which was the traditional way in which Sakyamuni's disciples showed him respect. The evolution of Buddhist sacred towers is interesting. The earliest shrines in honour of

7. A Chorten

Sakyamuni Buddha seem to have been stupas like the one at Sanchi in India—a huge dome with a rather small protuberance at the top. This was later developed in all the Buddhist countries in accordance with the national genius. In some, such as Thailand, the dome diminished and became more nearly cylindrical whereas the protuberance became a tall slender spire; in China and Nepal the pagoda was evolved from the spire and the dome vanished altogether. In Tibet and Mongolia, the stupa became the chorten. In design chortens vary only within narrow limits, so most of them retain the symbolical features indicated in the diagram below. The small ones often contain objects of special sanctity and rolls of exceedingly thin paper on which the essence of the Buddhist canon is inscribed.

Diagram 5
Key to the symbolism of a chorten

The photograph in the illustration shows a beautiful gold-plated chorten in the author's possession. Its symbology, which is typical of all chortens, is the same as the symbology of the diagram:

a, d, e, f and h represent the five elements, thus:

(a)	'mitre'-shaped or leaf-shaped	'ether', mind, spirit, void
(d)	umbrella-shaped	air
(e)	conical	fire
(f)	round	water
(h)	flat and square	earth

b and c represent the sun and moon.

g is a window-like aperture with a small statue of the Buddha inside

i represents the four stages of spiritual progress in the form of terraces.

j is incised with pictures of lions (symbols of the Buddha) guarding the jewel of wisdom (Dharma).

k is the support (the Sangha or Sacred Community).

The interpretation is that everything in the universe is composed of combinations of five elements of which the four material 'elements' (vapour, heat, liquid, solid) are ultimately absorbed in the subtle element, essence of mind. This essence is apprehended by means of the Dharma, which leads the adept, while still clothed by the material elements, through the ultimate stages of spiritual progress and up to Enlightenment.[1]

[1] The history of the author's chorten is worth relating. Its original owner, thought to be a wealthy Tibetan living in Lhasa, decided at all costs to save it from the invading Chinese. Entrusting it to a young monk who was about to make the dangerous journey through the mountains into India, he requested him to present it to any Buddhist layman he met who would undertake to fulfil certain conditions, the chief of which was that it should be permanently housed in a room where Buddhist rites are performed daily. Happily, when he reached the border town of Kalimpong, I was the person chosen to receive this precious gift. No sooner had I given the necessary (not at all onerous) undertakings, than he handed it over and prepared to continue his journey further into India. I noticed that, as it passed into my hands, he looked suddenly light-hearted—so much so that, although he was anxious to be going, I could not help asking one or two questions. All I could learn was that he felt relieved to have fulfilled the pledge made to the original owner. He had been much afraid of its being lost or damaged

on the journey and, at the same time, had found it an encumbrance difficult to hide about his person even when separated it into its component parts; for it is about two feet high, a foot square at the base and made of very heavy metal, but so delicately that it could easily be marred. Besides being firmly reticent about it, he refused to take any reward for his trouble, although his position was precarious, for he was destitute in a foreign land and unable to speak a word of Hindi. Eager to show my gratitude, I took from my neck a gold chain with a tiny Buddha-figure attached. With some demur, he accepted the Buddha-figure which was of no monetary value, but returned the chain of which the proceeds would have bought him some clothes, good meals and a train or bus ticket to his distant destination. He would not speak of the original owner, not even to tell me his name. I have never discovered why of all his possessions the chorten was, as far as I know, the only one he took pains to save from impious hands. Out of respect to his presumed wishes, I have left it in my will to a fellow Buddhist whose children, also Buddhists, will ultimately inherit it.

Part II
PRACTICE

Chapter I

ASPIRATION

General

From here onwards, this book is mainly concerned with practice, though theory and practice are so closely interwoven that no real division is possible and there are several passages where I have felt it expedient to recall points already made under the general heading of Background and Theory. However, my main purpose is to trace the progress of an initiate from the moment when he first sets foot upon the path to the time when, as an accomplished adept with many years of progress behind him, he is well on the way to becoming a Lama qualified to take disciples of his own. Of yet higher reaches of the path, nothing can be said, for no one who has not scaled those high peaks can have any conception of the purity of their rarefied atmosphere. Men with the hardihood and strength of purpose to climb so high are beings to whom all the splendours of this world are dross. Who can imagine the majesty of their thought or the brilliance of the wonders they behold?

The earliest stages of progress are clearly defined and vary within fairly narrow limits. First comes the day when a young man decides to make a gesture of his dedication to the spiritual quest. If he has been a Buddhist since birth, he has doubtless performed the simple ceremony of taking refuge in the Triple Gem—Buddha, Dharma and Sangha—many thousands of times, but on this occasion he goes to the temple and repeats the formula, not perfunctorily as in the past, but with a full heart. By doing so, he proclaims himself a Buddhist by conviction. Next comes the search for a Lama. If he lives in a small community separated by lonely wastes from the nearest town or monastery, he will probably have no choice. Carrying a few small gifts, he will present himself to the local Lama (who is likely to have been his schoolmaster for several years already) and make a formal profession of becoming his disciple. The Lama will bestow upon him a religious name and thereafter give him and some of his fellows rudimentary spiritual instruction. Then, if the boy shows promise, the Lama (who may be someone of middling education styled Lama only for courtesy's sake) may arrange for him to go elsewhere and study under a more highly qualified teacher.

What happens next to the youth will to some extent depend upon the sect to which his community belongs. If they are Gelugpas, he will almost certainly be sent to a monastery and spend many years on religious studies of a scholastic kind before he is given instruction in any but the most elementary forms of meditation. If his people belong to one of the Red Hat sects, he may go either to a monastery or to live with a Lama who may be a monk or a layman. In any case, the youth will be able to embark on Tantric studies early in his career. The ceremony of taking a teacher will be repeated, for the Lama who sent him away from home will have released him from his discipleship. When the time comes for the Tantric teaching to begin, an initiation ceremony will be held for a group of aspirants. The nature of the initiation will depend on circumstances; it may be at quite a low level, authorizing them to undertake a strictly limited form of Tantric practice; or it may be at a level far beyond their present status, bestowed with a view to allowing them to enter upon advanced practice when they are ready for it.

Following his initiation, the young disciple will spend two years or more performing the preliminary meditational exercises by which the ability to develop higher states of consciousness is acquired. Once these have been completed, if his Lama is satisfied with his progress, he will receive whatever further initiations are necessary for the mode of practice he intends to pursue, but several years or a decade may pass before he is adjudged fit to be initiated into advanced yogic mysteries involving a knowledge of the secret places of the body—the psychic centres and psychic channels.

In describing the kinds of practice to which these initiations provide access, I have dealt at some length with what may be called their liturgical aspects because it is a peculiarity of Tantric Buddhism to interweave meditation and devotion. The rites accompanying mystical practice are elaborate and colourful, some of the details having been borrowed from Tibet's ancient Bön religion, though most of them clearly had their origins at Nalanda and other places in India. The reasons for this unusual combination of mental practice and rites are manifold, but they can be summarized as falling into four categories: the belief that meditation unsupported by devotion can lead to a kind of spiritual pride incompatible with the effort to negate the ego; the Tantric insistence on involving body, speech and mind so that the adept will ultimately develop into what is called an Adamantine Being through subtle changes in his physical and mental constituents; the conviction that sensuous, aesthetic and emotional impulses are a valuable source of spiritual energy; and the discovery that some of the deeper levels of consciousness unapproachable through conceptual thought can be reached directly by means of appropriate symbols.

The result is that the spiritual exercises contain a good deal of substance that unsympathetic observers might be inclined to label hocus-pocus. The best answer to such criticism is that these colourful methods do in fact work; accomplished adepts do undoubtedly attain to states of consciousness and acquire curious psychic powers not easily attainable by other means. It should be emphasized that the rituals are never practised—unless by insufficiently instructed persons—in the hope of winning divine favour; from first to last, they are subtle aids to apprehension which derive their power from the mystical correspondence of the outer forms with hidden psychic forces and with the special states of mind that result.

Non-Buddhists who are interested in the Vajrayana as a science of mind control suitable for mystical realization and who believe that, shorn of their trappings, the methods could be used in a universal setting may not be much interested in the liturgical details; and those who find any form of liturgy distasteful may be even more impatient with them. However, the nature of the Vajrayana is such that all parts are interconnected by a hundred strands. Besides, there are aesthetic reasons for including samples of the beautiful liturgy. In the Tibetan original, much of it is in the form of verses, often with trochaic lines of seven or nine syllables, which are recited to the accompaniment of cymbals and drums in tones deep as the resonant bass voices in a Russian choir. Rendered in English prose without the musical accompaniment, the passages lose force, but something of their beauty can be inferred.

In all that follows, the background of the spiritual practice is likely to be two scenes. The first is the hall of a temple where the Lamas have assembled—men with the calm, inward look of those long used to contemplative exercises. Clad in robes of maroon with touches of yellow ochre, they sit cross-legged on their prayer-cushions surrounded by a profusion of brightly coloured symbols of their faith, eyes half-closed in rapt contemplation of the sacred visions being conjured from their minds. Points of flame and clouds of incense rise from the altar and the hall vibrates with their sonorous chanting, the clash of cymbals and the throb of drums. The atmosphere is marvellously conducive to the reverential awe proper to the contemplation of a sacred mystery. The second picture is that of an adept seated alone in a solitary cave bare of adornment or in a shrineroom which reproduces in miniature the temple scene. All around is silence, broken by the solemn murmur of his voice and punctuated at intervals by the thrilling tones of his vajra-bell and the rattle of the whirling pellets attached by thongs to a clapper drum fashioned from the craniums of two skulls placed back to back. These sounds and those of the belly-deep chanting, cymbals and giant drum used during gatherings are not easily described; their effect is not that of music but close to the elemental sounds of nature. Perhaps the only musical sounds at all analogous are those of the Kabuki and No plays of Japan; certainly there is nothing of the cloying sweetness of church music, nor anything resembling such dirges as 'Remember, o thou sinful man, how thou art dead and gone'.

Both these pictures would be misleading if their solemnity gave the impression that Vajrayana followers are long-faced, humourless bigots who suspect that joy is sinful. Tibetan humour is irrepressible. Even at the height of a moving ceremony attended by breathless awe, if something laughable occurs, the sacred surroundings will not constrain them to smother their laughter. Since their religion is interwoven with their lives, religious practice does not cease outside the temple, nor are normal reactions abandoned in the temple.

The Refuges

'I go for refuge to the Buddha;
I go for refuge to the Dharma;
I go for refuge to the Sangha.'

All Buddhist practice starts with 'taking refuge'. First pronounced as an affirmation of intention to live as a Buddhist, it also forms the beginning of every temple ceremony and is repeated morning and evening in the household shrines. These words of homage are recited thrice with three or nine prostrations, ending forehead to the ground.

The Buddha, the Dharma and the Sangha are collectively known as the Three Precious Ones or Triple Gem. In their most widely accepted sense, they stand for the Enlightened One, the Sacred Doctrine and the Sacred Community (of monks); in their special Mahayana sense, they also mean the Principle of Enlightenment, Universal Law and the Community of Those who Have Attained (known variously as Bodhisattvas, Pratyeka Buddhas, Arahans, etc.). To this exoteric definition, the Vajra-yana adds an esoteric one, thus:

Buddha: The Enlightenment Principle as represented by the line of Gurus stretching back to Sakyamuni Buddha and by what is now present in the form of a statue or living Guru.

Dharma: The Enlightenment Principle as existing in the adept's heart and as identical with the Yidam.

Sangha: The Enlightenment Principle as identical with the Dakini, the urge to seek Liberation for ourselves and all beings, and as the ultimate reality (i.e. void, undifferentiated nature) of all the myriad forms of life.

133

These interpretations and a few more subtle ones disclosed only to initiates are not mutually exclusive. They afford an example of the manner in which the Vajrayana, without rejecting the more ancient Buddhist doctrines, reveals them at several levels of truth.

In practice, Vajrayana rites generally require the taking of four or even five refuges—refuge in the Triple Gem as described above, prefixed by refuge in the Guru (the source of our knowledge of those three) and sometimes followed by refuge in the Yidam or 'Buddha in the heart'. In Sanskrit, the fivefold formula is:

'Namo Guru-bé, namo Buddhaya, namo Dharmaya, namo Sanghaya, namo . . . .',

in which the dots stand for the name of the adept's Yidam.

The purpose of frequent repetition of the act of refuge is mantric (i.e. it is thought to induce a psychic response by deeply impressing on the mind the absolute need to seek Enlightenment through the Dharma). Though success in attaining Liberation must depend on their own efforts, it is the Enlightened One's teaching which makes it possible. The Tantric manner of taking refuge is to repeat a longer formula than the one given above while visualizing an assembly blazing with light and emitting coloured rays in all directions; some of the rays enter the crown of the adept's head and fill his whole body with light. The Buddha and Sangha together with the Guru and the Yidam are seen as resplendent living beings; the Dharma is revealed as a pile of magnificently decorated volumes emitting mantric sounds. Surrounding the adept, heads bowed towards the objects of refuge is a great concourse of sentient beings. The full manifestation of such a vision requires long preparation. There are detailed instructions for evoking a great gathering of Buddhas, Bodhisattvas, Gurus, Yidams and Dakinis bearing witness to the act of taking refuge. To behold them all, perfect in every small detail, requires more than a feat of memory and concentration; indeed it is scarcely possible without entry into a deeper than normal state of consciousness. When refuge has been taken, all these divinities and the whole concourse of sentient beings 'rise up like a flock of birds disturbed by a sling-stone' and merge with the five objects of refuge; these in turn merge with one another until 'all are absorbed in the primal condition of undifferentiated Dharma-kaya'.

The Bodhisattva Vow

Very early in his practice, the adept-to-be takes the Bodhisattva Vow, which is thereafter renewed daily. He pledges himself to strive whole-heartedly to win Enlightenment but not to enter Nirvana while other beings are left struggling in Samsara's 'bitter ocean'. Between the moment of Enlightenment and the time, perhaps millions of aeons hence, at which he will enter Nirvana in the wake of all beings, he intends to remain in Samsara undergoing rebirth in forms conducive to his efforts to guide others to Liberation. This concept is pleasantly illustrated by statues of the much-venerated Bodhisattva Avalokitesvara (also called Chenresigs) in the form of a horse. The thought of vowing oneself to millions or billions of aeons in Samsara is appalling. The frightful fate of the Wandering Jew and of the captain of the *Flying Dutchman* pales beside it; however, space and time are dimensions whose effect is apparent only at the cruder levels of existence. It is possible that to an Enlightened mind the prospect of aeons of labour is less forbidding.

Bodhisattvahood is not easily won. It requires unbounded compassion for the beings in the six realms of existence. In particular it is taught that, prior to taking the vow, the adept must resolve to acquire six virtues. First comes dana (giving) which, in this context, means the adept's total self-surrender for the sake of his vow. The second is sila (morality), not merely in its conventional sense of restraint and harmlessness, but in the special Tantric sense that all thought of failure must be renounced as immoral because it implies a doubt of the adept's own Buddha-nature. The third is ksanti (patience) which enables him to suffer any revilement or setback without diminution of compassion or assurance. Next comes virya (zeal) which overcomes both obstacles and lethargy. The fifth is dhyana (meditation) which he must continue to perfect. Last, by cleansing himself of the dross of attachment and repulsion, he is to free his mind for the influx of prajna (wisdom). Having thus resolved, he prostrates himself before the sacred images or the Triple Gem and fervently vows to dedicate the whole of his present and future existences to liberating sentient beings. This done, he must acquire a Guru.

On the face of it, the list of six virtues is that of Mahayana Buddhism as a whole, but the definitions of giving and morality have a special Tantric flavour, i.e. the two physical virtues are supplemented by virtues of mind.

Obtaining a Guru

If the purpose is merely to learn a little meditation, the choice of a Guru (in the few places where they are abundant) presents no problem. If on the other hand the intention is to learn some high yogic practices or to attempt the Short Path through a shattering revolution of the mind and dangerous manœuvring of the adept's consciousness, then the matter becomes graver than the choice of a specialist to operate on someone hovering between life and death. The risk is so great that the Short Path and the more advanced yogic exercises should never be attempted without the guidance of a Lama in whom absolute faith can be reposed.

'When the pupil is ripe, a Master appears' is an old adage that may well have been true, but in the West, or in Communist China and Tibet for that matter, it must sound more like a pious hope than a statement of fact. In Europe and America, coming in contact with an accomplished Lama must often seem a sheer impossibility, short of emigrating to the Himalayan foothills where, to say nothing of having no means of livelihood and the difficulty of getting permission to stay, the language problem would take years to surmount. However, the dearth of teachers is gradually abating. Besides the trickle of Tibetan Lamas coming to settle in the West who will in course of time master the languages of their adopted countries, there is also a growing handful of Western people who will presently

be qualified to undertake at least some of the Guru's responsibilities. Besides the great German Acharya, the Lama Govinda,
they include an English Kargyupa monk now in Sikkim, a young
English layman fully initiated into the most secret practices
of the Nyingma sect and an English girl who has already
spent some four years as a nun of the Kargyupa sect studying
under excellent teachers; all three should, about ten years from
now, be well qualified for teaching by their degree of meditational attainment. There must be many others unknown to me.
The increase in the number of teachers will of course gather
momentum, as each Lama will no doubt instruct numerous
disciples, the best of whom are likely to become teachers in
their turn.

For those able to live in countries bordering the Himalayas
where the Tibetan refugee communities include many renowned
teachers, there are no special procedures for choosing a Guru; a
greater difficulty is to win his acceptance. However, it is not
wise to choose in haste. Popular esteem is in itself no sure
guide to excellence. The universal avidity for marvels is shared
by ordinary Tibetans and there may be some Lamas who, by
successful practice while their aim was still high, have acquired
extraordinary powers that have enhanced their reputation
among the common people and tempted them to be satisfied
with the progress achieved. I do not know if this is so, but
experience with Indian swamis and Chinese monks has taught
me to be wary of teachers who are not disturbed by fame.
Minor miracles can be seen and appreciated by everybody,
whereas the appreciation of good teaching is limited to those
far enough advanced to know good from indifferent.

Into the hands of our Lama we place our well-being and
perhaps our sanity. This is not a step to be taken light-heartedly.
Whether a Lama's spiritual attainments are of high quality is,
however, often discoverable in a simple way. All men of
advanced mystical attainment, by their mere presence, communicate an inner stillness. It is this rather than reputation,
bearing and conduct that offers the surest guide. To judge
conduct, we must know for sure the motives and surrounding
circumstances. A man seen to leap from concealment and

throw himself upon a passer-by will be taken for a brigand or rapist, yet he may be someone with prior knowledge of an imminent explosion ready to offer his life to protect a stranger's. If the explosion takes place, he will probably be killed. If something prevents it, who will credit the purity of his intention? There are many Tibetan stories of the unorthodox behaviour of Lamas, including the great Guru Rimpoché himself, which point to this moral.

Intention is often hard to judge and this applies no less to the selection or acceptance of disciples than to the choice of a Guru. That Tibetan Lamas are apt to put would-be disciples to severe tests is well known. There are many stories of ascetics in isolated hermitages who, foreseeing the approach through the mountains of young seekers after wisdom, conjure frightful blizzards and snowstorms to test their resolution. The most famous story of this kind concerns the poet-ascetic Milarepa in the early days when he longed to take Lama Marpa as his Guru. As the devout Milarepa had an unsavoury past, Lama Marpa was, to put it mildly, hesitant. Three times he ordered Milarepa to build a house single-handed and three times, when it was not yet finished, commanded him not merely to tear it down but to restore all the stones and earth to their original places! Not content with that, though Milarepa's back was now covered with sores from carrying baskets of stone, Guru Marpa administered some good beatings and ordered him to set to work upon a fourth house and then a fifth. Poor Milarepa often gave way to despair and ran off, but always returned because he believed that Lama Marpa had received from the Indian sage Naropa knowledge of the only sure way to attain Liberation in this life. The story ends happily with Milarepa becoming Marpa's best-loved disciple and the inheritor of his precious knowledge. Perhaps there will be no Western Milarepas. The modern Tibetan Marpas make generous allowances for our lack of training.

Even so, having found a suitable teacher, the disciple must, like Milarepa, be prepared for rebuffs. Some Lamas are so happy to welcome disciples who will one day spread the Dharma in foreign lands that they make everything as easy as possible.

On the other hand, if they greatly value a man and have high hopes of his success, they may be inclined to impose rigorous tests before opening their hearts to him. My own experience has been that some received me warmly from the first, whereas others subjected me to varying periods of polite but firm discouragement. Unhappily this is nothing to go by, for I have never had the good fortune to be with one of my teachers long enough to discover if he was prepared to place his knowledge unreservedly at my disposal.

The Guru

Once accepted, the disciple's obedience must be absolute; thenceforward, for as long as the spiritual compact remains in force, he must not presume to question his Lama's actions or harbour doubts of their fitness—which is the very reason why the selection on both sides needs such care. Unless he asks permission to withdraw from his discipleship, he must honour the Lama as he would honour the Buddha himself. In the Tantric view, this is of prime importance; indeed, in *any* view, it is vital because, when advanced practice is going forward, to dispute with the Lama would be like failing in implicit obedience to a captain piloting his ship past jagged reefs in a storm-tossed sea. Those to whom absolute obedience is repugnant are not qualified for the attempt.

Another reason for the adept to honour his Lama above all other men is that the Lama has received his heritage of wisdom from a line of Gurus stretching back to Sakyamuni Buddha and proposes to make his disciples the heirs of this treasure. In his Lama the adept reveres all the Gurus of that lineage. Furthermore there is the 'empowerment' received at the Lama's hands. 'Empowerment' is the literal meaning of the word elsewhere rendered 'initiation'. Vajrayana followers hold that the Guru transmits not only knowledge but also his acquired and inherited spiritual power. Occasionally, when the Lama touches his disciple's head with his hands (or as a mark of great favour, with his own head), a sensation of mild electric shock races from the crown to the tip of the spine and to the extremities. Possibly this is wholly imaginary and yet it seldom occurs when looked for.

The first instructions received from the Lama concern the preliminaries to the main practice—preliminaries so formidable as to frighten off the light-hearted, but never under any circumstances to be dispensed with. Though teaching about a sadhana may be given before the preliminaries are begun, this is on the understanding that no use will be made of the knowledge until the course has been completed—a matter of two years or so for beginners. In any case, the explanation of the sadhana's inner meaning is generally reserved until the main practice is underway. Exceptions are sometimes made if the disciple is a foreigner unable to stay long in the vicinity. In that case, his Lama may be inclined to give explanations at several levels right away, but the true meaning may prove illusive until understanding has been developed by practice.

During the time, long or short, that the disciple remains near his Lama, he must be prepared to serve him to the utmost, whether or not any specific demands are made. On entering or leaving a room where the Lama is seated, unless this happens several times a day, disciples prostrate themselves three times, then kneel at his feet awaiting the touch of his hands upon their heads. While in his presence, they must behave with decorum, not smoking, sitting carelessly, raising their voices or laughing too long and loud, although there is no call for long-faced solemnity—indeed, it is hard to imagine Tibetans remaining solemn. On meeting the Lama in the street, his disciples run to him and press their heads against his robe. Though others criticize him, they must never doubt the fitness of his actions. 'It is better for a man to cut out his tongue than to join in criticism of his Lama; for, by virtue of his teaching of the Dharma, he stands in the Buddha's place; to slander him is like slandering the Buddha.' His faults, if any, must be no concern of his disciples.

If a disciple is seriously dissatisfied with his Lama's conduct, he may prostrate himself and formally request leave to withdraw from the compact. By and large, however, a lively fear of the consequences would restrain Lamas from initiating people into advanced Tantric practice unless they felt qualified for the task, so occasions for such withdrawals are rare.

Westerners unused to oriental concepts of politeness sometimes find it embarrassing to prostrate themselves. Asians, however, honour elders and superiors in this way as a matter of course; there is no thought of degradation. The Lamas do not *exact* such homage and would not, I suppose, mind its omission; it is freely given because it is the custom and because it has value. Besides being a salutary check on pride and therefore egoism, it promotes the frame of mind needed for ensuring prompt assent to instructions profoundly affecting the disciple's mental and spiritual welfare.

The returns made by the Lama are held to be out of all proportion to the value of the service and devotion received. To qualify as a teacher he may well have spent some twenty years at a monastic university and worked indomitably to acquire his high knowledge. If he is from a poor family, which is more often the case than not (unless he was rescued from poverty as a child through being recognized as a Tulku), he probably suffered severe hardships during his training. His gifts are beyond his disciples' power to requite. Moreover, though he may permit some laxity in them, he will generally observe his own responsibilities meticulously. In becoming their Guru, he has taken upon himself more than a parent's duty: if their misuse of Tantric methods should endanger their lives or sanity, to say nothing of prejudicing their chances of swift Enlightenment, he will hold himself to blame. In course of time, he often comes to feel a lively affection for them and may demonstrate it in touching ways.[1]

Homage to the Guru must form the starting-point of the sacred practice and continue until the summit is attained.

[1] Tibetans carry their eating utensils thrust within their robes above the sash. Once I went to take leave of a Lama under whom I had been studying for about three months. Busy with rites at a temple some distance away from his dwelling, he was snatching a meal when I arrived. My departure was unexpected and so, disconcerted at having no gift to offer, he wiped his spoon of heavy beaten silver, wrapped it in a fragment of silk and handed it to me with a smile. The gift was of no great value but he was a refugee with few possessions and had given me one of the most useful, to say nothing of having to finish his meal by eating with his hand!

The Adept as the Buddha

Next to Sakyamuni Buddha, 'the original teacher', the disciple respects his Guru as the living embodiment of the principle of Enlightenment. That is easy to understand. What is less to be expected is the injunction that the adept must also recognize the Buddha as himself! The reflection 'I am the Buddha' is significant at several levels: (1) the Buddha and all sentient beings share the same nature of undifferentiated void; (2) as certain seeds are potentially mighty trees, so are all beings embryo Buddhas and, beyond the realm of time, potentiality achieved does not differ from potentiality to be unfolded; (3) the Buddha as the principle of, and urge to, Enlightenment penetrates the universe and is present in each sentient being.

In the text called Tak-nyi, this reflection is expressed: 'I am the expounder and the truth expounded. I am the hearer. I am the Teacher of the World. I am the worshipper. I am he who has passed beyond the six states of existence. I am the Blissful One.'

It is a reflection essential to the adept's progress. It obliterates fear of failure and banishes the kind of remorse that is not permitted to Tantric adepts—remorse in the sense of being dismayed by the weight of karma resulting from past errors. It rescues him from idolatry—the Theist dualism of worshipper and worshipped. It resolves the contradiction within the Mahayana between belief in self-power and other-power as a means to Liberation. It encourages him to try to behave in a manner worthy of his Buddha-status. It helps to negate ego-consciousness and promotes compassion and forbearance, for, if 'I am the Buddha', the same is true of every being, who therefore should be offered unlimited love, patience and assistance. For these and other reasons, it must be meditated daily and is symbolized by two rows of offerings placed upon the altar in reverse order so that they are offered simultaneously to the worshipped and the worshipper.

Nevertheless 'I am the Buddha' can be an exceedingly dangerous reflection. If improperly understood it can lead to overweening egoism and to libertinism worthy of a power-crazed bandit who cynically believes himself to be above the law. Therefore it must be meditated with the greatest circum-spection and false pride counteracted by daily acts of reverence before the Guru and the Triple Gem.

Initiation

The term 'initiation' (Sanskrit, 'abhiseka': Tibetan, 'wong') embraces the idea of 'besprinkling' and also of 'empowerment'. The besprinkling with holy water links it with Christian baptism and also with the Hindu rite for crowning monarchs, but a Tantric initiation is not bestowed once and for all. On the contrary, there are Tibetan laymen who eagerly *collect* initia-tions for reasons varying from serious intent to receive the instruction that follows to something quite different—namely, a wish to secure a share of the power transmitted from genera-tion to generation by the initiation rite. For, just as Hindus once held that the abhiseka conferred divinity upon a prince, so do Vajrayana followers hold that a sacred power enters their bodies and there remains.

In the Vajrayana, an initiation is invariably required before a Lama communicates a new level of knowledge or new practice to his disciples. There are therefore many different initiations, most of which are given either separately or together at four different levels of understanding and practice. The levels are:

1. *The Vase Empowerment* which cleanses the body-faculty of karmic hindrances and obscurations of the psychic channels, authorizes the visualization of deities and, like the other three levels, has certain results which cannot be revealed.

2. *The Mystical Empowerment* which cleanses the speech-faculty, permits the flow of vital breath (cf. the Chinese Ch'i or K'i), enhances the powers of speech so that the mantras can be used effectively and has certain other results.

3. *The Divine Knowledge Empowerment* which cleanses the mind-faculty, permits special practices (including those of Hathayogic type) and has certain other results.

4. *The Absolute Empowerment* which leads to recognition of the true essence of mind—symbols can henceforth be tran-scended and the identity of subject and object directly experienced.

It authorizes the practice of Atiyoga and has profound mystical results.

The first three empowerments belong to the sphere of relativity and authorize various means for dealing with the klesas (karmic obstructions roughly equivalent to what in Christian terminology is called sin). The fourth empowerment belongs to the realm of the absolute and cleanses not merely the faculties of body, speech and mind, but also 'the basis of personality'—cognition.

Each initiation may be regarded as conferring four types of benefit: (1) cleansing obscurations; (2) conferring power; (3) permitting access to a body of teaching and practice; (4) authorizing the adept to address himself in particular ways to certain of the mandala deities. There are some minor differences in the initiation rites of different sects; the deities personifying universal forces may have different names and forms, but all initiates are aware of their real identity. The first and second of the benefits derived make some people keen to receive as many initiations as possible even if they lack the time, inclination or ability to make use of the more important benefits. There is indeed a special category of initiation which does nothing but cleanse obscurations and confer power. A good example is the Longevity Empowerment (Tsé-Wong) which, if taken frequently, is thought to prolong life. It calls to mind a rite of the Russian Orthodox Church performed by chapters of seven priests who anoint the sick with holy oil to help them recover.

Generally the selection of an initiation is made by the Lama to suit his disciple's aptitude, but there is nothing to hinder people asking for one of their own choice. Whether such requests are granted depends upon the degree of secrecy involved and, if follow-up instruction is required, upon the Lama's having time to spend perhaps weeks or months on the task. I have once or twice been allowed to take part in initiations mainly intended for others, merely in the hope that one day I shall have the time and opportunity to receive the special instruction to which they provide access. Probably in the days before Tibet's ancient pattern of life was disrupted, things were not made so easy. In any case, however many initiations one can boast, spiritual progress cannot be counterfeited; others can be taken in, but not a man's own Lama or anyone else who is qualified to judge.

A major initiation may involve some other matters which should be briefly mentioned. Perhaps the Guardians of the sect will be invoked and the disciple will undertake to make them certain offerings at appropriate times. Thereafter, out of a healthy respect for the Guardians, he will be careful not to contravene the terms of the Samaya-pledge which binds the initiates to their Lama and to one another as Vajra-brothers-and-sisters. The Samaya-pledge covers three spheres of action—body, speech and mind; it has different meanings according to the level of the initiation, but always includes an undertaking to keep silent about certain matters for fear the uninstructed misconstrue them and suffer harm or misrepresent their inner truth. The need for this can be judged from the hair-raising nonsense written about Tantric Buddhism by writers like Waddell without access to the oral instruction that reveals the true significance of what is set forth in the Tantric texts. The Samaya-pledge cannot be lightly broken, but means are taught for repairing infractions within a maximum limit of three years.

Precisely what occurs at an initiation cannot of course be revealed in detail. The rite is likely to last about three hours and the atmosphere to be quietly awe-inspiring. The low-voiced intoning of the Lama, punctured by the rattle of his clapper-drum and the high note of his vajra-bell alternates with the clash of great cymbals and the thunder of a giant drum that make the walls of the building tremble. Meanwhile, the initiates earnestly try to enter the state of consciousness required for clear visualization of what is being revealed. They are besides taught the mantras, mudras and visualizations required for practising the sadhana(s) appropriate to the initiation. The rite is moving enough to cause some tension and, by the end, everyone, especially the Lama, is fairly exhausted. Yet with all this solemnity, there is no false sanctimony. I remember how the laughter rang out when some initiates made ludicrously unsuccessful attempts to emulate lions and elephants!

Following the initiation comes the 'Lung' or ceremonial reading of the texts which the initiates are thereafter authorized to study. This may last some eight hours a day for a week or so. The vital oral teaching which begins with the Lung may continue for several years.

Chapter II

THE PRELIMINARIES

Purpose

At the time of his initiation, the pupil receives a new name from his Lama which he will use henceforth for religious purposes. As an initiate, it will be proper to refer to him as the devotee during this chapter and to reserve the title adept for the following chapters; for, until he has completed two years or so of preliminary training, he will certainly not be an adept in the true sense of the word.

The progressive conquest of the ego and opening the innermost recesses of the mind to the flow of intuitive wisdom (prajna) constitute an immense achievement, even if they stop far short of Liberation. Without intensive preparation, it is vain to attempt so gigantic a task. Just as artists, however talented, seldom achieve near-perfection until they have been through a hard apprenticeship, just as doctors of medicine and psychiatrists are bound by law to qualify before venturing to practise, so too are students of Tantric methods compelled in their own interests and those of future generations to undergo a long course of training. The nature of the sacred practice is such that they have to become both artists and psychologists in order to succeed—artists able to conjure in their minds living pictures more life-like than dreams or visions, psychologists with so intimate a knowledge of the functioning of their minds that they become masters of their thoughts and emotions.

It is remarkable that the few books in English with much to say about Tantric Buddhist practice generally fail to mention the initial training. A newly initiated novice preparing to embark on his first sadhana is generally given five or six preliminary exercises each of which he must perform no less than *one hundred thousand* times! If he works at them every day

147

from dawn to long after dusk, he will be able to complete them in less than two years, which is about the minimum period for what may be called elementary training. (As we have seen, preparation for becoming a Lama is more likely to take some twenty years.) Thereafter, the novice will be able to perform most of the sadhanas without need for further preliminaries. Even if, later on, he studies under a Lama of another sect which prescribes slightly different preliminaries, it is not likely that he will be required to start all over again, for by that time he will almost certainly have achieved the results for which the preliminaries are intended.

Though most of the exercises can be completed in a few minutes, the need to perform them a hundred thousand times makes them add up to a prodigious effort. At first sight they may give the impression of being mechanical, tedious and unproductive which is quite misleading. They cannot be performed mechanically, for that would be tantamount to not performing them at all; they will not be found tedious because they soon lead to mystical contemplation that becomes a joy; and, so far from being unproductive, they constitute the first assault upon the barriers of faulty sense perception which hide from the devotee the sacred mystery he is longing to behold. On the other hand, a research scientist who does not believe in the goal but wishes to master the practice so as to be able to evaluate its psychological results will find these preliminaries not only intolerably tedious but barren too; for, without eager faith, they are bound to be mechanical and therefore fruitless.

People who advocate the use of drugs such as mescaline as a short-cut to yogic experiences otherwise requiring years of effort may argue that they can come as close or closer to the sublime mystery without expending any effort at all. That is sometimes true enough, but they are unable to foresee or control the experience that unfolds when they have taken the drug and may as often as not achieve results which, if not terrifyingly unpleasant, are at best irrelevant to what is intended. They cannot hope to emulate accomplished Tantric adepts who are able to contemplate the mystery at any time they wish. It remains to be seen whether a *combination* of the Tantric preliminaries with the use of psychedelic drugs (not taken until after the training has been completed) would have the desired result. It is probable that someone is working on this now.

The cumulative effect of the preliminaries is to prepare the faculties of body, speech and mind for the more advanced kinds of visualization and, if required, for performing the exceedingly difficult psycho-physical exercises which, under certain circumstances, are believed to lead to Liberation in this life. The mind becomes a stage which can be lit up at will for enacting the brilliantly coloured, vivid transformation scenes which cut through the sense barriers and permit mystical union with the sacred Source; simultaneously, the ego-consciousness is so reduced that, even in dealing with everyday matters, the adept acts in more or less strict accord with the concept of egolessness, responding to needs and circumstances as simply and unthinkingly as a tree responds to the need for sunlight and moisture.

Without the prescribed training, the benefit of the sadhanas would be lost and the total reorientation of mind and attitude could scarcely be accomplished. As people who experiment with Zen or Hindu yogic practice often discover, it is exceedingly difficult to achieve by a simple act of will a state of unwavering concentration that lasts for minutes or hours. Unless they are singularly gifted—in fact, 'natural mystics'—they find the mind as hard to control as a caged bird that has escaped and is fluttering among the garden trees in two minds about whether to come back to an unfailing source of nourishment at the cost of surrendering its liberty. The Vajrayana preliminaries offer a way of gaining firm control, whereafter the main practice becomes very much easier and more fruitful.

Some of the preliminaries do not seem obviously conducive to those effects and may be thought to resemble the devotional Paternosters and 'Ave Maria's of the Catholic Church. No doubt their content *is* partly devotional, which is to be expected of deeply religious men; however they have two important characteristics which distinguish them from prayer as ordinarily understood: they are accompanied by yogic visualizations and they are believed to derive their effectiveness from the mind of the devotee, rather than from the grace of the divine being addressed. Some of the preliminaries include the repetition of mantras which are very different from prayer in that the words are not pronounced for the sake of their meaning but for the 'power of their sound' which affects the mind at a deeper level than that of conceptual thought.

The Grand Prostrations

The various preliminaries are performed concurrently by doing a certain number of each in turn every day. They invariably include one hundred thousand grand prostrations, which are much more rigorous than prostrations of the ordinary sort. The latter consist of standing with the feet together, raising the joined palms to head, lips and breast, then bending down and placing hands, knees, elbows and head on the ground in that order, the whole sequence being performed thrice. This is the normal triple salutation to the Guru and to statues of the Buddha, which also constitutes the beginning and conclusion of every rite. It is universal throughout the Buddhist world except that, with other Mahayana sects, the joined hands are placed only before the breast and, among the Theravadins, the three prostrations can be performed from the kneeling position. For a grand prostration, the initial stance is the same; but, instead of falling to the knees and touching the head to the ground, the devotee swiftly slides his hands along the floor in front of him until he is lying prostrate on the ground with his limbs stretched out to their fullest extent; whereupon he bends his arms at the elbow and joins his hands above the head in salutation.

This exercise, repeated in bouts of one or two hundred in succession, is tiring; what is more, unless the ground surface is smooth enough for the hands to slide easily forward it is ungraceful; on an irregular surface it is scarcely possible at all and, if the floor is of inferior wood, splinters may wound the hands. So devotees prefer to use a special apparatus consisting of a wide board some seven feet long and raised about three inches at the further end. The board is well polished and, on either side at the points where the hands first come in contact with it, are two pads of cloth. The devotee grasps these pads and pushes them so that they slide towards the further end as his arms and body shoot forward.

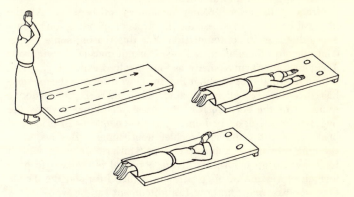

Diagram 6
The method of performing grand prostrations

Even with this useful aid, a hundred successive grand prostrations at a time are likely to tax the beginner's strength and he may, until he becomes accustomed to the practice, have to be content with a more modest number. If a board is used, it is not necessary to point it towards a Buddha-statue or reliquary tower—though this is done if convenient. The accompanying words and visualization make it a properly devotional exercise wherever it is done. Usually the words are: 'I, so-and-so, on behalf of all sentient beings and freely offering my body, speech and mind, bow to the earth in adoration of the Guru and the Three Precious Ones.' So saying the devotee visualizes a concourse of divine beings similar to those evoked during the taking of refuge. Rays from their resplendent persons penetrate in all the ten directions,[1] giving comfort to the six orders of

[1] The zenith, nadir and eight compass points.

sentient beings and entering the adept's own body, which is transformed to refulgent crystal. In this context the Three Precious Ones personify the shining void with which mystical union is sought. With progress, the visualization becomes increasingly lucid and detailed.

Grand prostrations confer a number of benefits. At the physical level, they redress the ill effects of spending long hours every day rapt in contemplation. For this reason, some adepts continue with them all their lives. It is not unusual for vigorous Tibetans to perform as many as four hundred every day. There is no doubt that those ancient Buddhists who devised the exercise had this remedial effect in mind. Then there is the symbolic humility of the act which contributes something towards the negation of the ego, for humility is the conqueror of pride and pride constitutes the ego's chief nourishment. Besides, it is thought proper for a being lost in Samsaric delusion with a long way to go before his divine potential is realized to give formal expression of his gratitude to the Guru and the Triple Gem for teaching him how Enlightenment can be won.

More important than either of these is the part played by the prostrations in combining the two Mahayana concepts of self-power and other power. Meditation performed without accompanying devotional practice will inevitably lead to the error of thinking: 'I have made this progress. This is *my* achievement.' From beginning to end of the Vajrayana practice, there is this twin approach: the concept of self-power, in that a man can be liberated by no one but himself; and that of other-power, in that his Liberation is accomplished by a power that vastly transcends the little 'I', which he must give up regarding as his real identity. On the other hand, the humility is not that of a 'miserable sinner' craving divine mercy, for at an early stage the devotee has been made aware of his own divinity that derives from the identity of his true nature with that of the Triple Gem. Though lying flat on the ground is a gesture of total surrender, in the Buddhist view a human being who has made that surrender is much to be envied by the gods lolling at ease in their cloud-girt palaces near the apex of Mount Sumeru; for gods, when their stock of merit is exhausted, tumble back into the lower realms; lacking a human body, they have no vehicle of Enlightenment and must await the good fortune of 'rebirth as a human being in a country where the Buddha-Dharma is proclaimed'.

The Refuges

In the chapter entitled 'Aspiration', the taking of refuge was described in some detail, for it must of course precede all practice including the preliminaries. It is the very first step of the path. Nevertheless it has to be recalled here, for one of the essential preliminaries consists of performing the act of refuge one hundred thousand times. As it would take many years to complete that number if the entire visualization had to be repeated that many times, the rite is reduced to manageable length by the simple means of visualizing the great concourse of deities as described earlier and then repeating the *formula* of refuge perhaps several hundred times at a sitting. Even so, it cannot be rushed; the formula must be repeated each time with great sincerity and the visualization continued throughout.

It is usual to preface each sitting with another rite entitled 'Calling upon the Lama to Arouse His Compassion'. The devotee performs three prostrations in front of the shrine on which incense tapers and butter-lamps or candles have been lighted, then seats himself cross-legged upon a cushion and thoughtfully recollects his good fortune in possessing the two essentials for Enlightenment—a human body and some knowledge of the Dharma. Next he reflects upon the folly of squandering this precious opportunity. Vividly he reviews the hindrances and dangers besetting his path and the formidable sufferings of those born into the animal state or still lower realms. To assist him, he may be provided with a text in which these reflections are set forth in movingly poetic style. Some extracts from this rite[1] as performed by the Nyingmapas are as follows:

[1] This text and some of those that follow were translated by John Driver and put into metrical form by the author.

'The Kesar flower of Faith blooms in my heart;
Lama most gracious, only Refuge, rise!
Bestow protection on this wretched being
Whom karmic deeds and klesas fierce oppress
By taking seat upon the ornament
Of Mahasukha-chakra o'er my head;
My recollection and awareness rouse!
This day I've won new respite, being safe
From hell; from birth midst pretas, brutish beasts,
Long-living gods, barbarians, heretics;
From Buddha-less worlds; from idiot's sad state—
Those eight conditions most innopportune!
As human being with faculties complete,
Born in a central land, my livelihood
Not ill; with faith in Dharma, I possess
All five endowments of the personal kind.
A Buddha has appeared; His Dharma's preached;
It still remains, and I have entered it;
With holy counsellor for guide, I own
The five endowments which from others stem.
Yet, though I've gained a state that's all-endowed,
I scorn the uncertain tenure of a life
That hangs upon conditions so diverse.
Indeed I'm bound to pass to lives beyond.
O Guru, Thou who knowest well these things,
My thoughts I pray Thee steer towards the Law;
Spare me, All-knowing Prince, low devious paths.
My mind is single, Lama, as Thou knowest.

If on this day I do not profit from
The firm support these respites render me,
I'll later lack support for liberation!
If merit's squandered in one happy life,
Then after death I'll stray through sad rebirths.
Unable to distinguish right from wrong,
Reborn in lands where Dharma is not preached,
I'll find no holy counsellor, alas!
How many and how varied are mere beings!

This thought makes human birth seem rare indeed.
And when we contemplate how men themselves
Live sinfully without the Dharma's pale,
The living of a Dharma-guided life
Will seem as rare as stars that shine by day.
O Guru, Thou who knowest well these things,
My thoughts I pray Thee steer towards the Law;
Spare me, All-knowing Prince, low devious paths.
My mind is single, Lama, as Thou knowest.

Suppose I have attained the jewelled-isle
Of human birth—sound physical support—
The wretched mind will ill support my aim,
I'm ruled by evil company and, worse,
The poisons five grow turbulent within;
Of if bad karma bring disasters down,
If sloth distract me, or I'm made a slave;
Or if my Dharma-following's mere pretence,
Of if I take the Refuges through fear,
Or I do stupid things, these are the eight
Inopportunes of adventitious source.
Now when these Dharma-foes beset me close,
O Guru, Thou who knowest well these things,
My thoughts I pray Thee steer towards the Law;
Spare me, All-knowing Prince, low devious paths.
My mind is single, Lama, as Thou knowest.

Not to regret our life's inherent woe;
To lack the jewel of faith; to be ensnared
By craving's noose; steeped in vulgarity;
Shameless though sinful; nurtured by evil means;
With vows all marred; and rent the Samaya-pledge—
Such are the eight engrained inopportunes.
Now when these Dharma-foes beset me close,
O Guru, Thou who knowest well these things,
My thoughts I pray Thee steer towards the Law;
Spare me, All-knowing Prince, low devious paths.
My mind is single, Lama, as Thou knowest.

Though free just now from illness and from woe,
And not as yet enchained in servitude;
What if, despite this circumstance so fair,
These gains are squandered through my idleness?
How think of pleasure, henchmen, kith and kin,
When e'en my precious body's dragged from bed
To be devoured by foxes, vultures, dogs?
What anguished fears the bardo-state must bring!
O Guru, Thou who knowest well these things,
My thoughts I pray Thee steer towards the Law;
Spare me, All-knowing Prince, low devious paths.
My mind is single, Lama, as Thou knowest.

From failing to restrain my evil-doing
While setting foot upon the sacred Path;
From lacking urge to benefit my fellows
Though now inside the Mahayana Gate;
From sloth in all the meditation stages,
Though four initiations were bestowed—
O Lama, pluck me from such erring ways!

From pride in views before I've understood;
From meditation marred by wandering thoughts;
From heedlessness of faults in action's sphere—
O Lama, save me from the state of "Dharma-bear".[1]

From thirst for dwellings, clothes and property,
Though I may have to die when next day dawns;
From failing in aversion to this life,
Though my remaining years grow ever less;
From boasting of my intellectual gains
While yet so far from learned in the Law—
O Lama, save me from such nescience!

From being immersed in bustle's trivial round,
Though splendid chances crowd upon my way;
From timber-like rigidity of mind,

[1] i.e. from being a hypocritical follower of the Dharma.

When choosing to rely on solitude;
From talking glibly of the vinaya,[1]
Though still a prey to anger and desire—
O Lama, draw me from these worldly ways.

O Lama, rouse me from my sluggish sleep!
O drag me quickly from this dungeon deep!'

Having recited this text three times, the devotee then visualizes the concourse of deities and recites one of the brief formulas for taking refuge perhaps a hundred and eight or a thousand and eighty times at a sitting; thereafter he contemplates the deities merging into one and thence into the formless primal condition of the undifferentiated Dharmakaya, whereat he himself enters samadhi.

The Generation of Bodhicitta

'Bodhi' means Enlightenment and 'citta' connotes both of what in English are called mind and heart (the seats of the intellect and emotion). The whole word therefore means literally 'Enlightened mind-heart', but the title of the rite is best rendered 'the attainment of an attitude of mind compounded of Buddha-like wisdom and Bodhisattva-like compassion for sentient beings'. The first part consists of cultivating what are known as the Four Immeasurables or Brahma States, namely impartiality, friendliness, compassion and sympathetic joy, which, according to a Nyingma text, is done as follows:

The devotee first reflects upon his friends and enemies, noting how enemies may by right treatment be made a source of blessing and how friends can become a hindrance to progress, as inordinate affection for them is likely to lead to further rebirths. Starting with one or two persons in mind, he gradually extends his reflections to include all beings in the universe, meanwhile cultivating an impartial attitude towards them so that the distinctions between close friends and distant acquaintances or between friends and enemies vanish. Thus impartiality is gradually achieved. Next he contemplates all sentient beings

[1] Rules of conduct.

together and, with a yearning like that of a parent towards erring children, ardently desires their well-being. Thus friendliness which longs to confer benefits by whatever means is achieved. Next, to fortify his compassion, he meditates upon the lot of some cruelly afflicted being such as a malefactor on the eve of execution or an animal in the hands of a butcher reeking with the blood of its pitiful kind. He thinks of this sad being as a mother thinks of her child, his heart full of love and pity such as flesh can hardly bear, saying: 'Ah, would that he could be spared this horror!' Then gradually he turns his mind to those in other evil states and to all who are working out their karma under painful circumstances. This part of the meditation leads directly into samadhi which is attained by visualizing the universe of suffering beings as expanding and expanding into nothingness. Upon emerging from samadhi, the mind attains sympathetic joy by being directed towards all those beings, especially enemies, who are enjoying present happiness. Free from envy, he rejoices in their joy and ardently desires its increase and continuance. By extending to infinity the number of happy beings contemplated he enters samadhi again.

Upon his withdrawal from samadhi for the second time, the actual generation of Bodhicitta commences. Longing for the Liberation of all beings and praying that his own deliverance from Samsara shall take place after theirs, he visualizes the sentient universe as composed of myriads of beings all of whom have been his own parents in former lives. They include gods, asuras, humans, all kinds of birds and beasts, reptiles and insects, as well as ghosts and demons.

From a heart full of deep compassion, he reflects:

'Of all these beings there is not one who has not been my parent. My present parents have reared me lovingly, lavishing upon me good food and raiment—while they and my former parents remain in the round of life and death, why should I be one to be delivered? I must set my thoughts upon the highest Enlightenment and therefore upon emulating the holy conduct of a Bodhisattva. I shall strive and strive until no single being remains in the round.'

158

Thereupon he recites a short verse movingly expressing his aspiration, perhaps repeating it some hundreds of times as a contribution towards completing the preliminaries. One such verse runs:

'Hoh!
Through divers semblances like moon in water,
The beings wander in Samsara's thrall.
In order to repose their minds in realms of light,
I from the Four Immeasurables beget the Bodhi-Mind.'

When the recitation ceases, the devotee visualizes the deities of the mandala as appearing before him and then becoming absorbed into his own body, whereat Bodhicitta is born like a flash of light in his own consciousness and, for the third time, samadhi supervenes.

The conclusion of the rite consists of meditating upon ways in which the devotee can train himself to be of service to others and the means of acquiring intuitive wisdom (prajna) by reflection upon the intrinsic emptiness of all entities (dharmas). This is the beginner's manner of generating Bodhicitta. With the most advanced methods, no set practices are required.

The Vajrasattva[1] Purification

This rite is performed first as a preliminary and later as a means of purification that can be resorted to from time to time throughout the adept's life. Whenever he infringes any provision of the Samaya-pledge, it is essential to perform it time after time until certain signs convince him that the pledge has been repaired. The longer the time that has elapsed since the infraction, the more thorough and lengthy the purification must be. If three years have gone by and no purification has taken place, the pledge is impossible to repair in this life and the erring adept must accept the fearful karmic consequences.

To readers unable to accept the vital doctrine underlying it,

[1] Vajrasattva or Adamantine Being is the name given to one of the figures in the heart of the mandala—the Buddha principle in the visible form nearest to the subtle, undifferentiated Dharmakaya form.

the rite will seem at best a useful psychological exercise; but Vajrayana initiates recognize it as a source of illimitable cleansing power. Just as the whole universe is manifested by mind, so is an endless succession of mental objects created by the individual mind. If the distinction between mind in these two senses were real, there would of course be a great difference between, say, a bronze kettle and the mental concept of a kettle, but to an initiate it is clear that this distinction is illusory. Dreams help to make this point of view more easily acceptable. There can be no doubt that the objects in a dream are mental creations, yet to the dreamer they are as real as the walls of his bedroom when he awakes. The efficacy of purification by means of the visualization of Vajrasattva derives from the identical nature of mental creations appearing as objects in a man's environment and those appearing as concepts in his mind.

When this rite is used as a preliminary, the part which has to be repeated many times in succession so that the repetitions amount to a hundred thousand by the end of about two years is the 'Hundred Syllable Mantra' of Vajrasattva. This, though it has a recognizable meaning when rendered from its Tibeto-Sanskrit form back into the original Sanskrit, is used—like all mantras—in an ejaculatory manner and the meaning of the words, unrecognizable from the pronunciation, is of no consequence at the level of conscious thought. Yet it would be wrong to say that the choice of mantra is of no consequence, for substitution of another mantra or of arbitrary strings of sound would not do. The way it is recited is of great importance; the sound is held to produce certain vibratory effects to which the mind responds at a deeper level of consciousness.

A well-known Nyingmapa text used for the rite runs as follows:

THE VAJRASATTVA MEDITATION AND RECITATION

The impediment to acquiring the fullest mental realization of the Profound Path is the obscurations caused by evil deeds;

and the best way of purging these obscurations is to practise the Yoga of Vajrasattva. The essentials of the Four Powers involved in this are as follows:

(a) *The Power of the 'Support'*. This results from taking Vajrasattva as your Refuge, from possessing the Bodhicitta of Aspiration and from Entrance upon the Path.

(b) *The Power of Vanquishing Evil Karma*. This results from generating a fierce remorse for your impure karma and your sins.

(c) *The Power of Restraining Evil Behaviour*. This results from thinking: 'Henceforth, though it cost my life, I shall refrain from evil deeds.'

(d) *The Power of the Antidote*. This results from the Vajrasattva Meditation and Recitation as a remedy for your former deeds.

With full recollection of the purification conferred by these powers, you should join visualization and utterance in perfect union and begin by reciting:

> *'Ah!*
> Lowly myself, above my head
> Carpet of moon on lotus white.
> From *Hum* springs Lama Dorje Sem[1]
> White-shining in Enjoyment Form
> With Nyemma[2] and a vajra-bell.
>
> Be Thou my refuge; purge my crimes
> Which I with sharp remorse lay bare
> And henceforth, cost it life, abjure.
> At Thy heart a full moon glows.
> Around its *Hum* Thy mantra spins.
> Incited by these sacred words,
> From Yabyum locked in blissful sport,
> Clouds of Bodhicitta dew
> Descend like glistening camphor dust.

[1] Vajrasattva.
[2] The Yum.

> Whereby, I pray, may be erased
> All karma, klesa,[1] seeds of woe,
> Distempers and all demon-plagues,
> Sin's dark shadow, evil's murk—
> Both mine and all the Triple World's.'

Next, you should repeatedly recite the Hundred Syllable Mantra with attention, reverence and respect, not straying discursively from one-pointedness:

Thereupon the jnana-ambrosia[2] of Great Bliss, like molten moonlight, falls from the syllable *Hum* in Vajrasattva's heart and from the mantra encircling it. Thence flowing from their bodies, it enters by your own cranial orifice; whereat all illness in the form of pus and blood, all plagues in the form of horrid insects, and all sin obscurations in the form of smoke and vapour emerge from your pores and two lower orifices. Passing through nine earth-levels, they enter the belly of the (black) Lord of Death—that Yama of Deeds (in dreadful form)—who waits for them (surrounded by his horrid minions) with mouth agape (hungry for the oblations owed him for your sins). And thus you are redeemed from untimely death. Visualizing all this, you should continue repeating the mantra as long as possible. Finally, your four chakras being filled with shining-white ambrosia, your body and mind will be intoxicated with inexhaustible bliss.

Next, recite:

> 'Protector! Lost in darkest folly
> I've often transgressed the Samaya-pledge.
> Lama, Protector, be my Refuge!
> Mandala-Lord and Vajra-bearer,
> Embodiment of vast compassion,
> Lord of every sentient being,
> I go to Thee for refuge sure.'

'I now confess and disclose all my failures to honour the Samaya of Body, Speech and Mind, both main and subsidiary.

---

[1] Karmic accretions, defilements.

[2] Wisdom visualized as a milk-white non-substance.

I therefore pray Thee cleanse me, purifying me of the stains caused by my falling into evil, and of all darkness and sin.'

At these words, Vajrasattva with glad and smiling countenance bestows forgiveness, saying: 'Son of good family, all the darkness of your sins and the evils of your shortcomings are cleansed.'

So saying, He dissolves into light and merges into yourself, whereupon you become Vajrasattva, like a reflection in a mirror, both apparent and void.

This rite, when it is used for purification by adepts who have completed the preliminaries, has a further step to it which is described in the following chapter under the heading Regular Rites and Meditations. When used as a preliminary, it ends with the merging of Vajrasattva with the devotee, who visualizes their unified form as being absorbed into the void, whereupon samadhi supervenes.

The Mandala Offering

In this context, the word mandala has a special meaning. It is not the mandala of peaceful and wrathful deities, but the mandala of the visible universe conceived of in transmuted form as a symmetrical mass of precious substances studded with jewels. In shape and composition it resembles the ancient Hindu conception of the universe, of which our world forms an insignificant part, although strangely the sun and moon bear the same relation to the whole as they do to our tiny world. As an offering, though symbolized by a few grains of rice contained in the devotee's hands, it is of infinite extent, for large and small have no meaning when the plane of relativity is transcended. Each 'continent' alone contains galaxies of stars and planets.

(Our world is one of millions situated in the southern 'continent'. Mount Sumeru reaches above Brahma's heaven.)

The rite in its most simple form is thus. The devotee seated before his shrine with its lighted lamps and incense tapers, picks up a handful of uncooked rice grains. With about half of them lying in each palm, he interlocks his fingers in a complicated mudra symbolizing the mandala of the universe. The two fourth fingers stand up back to back and pressed against each other to represent Mount Sumeru. The little fingers are crossed and each has the top of the thumb of the opposite hand resting upon its tip. The middle fingers are also crossed and each is embraced by the first finger of the opposite hand. This offering of rice and its container (the hands) are visualized as the universe composed of shining substances and adorned with piles of precious jewels, silken banners, silver bells and so forth.

Holding the offering in front of him, the devotee visualizes his parents seated to either side with his loved ones pressing close about them. Seated in the place of honour with their backs to him and facing the Buddhas are his enemies and all who wish him harm. To either side and behind is a great throng composed of sentient beings of every kind—in fact, all sentient beings in the universe. Facing them is the great concourse of deities with the Three Precious Ones, his Yidam and his Guru in the centre. Now he recites:

'I, on behalf of parents, loved ones, friends, enemies and all this great throng of sentient beings, offer all I have of body, speech and mind, all good qualities, actions and property, all my merit—past, present and yet to come—to the Buddhas of the ten directions. May all beings be spared rebirth into states of suffering; may they attain present tranquillity and swiftly achieve Nirvana.'

This reflection must be accompanied by a sincere intention to put himself and all he has at the service of others, as well as to endure any amount of suffering for their temporal and spiritual welfare. Offering the mandala constitutes a sacred pledge.

Next, with hands still joined in the mudra and the rice grains resting on his palms, he recites:

'*Om Vajra Bhumi Ah Hum!* Now let the ground be spotlessly

pure. *Om Vajra Rekhe Ah Hum!* Now let an iron wall arise with *Hum* in the centre. To the east, south, west and north lie the four continents interspaced with four pairs of lesser continents, and also the Mountain of Precious Substances, the Wishing Tree, the Wishing Cow, the Unploughed Harvest, the Precious Wheel, the Precious Jewel, the Precious Queen, the Precious Minister, the Precious Elephant, the Precious and Best of Horses and the Precious General. Also present, are the Great Treasure Vase, the Lady of Gestures, the Lady of Garlands, the Lady of Song, the Lady of Dance, the Lady of Flowers, the Lady of Incense, the Lady of Lights and the Lady of Perfume. There are besides the Sun and Moon, the Umbrella of Precious Substances and the Banner of Victory.

'These same possessions of gods and men, lacking nothing, I now offer to the Glorious Holy Lamas my immediate Teachers and their predecessors in the Sacred Line of Succession, and to the Deities of the Mandala and to the Yidams, together with the whole Assembly of Buddhas and Bodhisattvas.

'I pray you out of your compassion to accept these offerings for the sake of all sentient beings. I pray you, having accepted them, graciously to bestow your blessings upon all.'

A simpler and in some ways more beautiful version often used is:

> 'We have strewn upon the earth sweet scents
> And scattered flowers,
> With Mount Sumeru,
> The Four Continents,
> The Sun and Moon
> As ornaments—
> All these we offer from our hearts
> To the Buddhas everywhere.
> To the end that every being
> May be reborn in happy state.'

Then, pronouncing the appropriate mantra, the devotee tosses the rice grains high into the air and thus completes the offering. If this is done as part of the preliminaries, the mantra (which contains less than twenty syllables) may be repeated a few hundred times at a sitting and the throwing of the rice grains imagined after the first time, so that one hundred thousand recitations can be completed within about two years.

Such a rite can be viewed in several ways. At the most elementary level—that of those non-initiates who are simple folk—it is closely analogous to making an offering to God in the hope of pleasing Him and obtaining His favour. This conception, though not fully in accord with Buddhist teaching, forms part of the vast range of skilful means for attracting as many people as possible to the Dharma. In all Buddhist countries the peasantry by and large *do* think of the Buddha very much as Christians and Hindus think of the deity. The more subtle and mystical Buddhist beliefs are hard for them to comprehend and, if they choose to conceive of the Buddha more or less as a god, there is no harm. It makes them glad to accept the Buddhist rules of restrained and compassionate conduct and many of them will presently reach a stage at which they can be taught to understand a more orthodox concept of the Buddha. When an initiate, albeit still at a relatively low level of understanding, uses verses of this kind, he knows that the merit accruing from the offering is not bestowed upon him by the Buddha in the form of grace to reward his piety, but arises from the alteration to his own mentality that results from reiterated verbal expressions of a genuine aspiration to expend his wealth, time and energy on other sentient beings. The repetition of this formula of aspiration drives deeply into his heart the need to pursue his high goal without a thought of selfishness and this tends, at least in a small measure, to the diminution of the ego. Furthermore whoever recites the formula several times a day with true sincerity will, when confronted with opportunities to be helpful, scarcely forgo them thoughtlessly, still less deliberately neglect to make the most of them.

As to the form of the rite, it can be argued that the universe does not belong to the devotee and that he is 'getting off very cheaply' by substituting a mentally created idealized replica in place of what is not his to offer. However, at the lowest level of understanding, what the offer really amounts to is a pledge to utilize without exception for the benefit of others whatever tiny fragments of the universe come into his possession. From the Tantric point of view, on the other hand, there is absolutely nothing which is not his own, since each sentient being contains within himself the whole universe. This is so because mind is not subject to space limitations and the mind of each being—though apparently cut off from mind as a whole by the karmic accretions constituting his individual personality —is in fact identical with mind, the container of the universe.

Others

The preliminaries outlined so far are common to all the sects and are seldom replaced by others when prescribed for serious-minded initiates of the kind we are discussing. There are usually a few additional preliminaries which vary among the sects or with individual teachers.

To keep count during the preliminaries and in general for the recitation of mantras, rosaries are used. They consist of a hundred and eight beads with the first seven and the first twenty-one marked off by extra beads of a different size and colour. To the large bead at the head of the rosary, two cords are attached and on each of them there are ten tightly fitted discs of bone or metal which can be slid up and down but grip the cord so tightly that they will not move unless pushed. Each bead on the rosary itself is moved to record a single recitation; the discs on one pendent cord are for recording hundreds and those on the other cord for recording thousands. The number a hundred and eight is borrowed from ancient India and is said to correspond to some heavenly bodies of special importance in astrology. In practice, each set of a hundred and eight repetitions is counted as a hundred and the remaining eight thrown in for good measure in case some beads have inadvertently slipped through the devotee's hand. Rosaries can be of any suitable substance, but the most favoured kind are those made of so-called Bodhi-seeds[1] each of which has on its yellow surface one large dot (the moon) and many small

[1] These seeds do not come from the Bodhi Tree (*Ficus religiosus*) under which Sakyamuni Buddha was Enlightened, but from another plant.

ones (stars). Coral, agate and various precious stones are used for the head-bead and for the markers that follow the seventh, twenty-first and sometimes the forty-ninth or fifty-fourth bead.

Devotees not on the Short Path and without much time to spare from occupational and social responsibilities can at best perform a very simple kind of sadhana, so they are sometimes given simpler preliminaries. The simplest of all consists of repeating a single mantra of perhaps half a dozen or a dozen syllables—but with the proper visualization. That is why in the Himalayan regions one so often sees Tibetan lay folk from whose lips comes a continuous low hum of mantric sound. No doubt their devotions are in some cases mechanical, but it is taught that mere recitation without either visualization or a special state of mind is of little value, except that it will have the effect of making the mantra come to mind at moments of crisis. The mantra is clung to as a means of inducing the proper state of mind for passing into the bardo at moments when sudden death is likely to occur.

Most Tibetans, even illiterates, are well aware of the need to use the mantras in the proper way. Those well schooled in the practice learn to give just as much attention to their manual tasks as is necessary for performing them; the rest of their thought is given to maintaining the state of consciousness on which the efficacy of the mantra depends. So their minds are calm and still below the surface ripples caused by the task in hand. It is said that some of them can carry on lucid conversations without disturbing their inward contemplation. Anyone who has been deeply in love should have no difficulty in believing this, for lovers easily perform their daily tasks and talk about trifles with the image of the loved one constantly in mind.

Chapter III

GENERAL PRACTICE

Introductory

With his mind fortified by the psychic changes wrought by the preliminaries, the initiate may now be properly called an adept. Though not far beyond the gateway of his journey, he is at least qualified to advance swiftly. Already he has learnt how to activate the latent forces proceeding from beyond the level of everyday consciousness. The next step is to make fruitful use of them.

This chapter deals with the basic practice that forms a background for special techniques of the kind set forth in the chapters that follow. To people unfamiliar with the theory underlying Tantric Buddhism, the daily practice may well seem an extraordinary medley of exalted conduct and meditation on the one hand and of 'magic' and 'superstition' on the other. In a sense that is so, for some of the current practices were evolved from pre-Buddhist rites in accordance with the Tantric technique of bending everything available to the one high end. To some extent the incorporation of ancient 'superstitions' (but with their content subtly altered) reflects an intention to provide for simple people incapable of grasping abstract psychological concepts. Another reason is that, even in their original form, such 'superstitions' are not to be despised. If it is not possible to demonstrate their worth, that is because modern education, while revealing so many truths of which our ancestors were ignorant, has at the same time inhibited our appreciation of much that they knew well.

Still another cause of misunderstanding is the Tantric technique of employing several levels of practice and understanding simultaneously. That is to say, an initiate who has reached the fourth and highest stage does not usually abandon the practices and concepts used at the lowest. Taught to see everything in four ways, he brings to bear all four levels of understanding at once or selects the one best suited to the needs of the moment. This will often appear (and be) illogical; but, as all those with experience of Zen and other forms of mysticism will agree, logical thought is actually a barrier to mystical attainment. This is so because ultimate truth transcends logical thought. For example, logic demonstrates that the one cannot simultaneously be the many and vice versa, whereas during profound mystical experience it becomes brilliantly apparent that the one *is* multifold while yet remaining one. The application of four apparently contradictory levels of understanding to the same phenomena will become clearer when the section on Yidams is reached. There are times when it is convenient to think of them as independently existing deities, others when they are seen as emanations of the adept's own mind, and yet others when they are recognized as void.

A Westerner attracted by some of the lofty aspects of Tantric Buddhism once exclaimed: 'Splendid; I go for that mystical stuff about the void and the non-ego in a big way, but the last thing I need is a little old god or goddess sitting in my heart.' He may have been right. On the other hand, though he goes for 'all that stuff about the non-ego', does it get him anywhere, or does he pass his life with 'a little old ego' of enormous weight pressing on his chest each time he wants to fly? There are Tibetans who have amply demonstrated that, with 'a little old god or goddess' in their hearts, they have become great yogic adepts able to draw immense resources from mystical communion and no longer subject to the tensions and anxieties generally regarded as an integral part of the human state. Their example suggests that it is worthwhile to put aside all preconceptions before evaluating the Tantric practice.

With initiation and the preliminaries behind him, the adept has become a man apart, vowed to Bodhisattvahood for the sake of all beings. The speed of his progress will depend on the type of adept. Monks, hermits and others free to devote themselves to the task day and night will probably undertake all the practices listed in this chapter, together with some sadhanas or the psycho-physical yogic practices described later. Laymen,

170

unless they are Nyingmapas with wives similarly dedicated, have to do the best they can in the light of their other responsibilities. They are free to choose how much of their Lama's instruction they will work upon. For those who have the courage to attempt the Short Path, it is considered very nearly essential to take monastic vows or to live apart in some solitary place, or else marry Nyingmapa-style but sever all social and occupational ties. Laymen unable to renounce the world must, with very rare exceptions, set themselves a more modest goal for this present life.

Custom inclines one to speak of adepts as male, but adepts of the other sex are not uncommon, though I have yet to meet a woman on the Short Path. For all that Bodhisattvas[1] are sometimes portrayed in female form, the canon does not speak of women attaining Liberation in this life. It is generally held that, however great her progress, a woman must be reborn a man before achieving the final goal. On the other hand, at least one of the Tulkus or recognized sacred incarnations is a woman. Dordje-P'agmo, an incarnation of the Indian Devi, Vajra Vakari, has for centuries been Abbess of Samding, from whose windows she used, before the Communists came, to look down upon the waters of the wild, scorpion-shaped Yamding Lake. It would seem that, if women seldom achieve a status close to that of an Enlightened One, it is because they *do* not, not because they *cannot*. Unfortunately, the English language, unlike Tibetan or Chinese, lacks a singular pronoun denoting either sex, so I must perforce speak of adepts as though all of them were male.

The life of a dedicated adept involves much more than observing such cardinal Buddhist virtues as right livelihood, right meditation, restraint and avoidance of wilful harm to sentient beings. All of these may be taken for granted. Even spending hours a day rapt in contemplation leading to mystical communion is not enough. The prime essential is for his mental attitude to be firmly based on recognition of Samsara as Nirvana, of sentient

---

[1] Female Bodhisattvas are not necessarily, of course, the incarnations of women who attained Enlightenment. Bodhisattvas appear in whatever form, male or female, human, animal or demon, suits their purpose.

beings as potential Buddhas, and of the voidness of the ego. His thoughts, words and actions should all proceed from these realizations. Meditation divorced from right conduct, or meditation and right conduct divorced from right attitude would be as useless as playing aimlessly with a set of elaborate tools.

There is, in the Tantric view, little to be gained from piling up the hours spent in purely devotional practice and good works. These at best lead to acquiring a substantial stock of merit that will alleviate a small part of the unsatisfactoriness of this or the next few lives. There is no difference in result between a man whose stomach is an inch or two too big to allow him to escape from a fire by crawling through a narrow hole and one who has a mighty paunch. If there were a Supreme God, as Christians see Him, He might be merciful in His judgement on men who had made sincere but desultory efforts to be virtuous, giving them credit for their good intentions and making allowances for their failure to act accordingly. As it is, well-meant efforts will avail the adept nothing; either he succeeds in going some way towards negating the ego and breaking down the obstructions to the flow of intuitive wisdom, or he does not. If not, then his labour is in vain, except that his pious practices will have left him rather less leisure in which to build up bad karma. In short, there can be no reward for exalted aspiration; effective *practice* engaging body, speech and mind is the only means to success.

In books about the Vajrayana, descriptions of rites and visualizations are bound to occupy a disproportionate space because they can be set forth in detail and do not vary from day to day, whereas the adept's reactions to events are as multifarious as the events themselves. All that can be said is that, ideally speaking, each moment of life should be properly employed. There are instructions for every sort of contingency. If properly carried out—as it must be in the case of a Short Path adept— then the practice governs: walking, sitting, standing and lying; being awake or asleep and dreaming; talking, laughing and joking; bathing, dressing, urinating and excreting; working, praying, playing, eating and (if he be not a monk) love-making. There are no occasions when these dedicated men need not be mindful of what they are doing or cease making use of it for their spiritual progress.

This appears to be a mighty task—and so it is, but it is less daunting than it seems because, once the means are known and the right attitude has been cultivated, much of what has to be done happens of itself. A carefully brought-up Quaker youth does not have to remind himself to be truthful—he is naturally so, truthfulness having become his second nature. So it is with the very comprehensive spiritual duties of Tantric adepts; the proper thoughts, words and actions presently come to them effortlessly. Naturally few of them achieve this ideal without relapses. It may be supposed that the wisest and most devoted Lamas now and then allow their minds to slip from the task, unless they are truly extraordinary men like Milarepa.[1] Happily, there is no humourless intensity about them. Advanced adepts are invariably relaxed and gently gay, fond of laughter, affectionate and uncensorious. Where there is tight-lipped solemnity, something has surely gone wrong with the practice. Of the dozen or so notable Lamas I have met, all struck me as charmingly light-hearted. Their ready smiles were not the calculated smiles of politicians or of businessmen anxious 'to win friends and influence people', nor professional smiles that look like grimaces, but the unmeditated smiles of men at peace with themselves who are glad to find you happy in their company.

Daily Practice

Waking early in the morning, the adept communes with his Yidam, gets up, moves his bowels, bathes and dresses, for all of which actions there are appropriate mantras and reflections. Then he goes to his shrineroom to perform his morning meditations and devotions. During the course of the day, his devotions (including several performances of his sadhana and perhaps some yogic exercises), his work, his recreation and his relations with other people are all kept largely free from egocentricity and transmuted into the blissful play of a divine being surrounded by divinities in an environment where

[1] See *Tibet's Great Yogi, Milarepa*, edited by Evans Wentz, Oxford University Press.

everything is seen as a magical emanation of the pure, shining non-substance of the void. In the evening, regardless of how much of the day has been spent in his shrineroom, he returns to it for his evening devotions and meditations. On going to bed, he communes with his Yidam and, if he knows how, prepares to perform the yoga of dreams.

Foreseeing that, during my working life, I should have difficulty in observing more than a few fragments of such a pro-gramme, I took separate opportunities to ask a Mongolian Gelugpa (Yellow Hat) Lama and my principal Nyingmapa Guru what are the prime essentials. Their replies are not altogether comparable because, at that time, the former was teaching me Guru-yoga, the aim of which is to identify the adept's body, speech and mind with the Body, Speech and Mind of the Yidam, whereas the Nyingmapa was expounding the sadhana of the Essence of the Profound Meaning, so he did not, in the context of daily practice, stress the importance of the Yidam so strongly. This should be borne in mind in studying their replies. The Gelugpa Lama answered:

'On rising, listen for the Yidam's voice. Reflect on the good fortune of being alive and able to make progress towards the goal. Reflect on the consequences of death while still in a state of delusion. Resolve to hear all sounds as the Yidam's voice, to see your entire surroundings as Nirvana and to recognize all beings as deities. Visualize the Yidam and repeat her mantra not less than a hundred and eight times.

'Throughout the day, offer all good things—fresh fruit, good tea, new garments—to the Yidam. Constantly remind yourself of the proper way to hear all sounds, see all sights and welcome all beings. Recollect the mantra which means: Spotlessly pure are all dharmas and spotlessly pure am I![1]

'When eating and drinking, visualize your body as the Yidam's and the food and drink as offerings. If flesh is eaten, repeat the mantra of happy rebirth seven times, and earnestly desire that the sentient beings slaughtered for man's enjoyment will be reborn in higher states.

[1] Pure in the sense of void and, except relatively, free from stain.

'Before sleeping, place the palm of your right hand under your cheek and visualize your Yidam seated where the pillow is, her legs supporting you. Full of joy and security, repeat the Yidam's mantra several times and fall peacefully asleep.

'During your devotions, if circumstances do not permit performance of the Yidam's sadhana, at least do not omit the prostrations, offerings, confession, generation of Bodhicitta, meditation on the Yidam, entering into samadhi, dedication of merit and offering of good wishes to all beings.

'There are no hard and fast rules, but the emphasis should be upon reverence for the Yidam, Guru and Triple Gem; the attainment of samadhi and prayer for the dispersal of merit to others.'

The Nyingmapa Lama prescribed:

'Taking the Four Refuges [the Guru and the Triple Gem];
The generation of Bodhicitta;
Confession and meditation on Vajrasattva;
Samadhi, entering into void;
Dedication of the resulting merit and offering of good wishes to all beings.'

He also taught that, when eating, the adept should visualize himself as Vajrasattva and make offerings to his own mind-body as to the great mandala of peaceful and wrathful deities which emanates from the void through Vajrasattva. The adept's five skandhas (form, sensation, discernment, mental discrimination and cognition) and his five dhatus (solids, liquids, heat, energy and space) are the five Jinas and their consorts. His senses (sight, hearing, etc.) and their objects are the mandalas of the eight Bodhisattvas and their consorts. His four limbs are the Four Fierce Gatekeepers and their consorts[1] and, at the same time, are equated with wrong views—the right leg with belief in permanence, the right arm with belief in annihilation, the left arm with belief in ego-entities, and the left leg with belief in phenomena as signs. In thus meditating and at all other times, the klesas or karmic hindrances should be recognized as possessing, like everything else, the nature of void.

[1] The names of three of the Gatekeepers' ladies are Lady Non-Permanence, Lady Non-Annihilation and Lady Non-Ego. The fourth lady is not characterized.

The Importance of the Yidam

The function of the Yidam is one of the profound mysteries of the Vajrayana. At the time of the adept's first initiation, his Lama will have allotted him a Yidam from among the peaceful and wrathful deities of the mandala. Especially during the first years of practice, the Yidam is of immense importance. Yidam is the Tibetan rendering of the Sanskrit word Istadeva—the indwelling deity; but, whereas the Hindus take the Istadeva for an actual deity who has been invited to dwell in the devotee's heart, the Yidams of Tantric Buddhism are in fact the emanations of the adept's own mind. Or are they? To some extent they seem to belong to that order of phenomena which in Jungian terms are called archetypes and are therefore the common property of the entire human race. Even among Tantric Buddhists, there may be some division of opinion as to how far the Yidams are the creations of individual minds. What is quite certain is that they are not independently existing gods and goddesses; and yet, paradoxically, there are occasions when they must be so regarded. There may of course be many Tibetans who, at the outset of the practice, do not recognize the Yidams as projections of their own minds; and their Lamas may find it expedient not to reveal this fact right at the beginning, especially to people accustomed to worshipping gods and goddesses who might not be able to summon up unquestioning faith in their own mental creations.

The Yidam is in fact the tremendous inner power whereby the adept negates the ego and attains Enlightenment. Possibly there is some correspondence with the Christian concept of the Holy Ghost as divine power dwelling within the heart. However, in appearance the Yidams look like gods and goddesses: very detailed instructions are given so that the adept can exactly visualize the appearance of the one he cherishes, so the question arises as to why it is necessary to personify this inner power, all the more so as the Yidam is not an elementary 'prop' to be discarded close to the beginning of the journey. Adepts are taught that, even when nearing the highest level of spiritual progress, they should continue their practice at all four levels simultaneously. They will therefore variously regard their Yidams as: (1) having some of the characteristics of an external deity; (2) as being identical with themselves and yet with the void (i.e. both relative and absolute); (3) either as dwelling within or sometimes entering their hearts; and (4) as identical with pure jnana[1] (wholly absolute).

Perhaps the need for personification can be made clear as follows, taking into account people at different levels of understanding:

1. Devotees accustomed to thinking of their religious duties at the rather primitive dualist level of worshipper and worshipped may at first have difficulty in understanding the subtle concept of non-duality. It is easier for them to think in terms of an actual deity who has graciously come to dwell in the heart.

2. Those at a higher level of perception know very well that the Yidam is not a deity apart from the worshipper, but they find it expedient to act as though it were so. No one can conceive of the nature of the Dharmakaya and similar high mysteries without employing symbols, even if the symbols are not objects but names (i.e. sounds or groups of letters). People use words like 'Dharma' or 'God' a hundred times a day without stopping to reflect on their full significance. There is no real superiority in using a name rather than a form to symbolize something; indeed the two often go together. When a Christian pronounces the word 'God', he is likely briefly to envision a glorious-looking being with a beard, though he is quite aware that God is spirit and can scarcely have a beard. To penetrate to the depths of mind where logical reasoning and discursive thought are transcended, purely abstract symbols, such as words, are ineffective, hence the need for more concrete symbols perceptible to the inner vision.

3. As to what concrete symbols are most suitable, there are

[1] 'Jnana' is a Sanskrit word frequently used in Tantric writings. It is the pure void of which intuitive wisdom (prajna) is the function, related to it as sunbeams to the sun; in certain contexts, it can be rendered: 'original mind', 'ever-existing knowledge', 'intuitive knowledge', 'the five wisdoms', 'the play emerging from the void', 'the Two-in-One' (void and manifestation). It may also refer to our own spiritual knowledge and progress. It is sometimes visualized as a 'non-substance' white as milk or camphor dust.

present within the universal consciousness figures which, as it were, are endowed with form and life not wholly determined by the mind of the individual. These are embodiments of realities not present at the ordinary level of consciousness. (For example, there is one who has been variously intuited by people of widely divergent cultural backgrounds as the Divine Mother, the Blessed Virgin, the Compassionate Beloved, the Saviouress, Arya Tara or, in Tibetan, Jetzen Drölma—the most popular of Yidams. Catholic and Orthodox Christians have intuited her in their hearts and, conveniently equating her with Mary the mother of Jesus, adore her as the Queen of Heaven. Protestant Christians and Moslems have, rather sadly, denied themselves this form of comfort.)

4. Since intuitions of this kind lie readily at hand, great advantage can be taken of them. When Tantrists are instructed to identify their body, speech and mind with the Body, Speech and Mind of the Buddha, what this really means is the attainment of communion at all levels with the reality lying beyond the realm of distorted sense perception. As the Body, Speech and Mind of the Buddha are actually functions of the void, it is simpler in the first place to aim at identification with the triple faculty of a chosen deity who can be regarded according to the need of the moment as being material or immaterial.

5. Either from the first or at a very early stage of his practice, the adept realizes that these embodiments of realities present at the deeper levels of consciousness are not the gods and goddesses for which people of other cultures have mistaken them, but emanations of his own mind and, simultaneously, of the void-non-void which is the Dharmakaya—ultimate reality. They include forces such as wisdom, compassion, liberating activity and many more particularized emanations of these. Such forces are able to bring about the fulfilment of a need which is everywhere felt but seldom recognized for what it is. The youth pining for his beloved, the child crying for its mother, the idealist groping for some means of ushering in universal happiness—all of these are people longing for something not at hand, the presence of which, so they believe, would banish sorrow and discontent; but when the longed-for

8. Maha Arya Tara (the Green Drölma)

9. Yamantaka (the wrathful form of Manjusri Bodhisattva)

object is attained, full satisfaction remains illusive, for the true object of their longing is not what they supposed. Their thirst cannot be quenched by the (frequently changing) beings or ideals they take to be its objects, but only by its real object, the blissful state of at-onement which is called Nirvana. The Buddha principle, of which the Triple Gem is the primary embodiment and which expresses itself as the urge to Enlightenment, engenders compassionate means to draw them towards their true goal. Blinded by ignorance and karmic defilements, they think in terms of form, dimensions, colour, texture and therefore it is expedient to clothe the true object of their longing in forms perceptible to their minds and senses which will vanish in due course. In response to this need, the forces of wisdom, compassion and liberating action can be made to appear in embodied form. Cherished in the heart, the Yidams transform people's passions and inordinate desires into power and adoration free from stain. When the devotee has learnt to perceive his goal in its subtle form—not just conceive of it intellectually—the need for Yidams is gone and they dissolve into the void.

The Yidam is usually selected to accord with the devotee's wishes or temperament; e.g. sometimes the choice falls upon a wrathful deity such as the bull-headed, blue-bodied, many-armed Yamantaka who dances on prostrate corpses amidst a sea of flame. (This is the wrathful form of Manjusri Bodhisattva, embodiment of wisdom.) Sometimes a gentle female deity such as the White or Green Tara is deemed more suitable. A wrathful Yidam of terrible aspect is selected for those of fiery temperament who must be ruled by fear; for the Yidams, with power acquired from mind, soon come to control the people whose bodies they inhabit—whether through love or fear. To men of emotional temperament easily moved by the beauty of women, whether their adoration is already of an exalted kind or frankly sexual, a lovely female Yidam is given, one to whom the warmth of romantic feeling purified of its grosser content can be transferred. It is reported that in some particular cases the Lamas think it salutary for the Yidam to be worshipped for a time with undisguised sexual adoration, but I have not heard

179

of anyone receiving this teaching and am not sure that it is given. On the other hand, why not? The purpose of the Vajrayana is to employ whatever expedients exist to free men of ego-centred passions so as to liberate them quickly from the vicious karmic circle. If there are men who could be assisted by such means, there is no reason to suppose it would be avoided. Tantrists are not puritans; if in most cases they prefer chastity, that is because it is generally found more expedient for Libera-tion. Most often a female Yidam is used in such cases to con-centrate the power of the romantic urge, purify it of its physical component, and put it at the adept's disposal to assist in the conquest of this ego.

My Nyingmapa Lama's teaching about the nature and func-tions of the Yidam was as follows:

'The adept's chief Yidam, though no other than the play of his own consciousness, must in Guru-yoga be adored as the embodiment of the Guru, the Triple Gem, the Void. When, by powerful devotion, we behold the Yidam face to face, the internal is manifested and the external internalized. Absence of doubt is essential. When the Yidam is visualized, the adept must feel with deep assurance "I *am* Tara" (or whoever the Yidam may be).

'Devotion to the Yidam is of special value in preparing for death; for what appears then will be whatever one has exerted himself towards. If the Yidam appears—excellent! If the dying man can identify his body, speech and mind with Body, Speech and Mind, then all will most certainly be well. Or, if he recog-nizes the five chief wrathful deities which rise in his head at his death as the five Jinas, and recognizes the latter in turn as the five jnanas;[1] and if he remembers that, apart from the five aggregates—form, sensation, discernment, discrimination and cognition—four of which are in the mind, there is no man(self), he will be liberated.'

As to the manner in which Yidams are cherished, what I know is limited to Maha Arya Tara, for I have had no instruction

---

[1] Five aspects of the wisdom proceeding from the void.

regarding the others, but I do not doubt that the methods used with all the Yidams are broadly similar, though varied in accordance with the Yidam's peaceful or wrathful nature.

Those who practise Guru-yoga with Arya Tara as the indwelling 'deity' daily perform a Tara sadhana of the kind described in the next chapter and, in all their visualizations, she is the central figure into which all the other deities merge before she herself unites with the adept and the void in perfect samadhi. Throughout the day, all means of enjoyment are offered to her. At moments of anxiety or danger, her form is called to mind and her mantra repeated. All sounds are heard as her voice and all objects of perception equated with her. Yet it is never forgotten that she is an emanation of the void and that the adept's identification with her arises from the void- ness of his own real nature. After the evening devotions when he retires, he envisions a lovely Chinese-temple-like pavilion she has created of crossed vajras to enclose his bed. Above the pavilion revolves her green dharani, a circle composed of the written syllables corresponding to her mantra. Each time he wakes, this dharani descends and revolves around his head. This, besides inducing a sense of marvellous security, helps him to control his dreams or to observe them impartially as though another person were doing the dreaming. Whenever, as part of a dream, danger seems to threaten, the sleeper finds himself repeating the mantra that must be on his lips when he really comes to die.

The adept's emotional feelings towards his Yidam are warmly human. Her beauty like that of a lovely girl stirs his adoration, but it is of a sort that transcends physical desire. He knows that he is in fact adoring the active principle of compassion which, united with the Buddha-Wisdom, draws people irresistibly away from Samsara's toils.

It is clear that, in Guru-yoga, there is an obvious and inten- tional paradox. The Yidam is simultaneously regarded as a real entity—the Protector, the Beloved and yet as a creation of the adept's mind, a personification of the abstract forces of wisdom and compassion, and therefore synonymous with the

181

voidness of the ultimate Source. It is a psychological conjuring trick and its value is best demonstrated by the attitude and conduct of the people who perform it. It would not be surprising if psychiatrists were to castigate it as a sure way to insanity; yet Tibetans, almost every one of whom cherishes a Yidam, are by and large a people eminently sane and free from the stresses and complexes that wreak such havoc among the peoples of the modern world—particularly psychiatrists.

The Shrine

For Vajrayana rituals, the adjuncts vary from the most elaborate paraphernalia to nothing at all. The ascetics who inhabit secluded caves bare of all adornment do without ritual accessories or mentally create what is needful by act of mind alone or by visualization reinforced by appropriate mantras and mudras. (For example, to create lights, the hands are held palm upwards with the fingers curled and the thumbs pointing up from as near the centre of the hand as possible to suggest the wicks in butter-lamps; a mantra containing the word 'ahga' is pronounced and a multitude of brilliant lamps appear which remain burning throughout the rite.) For a practice that is essentially mental, there is no need for material adjuncts; on the other hand many people—at any rate Tibetans—find them helpful and shrines in temples and in private houses are generally elaborate. The shrines are likely to be situated in the top storey as, throughout Asia, it is considered improper to stand above whatever is accorded reverence.

A typical Buddhist household shrine consists of a high table or cabinet where the sacred symbols stand backed by scroll-pictures hanging from the wall, and a lower table set with offerings and implements. In front is a square cushion on which the adept sits cross-legged. Tantric shrines, linked like everything else to the triple faculty of body, speech and mind, generally contain three sacred objects. In the centre is a statue of the Buddha or of the Yidam representing Body; on the left as one faces the shrine, is a sacred text wrapped in maroon or yellow cloth representing Speech; and on the right is a miniature reliquary tower representing Mind. Alternatively, they represent Buddha, Dharma and Sangha. Pictures of Buddhas, Bodhisattvas and other deities hang behind with, perhaps, the likenesses of the Guardians etched in gold on black paper in a corner apart.

The essential offerings are of seven kinds (eight for Gelugpa adepts), namely: two bowls of water (symbolizing purity of mind and body), one of rice with a flower laid upon it (beauty), one of rice from which rises an unlighted incense taper (the Dharma's all-pervasiveness), one of oil containing a lighted wick (illumination), one of scented water (devotion), one of rice with a fruit upon it (gratitude) and, for the Gelugpas, one of rice supporting a tiny conch-shell (sacred sound). Often there are fourteen or sixteen bowls, i.e. two identical rows of offerings placed in reverse order, to indicate that the statue above the altar and the adept's own body are both representations of the Buddha principle. Often the bowls will be filled with pure water instead of the offerings specified. During the morning rite, this water is converted into the appropriate substances, by an act of mind accompanied by the appropriate mantras and mudras. There may also be other offerings, such as silver lamps filled with solid butter into the centre of which a stiff wick has been inserted (or, outside Tibet, yellow candles of mineral wax), vases of flowers, and incense smouldering in an oblong burner. The lid of the burner may have perforations forming the mantra *Om Mani Padme Hum*, so that the smoke rises in the form of its syllables, starting with *Om* and finishing with *Hum* as the tapers lying on a bed of ash burn towards their butts. The efficacy of the offerings resides of course in the effect of the symbolism upon the adept's own mind.

A kind of offering peculiar to Tibet and Mongolia consists of small figures made of butter and dough sometimes mixed with a red pigment; these are shaped in different ways for different categories of deities, each shape having its esoteric significance. Tormas are probably among the externals which Tibetan Buddhism inherited from the ancient Bön religion. Many Tibetans are expert at modelling not only tormas but much more elaborate figures from flour and butter or pure butter—

lifelike deities, amusing birds and animals or wicked-looking demons. If the Vajrayana ever spreads elsewhere, it will be interesting to see if this special art goes too.

As to ritual implements, the most important are the vajra-sceptre and vajra-bell held in the hands during certain rites while mudras are being formed by hands and fingers. Ordinary laymen are not taught how to use them, but it is well known that the vajra-sceptre embodies skilful means and compassion and that the bell symbolizes the wisdom with which means and compassion must be united. Another implement is the damaru or clapper-drum with sounding pellets attached to it by leather thongs; the furious rattle of this drum and insistent tinkling of the vajra-bell mark the separate stages of each rite. The former sounds like hail pelting fiercely upon the roof and, combined with the sound of the bell, creates a sense of terrible urgency, a reminder that not a moment must be lost in utilizing this precious opportunity of escaping Samsara's snare. It is this sound more than any other which dwells in the minds of people who have lived among Tibetans.

I have never seen in any book a detailed reference to the important part played by percussion instruments in the rituals of Eastern races, especially the Chinese, Japanese and Tibetans, but I know from my own experience that the elemental sounds produced by striking wood, stone, metal and stretched hide are conducive to those states of consciousness which the meditator seeks to enter. Something deep within ourselves responds to them, as to the eerier sounds of nature—the drip or gush of water, the drumming of hail and the crackle and crash of thunder.

In the introductory remarks to the texts of sadhanas, there are instructions to keep the shrine spotlessly clean and make it attractive to the invisible beings who may come thronging about the adept to join in the rites. The shrine should never be profaned by unsuitable objects, but there is no means of preventing the entrance of impious sentient beings. In most Asian countries, rats are plentiful and the daily scattering of rice grains during the mandala offering is an event known throughout the neighbourhood. Rats lurk behind the tankas (sacred

10. Ritual implements

scroll-pictures) and in the narrow space between the altar and the wall, waiting to pounce as soon as the rite is over.[1]

The shrine is used for morning and evening rites and also for meditations and sadhanas at the appropriate times of the night and day. (For example, the Arya Tara Sadhana must be timed to avoid overlapping the hours of dawn, noon, sunset and midnight. It is best performed in the hours before sunrise.) For someone with a shrine in his house not to perform morning and evening rites would be considered a serious breach of respect for the Triple Gem—an idea which perhaps lingers from pre-Buddhist times when deities were regarded anthropomorphically like the Christian deity.

Regular Rites and Meditations

The daily devotions are likely to include 'Calling Upon the Lama to Arouse Him' or some similar rite directed to the Guru; taking refuge; invocation of the Yidam; the generation of Bodhicitta; a brief Vajrasattva meditation for purification; entering the Four Immeasurables; meditation upon the Ten Evils and Ten Virtues accompanied by confession; meditation upon the voidness of the ego and non-duality; and entering samadhi. These form a background to the main sadhana on which the adept is working.

While the generation of Bodhicitta was performed as one of the preliminaries, a single verse formed the heart of the rite, but the adept will by now be working on a more subtle practice for generating absolute Bodhicitta, in connection with which there is a Nyingmapa poem that contains the very essence of Mahayana Buddhist thought.

> 'E Ma O!
> O wondrous Dharma most marvellously rare,
> Profoundest mystery of the Perfect Ones,
> Within the Birthless, all things take their birth,
> Yet taking birth is naught which can be born!

[1] Nothing can be done about this because of the powerful Buddhist objection to taking life. A few years ago, a nunnery in the Himalayan foothills had to be abandoned because so many rats infested it that, in winter when it was cut off by heavy falls of snow, the supplies of food used to vanish.

E Ma O!
O wondrous Dharma most marvellously rare,
Profoundest mystery of the Perfect Ones,
Within the Ceaseless, all things cease to be,
Yet ceasing thus, is nothing which can cease!

E Ma O!
O wondrous Dharma most marvellously rare,
Profoundest mystery of the Perfect Ones,
Within the Non-Abiding, all abides,
Yet, thus abiding, there abideth naught!

E Ma O!
O wondrous Dharma most marvellously rare,
Profoundest mystery of the Perfect Ones,
In Non-Perception, all things are perceived,
Yet this perceiving's quite perceptionless!

E Ma O!
O wondrous Dharma most marvellously rare,
Profoundest mystery of the Perfect Ones,
In the Unmoving, all things come and go,
Yet in that movement nothing ever moves!

Similarly the Vajrasattva purification will have had a section
added to the preliminary form. During the preliminaries, the
rite ended with Vajrasattva dissolving into light and merging
with the adept. It is now continued from this point:

Around the *Hum*, which is the life-essence of His heart,
shine the four syllables *Om Vajra Sat-tva* radiating light
in all directions; and the Triple World becomes Buddha in
the form of the Five Vajrasattva Families and Their field.[1]
Visualize your body as being of the nature of light and as a
replica of Vajrasattva. In your heart is a moon-disc bearing
a blue *Hum*; to the east (front), a white *Om*; to the south

[1] Normally Vajrasattva is at the centre or east of the o o̮ o, but in this case, he
is conceived of as fivefold with attendant Yum and Bodhisattvos, thus o⊕o.

(right), a yellow *Vajra*; to the west (back), a red *Sat*; to the north (left), a green *Tva*. From these letters blazing light-rays spread everywhere, filling immeasurable space and reaching the abodes of all sentient beings. (Among those beings, all of whom are present, your parents and chief enemies stand closest to yourself being similarly purified.) The offerings in the form of light from the glowing syllables are made to the Jinas of the five directions. They purify all worlds and all that is contained in them. Thus all worlds become Buddha-fields and all sentient beings become Vajrasattvas of the five sacred colours, while all sounds are transformed into *Om Vajra Sat-tva Hum*, which you should continually repeat, syllable by syllable, as your thought passes from *Om* to *Vajra*, to *Sat* to *Tva* and to *Hum*. Observe that the heart of the Vajrasattva methods, which constitute the basic exercise of the mandala of peaceful and wrathful deities, requires the acceptance of all sounds as Mantra and of all perceptions as Buddha-fields containing countless Vajrasattvas.

The rite may end at this point, although there is a further section for advanced adepts. There is a note in the text to the effect that the inner meaning of the final section will become apparent as progress is made, and that one of the signs of successful purification is to dream of foul matters expelled from the body.

Apart from these ritual and meditative exercises which, excluding the sadhana, will occupy not more than three or four hours a day, the adept is adjured to follow the practices already described on getting up, eating, retiring and so forth, as well as to bathe, defecate and urinate with the proper reflections and mantras. Every moment of the day can be made to contribute to negating the ego and overcoming obstacles that inhibit the influx of intuitive wisdom. Dreams are important quite apart from the yoga of dreams, as some of them are clear indications of the degree of success attained.

As to general conduct throughout the day, this will depend on the type of adept, his personality and competence in Tantric practice. Hermits, yogis, monks, upasakas (laymen devoted to religious duties) and ordinary householders all have their separate ways of living. It is the ordinary layman who stands most in need of a knowledge of Tantric methods for turning klesa to good account. Hermits and monks are beset by fewer hindrances; yogis are so immersed in non-duality that they can do so as they please without fear of starting up a chain of karmic consequences; upasakas are generally abstemious men in firm control of their passions. With ordinary laymen it is otherwise. Involved in worldly pursuits, they face innumerable obstacles. Therefore they require detailed instruction in methods of transmuting their cravings and passions, even if their modest aim is to make enough progress to ensure rebirth in a state attended by the two precious endowments—a human body and knowledge of the Dharma.

Special Rites

There are days of the Tibetan lunar month dedicated to particular beings such as Guru Rimpoché and Arya Tara and days sacred to the adept's own Yidam and to the Guardian Deities of his sect, to say nothing of the annual festivals such as Losar (Tibetan New Year). For all of these there are special practices.

Then again, there are rites intended to bring about specific results such as healing the sick or bringing good fortune to a household or community. These, though a part of Tibetan Buddhism with counterparts in every Buddhist country, are from a Tantric point of view of secondary importance, but the rites employed may be of a Tantric nature. There are two views as to their efficacy. At the popular level, regular worship and propitiation of divine beings still survives from pre-Buddhist days. At a different level of understanding, it is recognized that effective psychic force can indeed be conjured up by people intent upon the worship or propitiation of gods and demons, so the practice is not actively discouraged. Anything which can instil into people's minds a veneration for spiritual forces is held to have some value.

The Chöd Rite

A Nyingmapa yoga widely practised from time to time by adepts of all sects is the Chöd rite, the name of which literally means 'Cutting Off'. Used for destroying passions and karmic accretions, it may have been evolved from a pre-Buddhist rite within the category of demon sacrifice, but it has been given a Buddhist content which brings it into accord with Mahayana doctrine. At first sight, it may look like a grisly charade, but in fact it is a rite that needs courage, especially as it has to be performed in the solitude of the high mountains. The more unsophisticated type of Tibetan adept has a lively faith in the existence of actual demons quite apart from the beings mentally created during a sadhana. He will firmly believe that, if he fails to impose the mantric safeguards properly, real demons will materialize and, taking him at his word, strip his flesh to stay their hunger!

In the opening stage, the adept in the form of a certain Goddess dances the dance which destroys erroneous beliefs. Identifying his passions and desires with his own body, he offers it as a feast to the Dakinis. Next he visualizes it as a 'fat, luscious-looking corpse' of vast extent and, mentally withdrawing from it, watches the Goddess Vajra-yogini sever its head and convert his skull into a gigantic cauldron, into which she tosses chunks of his bone and slices of his flesh. Then, by using words of power, he transmutes the whole offering into pure amrita (nectar) and calls upon the various orders of supernatural being to devour it. For fear they should be impatient, he begs them not to hesitate to eat the offering raw instead of wasting time on cooking it. What is more, he dedicates the merit of his sacrifice to the very beings who are devouring him and to all sentient beings in general wherever they may be. His final prayer is that the Uncreated Essence of the Pure, Unborn Mind will arise in all of them and that he himself will be able to complete his ascetic practices successfully. All this must be done in a solitary, awe-inspiring place and the adept must take care to master the rites that will keep him safe amidst a horrid host of blood-drinking demons. If he is skilled in visualization, he will actually behold these creatures and see his body being hacked and torn by Vajra-yogini.

Preparation for Death

The rites in connection with death are of very great importance and involve the co-operation of the dying man which is continued *after his death*;[1] for it is believed that, when the consciousness begins its wanderings in the bardo or intermediate state between death and rebirth, the words whispered by the Lama into the ear of the corpse can still reach him. In the first bardo stage dawns the Clear Light of the Void which, if the adept clings to it instead of cowering from it in terror, will immediately bring about his Liberation. But he is more likely to turn and flee. During the remainder of his wanderings in the bardo, throughout which his chances of Liberation or of a good rebirth progressively recede, the whispered advice of his Lama may still help him.

Daily practice in the art of dying is vital, whether to prepare the adept to receive his Lamas' final guidance or for fear that no Lama will be at hand when he comes to die. Of special importance is the teaching that the human state—the only vehicle for Enlightenment[2]—once lost is hard to regain. Unless careful preparation for death has been made, the consciousness will be reincarnated in non-human forms many, many times—perhaps for aeons—before the dual endowment of birth as a human being in a land where the Dharma is preached is obtained once more.

There are several ways of preparing for death, the choice depending on the devotee's skill and yogic ability. The easiest

[1] See *The Tibetan Book of the Dead*, edited by Dr Evans Wentz. Of special interest is the stress placed on the fact that all the deities of the mandala and the bardo emanate from within man's own consciousness.

[2] This does not mean that Enlightenment cannot be attained in one of the states succeeding death; indeed all Mahayana Buddhists, including Vajrayana followers, believe that it can be achieved in any of the mind-produced paradises specially created by the Blessed Ones for that purpose. What is meant is that the quest must be *entered upon* while in possession of a human body. If some progress is made then, Enlightenment at some period after death is not only possible but likely; relatively few people are capable of Enlightenment at the moment of death.

and most widely practised is to make sure that, whether the devotee is awake or asleep at the moment of death, the Yidam's mantra will spring to his lips and the Yidam's form be clearly visualized. If this happens, it is believed that the Yidam will conduct him through the bardo to one of the heavens projected from the minds of the Blessed Ones whence, after an interval varying from a few days to an aeon or more, he can enter directly into Nirvana or undertake voluntary rebirth in Samsara to carry out his Bodhisattva's vow. To ensure that his being asleep at the moment of death will not prevent him from uttering the Yidam's mantra, he may attempt to master the Yoga of the Dream State and thereby learn to control his dreams.

Another way, suited to more advanced adepts, is to study the Yoga of the Bardo State and, by that and other means, ensure that there is no break in the continuity of consciousness during the three successive states of dying, death and after death. If consciousness can be maintained and if the fruits of years of study of the Dharma are present in the memory, it may be possible to escape rebirth (other than voluntary rebirth as a Bodhisattva) by facing up to the brilliant radiance of the Clear Light during the first stage of the bardo.

The most difficult but effective way of all is to become proficient in the Yoga of Conciousness Transference, which will enable the consciousness to depart from the body just prior to death and take up its residence in a body of the dying man's own choice. However, this requires proficiency in an advanced type of Yoga that will be described in the next chapter. For one unable to perform it successfully and not yet ripe for Enlightenment, the best that can be hoped for is that, thanks to his careful preparation for the experiences of the bardo, he will not plunge blindly into the womb of an animal, supernatural being or unsuitable human mother, but choose birth in human form under circumstances that will favour his progress along the path.

As to the mind-produced paradises compassionately created by certain of the Blessed Ones (Buddhas, Bodhisattvas and others), it is said that rebirth there is attainable only by those who have at least made sincere efforts to heed the Dharma. If such a rebirth is attained, Liberation is sure, for those states

191

have been specially established to provide conditions conducive to progress towards Enlightenment. They are described as places where earth and trees are made of precious substances and where jewelled birds sing gloriously of the Dharma. It may be that the mind of the departed does indeed experience his surroundings in that form, or perhaps the descriptions of jewels and precious substances symbolize formless states in which the mind absorbs the saving wisdom that it was too cluttered with mundane knowledge to take in before.

Meditation in Cemeteries

Monks and yogis often spend some time meditating, as Buddhists have done since the very beginning, in graveyards or places where the bodies of the dead are compassionately offered to feed birds and beasts. This practice has two advantages. Meditation on decay and corruption effectively drives home the truth of transience and brings vividly to mind the unsatisfactoriness of Samsara; moreover it is said to banish carnal desire. For Tantric adepts, there is a much greater advantage. Seated in meditation amidst bones and rotting flesh, with the stink of corruption in their nostrils, they seek to achieve a non-dual state of mind in which no distinction is made between objects of attraction and revulsion, all things being regarded as manifestations of pure, shining void. The horrors depicted in Tibetan iconography—corpses, skulls, bones, blood, daemonic forms and terrible weapons—besides having an esoteric meaning which equates them with the destruction of karmic hindrances—are intended to stress non-duality. The frightful Yamantaka, with his bull's head and necklace of skulls who dances upon corpses drained of blood, is no other than Manjusri, the tranquil embodiment of wisdom. In itself, the gleaming headsman's axe is as much an object of beauty and should be as undisturbing as the lotus in full flower.

Pilgrimage

Up to this point, the practices described have been mainly for monks or laymen of considerable ability with a reasonably high level of understanding. Many other methods have been devised for laymen who, however pious, have no leisure for frequent meditation or who cannot cope with any but the simplest practices. A kind of devotion very popular among Tibetans and Mongols of every class is pilgrimage. Tibet, Mongolia and north China are studded with sacred lakes and mountains, famous temples and reliquary towers to which, until the Communists came, pilgrims used to flock in thousands. I once met some Mongols who had spent years journeying on foot from the forests of northern Manchuria to one of China's sacred mountains, Wu T'ai Shan, and who intended to go home in the same arduous way. They had no money but had begged their way all along the route. In Thailand, one sees Tibetan traders who have travelled overland through India and Burma buying and selling along the way so as to be able to visit the shrines in the southern part of the Buddhist world. Such people are often illiterates with little understanding of the profounder teachings, but full of devotion to the Dharma and eager to express their love as best they can.

Some pilgrims, hoping to acquire merit, deliberately add to the hardships of the journey by kneeling down every three paces and touching their foreheads to the earth in the direction of the shrine they are approaching. This kind of discipline is permissible to Buddhists if it does not have harmful physical consequences, whereas flagellation or any kind of self-torture is strictly forbidden.

The climax of a pilgrimage takes the form of perambulation. This consists of walking slowly round the principal centre of devotion 108 or 1,080 or 10,800 times, perhaps stopping to make grand prostrations at every three steps. During perambulation, the mind is held still and an appropriate mantra recited to the rhythm of walking or breathing. As with everything else, body, speech and mind must play their part. People unable to go on long pilgrimages are fond of perambulating towers or temples in the neighbourhood. The practice is warmly recommended as, combined with meditation, it is a means of combating the ill effects of sedentary practice.

Special Uses of Mantras

Besides the mantras pertaining to the Yidam and to the daily performance of sadhanas and rites, the adept will be taught others for use on appropriate occasions. In particular, mantra recitation constitutes the main practice of farmers and artisans who need a form of devotion-cum-meditation for use at work. It is at once a simple and very effective technique. Of mantras used in this way, the Mani is by far the commonest and will serve as an example of them all. It consists of the six syllables *Om Mani Padme Hum,* to which so much meaning is attached that the Lama Govinda's attempt to explain them developed into a book of three hundred pages![1]

In common with all mantras, the Mani has *Om* as its first syllable. *Om* stands for the totality of sound and, indeed, for the totality of existence. Originally written *Aum*, it starts at the back of the throat and ends with the lips. It is chief among the sounds to which a mystical creative quality is attached. Translators who have rendered it 'O', 'Oh' or 'Hail' have obviously mis-conceived its meaning and its function. The A stands for con-sciousness of the external world; the U, for consciousness of what goes on inside our minds; and the M, for consciousness of the non-dual, unqualified emptiness of the void.

The next syllable is *Mani*, meaning the Jewel. It is equated with Vajra, the adamantine non-substance which is perfectly void and yet more impervious to harm or change than the hardest substance known to chemistry. *Mani* is the symbol of highest value within our own mind, the pure void which is always to be found there when the intervening layers of murky consciousness are pierced.

Padma (of which *Padme* is the vocative form) literally means the Lotus. It is the symbol of spiritual unfoldment whereby the *Mani* is finally reached.

Hum, like *Om*, is untranslatable. *Om* is the infinite and *Hum* is the infinite within the finite and therefore stands for our potential Enlightenment, the perception of the void within the non-void, Mind in the form of mind, the unconditioned in the

[1] *Foundations of Tibetan Mysticism*, Rider.

conditioned, the transcendental in the ephemeral, the subtle embodied in the dense. This above all other mantric syllables symbolizes the central truth of the Vajrayana—the truth of voidness enclosed within the petals of non-void.

Om and *Hum*, however, are much more than symbols. Properly used, they have the power to awake in the human consciousness an intuitive understanding of truths impossible to clothe in words. *Mani Padme*, the Jewel and the Lotus which form the body of the mantra, have, even at the surface level, a number of complementary meanings. For example, the Lotus stands for the Dharma and the Jewel for the liberating truth it enfolds; or the Lotus is the world of form and the Jewel, the formless world, the reality infusing form; and so on.

The Mani is the mantra sacred to Avalokitesvara Bodhisattva Mahasattva, who is known in Tibet as Chenresigs and is revealed there in male form; whereas in China and Japan, a similar Bodisattva in female form is known as Kuanyin and Kannon respectively. Avalokitesvara is the embodiment of the active principle of compassion and is therefore specially invoked by people in distress.

One way of using the mantra is to recite it while radiating thoughts of compassion to the sentient beings of the six realms. The syllables are intoned rather slowly; as each is pronounced, the thoughts are directed to the beings in the appropriate state of existence and the written form of the respective syllable visualized as sending forth brilliant rays to bring comfort to the beings there:

Om	white	realm of gods
Ma	green	asuras (semi-divine beings like titans)
Ni	yellow	humans
Pad	blue	animals
Me	red	pretas (tantalized ghosts)
Hum	black	hell

Superficially this may appear to be no more than an exercise in developing sympathy for others; but it is believed that, by virtue of the sacred syllables and by properly focusing his mind, the devotee enters mystical communication with the Bodhisattva

195

and thereby achieves power to make his compassionate thoughts effective. To one who beholds the entire universe as a mental creation, there is nothing strange in the notion of mind becoming reidentified with Mind and thus having a beneficial effect upon mind's contents; though it might be thought that the power of the effect must depend on the density of karmic obstruction between mind and Mind which the mantric force has to pierce. Or it may be held that this is immaterial, that the devotee by his own sincerity activates the immense resources of the Bodhisattva's power.

Another use of the Mani is in connection with the most simple kind of yogic breathing exercise. With each slow inhalation and exhalation, one syllable is silently pronounced and its written form visualized with such concentration that the mind is gradually led into samadhi in which all thought is replaced by object-free awareness.

By non-Tantrists, the Mani may be taken to be a string of sounds and symbols used as an aid to concentration. The Tantric view is that, since the mantra has a force which enables the devotee to tap the inner resources of his consciousness at a level where there is no thick barrier between his own and cosmic consciousness, he can draw upon great power whether to assist his spiritual development or to make compassionate thought a fruitful gift to others.

That Lamas, in thinking of the Mani as a source of cosmic power, may not be as far removed from the psychologist's position as might be thought is illustrated by the story of a semi-illiterate Chinese who, given the Mani to work on in his meditations, mistook the writing of *Hum* for a rather similar Chinese word meaning 'ox'. After practising with *Om Mani Padme Ox* for years, during which his spiritual progress was satisfactory, he learnt of his mistake from an acquaintance. Thereupon he set to work with *Om Mani Padme Hum* only to discover that he could make no headway. It seemed that his progress had deserted him, until he chanced to meet his Lama again. On the Lama's advice he went back to using *Om Mani Padme Ox* and all was well!

One aspect of popular Tibetan Buddhism which has drawn

disparaging remarks from travellers is the use of prayer-flags and prayer-mills which cause mantras to flutter in the breeze and dharanis to whirl in the streams. These travellers pour scorn on what they take for examples of mechanical religious practice carried to extremes. Even if that were so, one might be tempted to reply that flags inscribed with mantras of compassion are a pleasanter and more improving sight than the concrete structures shaped like torpedoes and rocket-bombs that adorn many cities in the West. As it happens, Tibetans do not suppose that wind or water power will assist them to reach Nirvana, leaving them free to spend their time in earthy enjoyment, for they are acquainted with the Buddhist teaching that Liberation is the fruit of a man's own effort. The prayer-flags and prayer-mills, set up by people with mantras constantly on their lips and in their hearts, testify to a sort of spiritual exuberance, to a longing for the whole universe to be full of sounds and symbols inspired by the Dharma with even the wind and the water contributing to the auspicious mantric dance. Where everything exists in the mind, what is the difference between words that are spoken and words that flutter in the breeze?

Chapter IV

THE SADHANAS

The General Content

In this chapter we tread upon holy ground and treat of a subject fertile in its scope for misunderstandings. The adept, with his powers of visualization heightened by the preliminaries and his mind disciplined by the daily practice, now embarks upon the sadhana selected by his Guru. His knowledge of the words and gestures of power must be exact, his skill in visualization considerable. For some sadhanas, he will need instruction in psycho-physical exercises that produce results which to the uninstructed must seem incredible; but this is a matter treated under the heading of advanced practice, although the term 'advanced' has but an arbitrary meaning in that the kind of mental practice now to be described can, if all other requirements are fulfilled, lead to Liberation in this life without resource to physical yoga.

The Lamas teach that such sadhanas are intended for adepts dedicated to bringing about the union of wisdom and means, of void and non-void consciousness, in order to be fully prepared for their task of assisting the Liberation of all beings. Unfortunately, the unscrupulous have discovered that, in other contexts, the sadhanas can be perverted to serve mundane ends; for the psychic force acquired and the power of mantras can also be used for ill, just as Milarepa in his unregenerate youth employed them to destroy his enemies and bring ruin upon their friends and neighbours.

That is why sadhanas are rarely if ever expounded to the uninitiated and why, in books for general publication, they must be set forth in such a way that no practical use can be made of them. Even in the Tibetan manuscripts and blockprints which the Lamas carefully guard from profanation, certain essentials are deliberately omitted and sometimes passages are jumbled so that they cannot be unravelled without qualified guidance; moreover the mystical language in which they are couched yields up the whole of its meaning only to those who have received the teaching that is 'whispered in the ear'. A few years ago, one English Tibetologist published a text which on the face of it requires the deflowerment of a young virgin as part of the rite; the translator seemed unaware that that text deals in veiled terms with a type of yoga that takes place within the adept's own body—'the very young virgin' being in fact the female power (or goddess) at the base of his spine which has to be yogically united to the male power in the chakra (psychic centre) in his head.

The aim of the sadhanas is to transcend duality—including the acceptances and rejections of the other vehicles of Buddhism —by achieving vividly conscious *experience* of the non-dual state. As already explained, the peaceful and wrathful deities invoked during a sadhana correspond to components of the adept's own being and are the forms they assume in certain states of consciousness, such as the state which follows death, certain dream-states and some of the states reached during meditation. Furthermore, for the successful performance of his sadhana, the adept—if he cannot actually perceive all sounds as mantra, all beings as Buddhas and the entire universe as Nirvana— must at any rate act and think *as though* these three truths were fully apparent to his senses. He must behold the universe as a vast expanse of spotless purity, as the 'container' or 'field' inhabited by 'deities', whose very nature he recognizes as pure void and whose immense power is the creative power of void manifested in its non-void emanations.

Similarly, the adept's reactions throughout the day to objects of the senses and the objects themselves must be recognized as 'deities enjoying deities and the void enjoying void'. In welcoming the sensations they arouse, he must avoid attachment to any particular object or perception of it. Enjoyment is not for him an evil, nor to be avoided, provided no attachment results. It becomes harmful if either depravation of it or, on the contrary, inability *to have the sanctimonious satisfaction of being rid of it*

199

causes regret. He must eliminate the idea cherished by Buddhists unable to transcend dualistic distinctions that taking this or rejecting that leads to merit or demerit. If he is far advanced, he will recognize that taking and rejection are impossibilities, since taker and the object grasped, or rejector and the object shunned, are identical. Taking, he takes himself; rejecting, he rejects himself which, of course, cannot be left behind. As the Tantric saying puts it: 'giver, gift, receiver—all these are one'. Whether or not his senses perceive this, the adept must be free from grasping; for as long as his mind remains like a cloudless sky, no harm can result from his relations with any object whatsoever. For such a man, nothing is commonplace, nor the human body a skin sack filled with horrid substances and with animal-like propensities—everything without exception is seen as a manifestation of pure, undifferentiated void.

The sadhanas provide the powers and the mental, psychic and (if necessary) physiological practices for attaining this result. By their performance, the adept gradually releases himself from delusions based on ordinary concepts and perceptions; he directly experiences and masters the psychic forces that can be used to transmute concrete-seeming emanations of the void back into their subtle state. The 'deities' which arise in his mind, though but abstractions of consciousness, assume for a time a very potent reality.[1] They are for him more 'real' than his material surroundings and it is essential that he repose perfect trust in their reality. By his union with them, the internal is manifested and the external is internalized. During union there must be no shred of doubt in his mind; he *is* Vajrasattva (or Maha Arya Tara, or whichever deity it may be). Therein lies the key to success.

Traditionally, each sadhana has seven branches, though what constitutes a branch may differ slightly from sect to sect. A common list is as follows:

1. Taking refuge in the Triple Gem.
2. Generating Bodhicitta.

[1] This is not surprising for, though the deities are formed by his own mind and are but symbols representing various stages of progress and (in their wrathful form) retrogression along the path, this does not mean that they are *less* real than

3. Making a protective enclosure—the 'universe' of the deity or deities to be visualized.

4. Evoking the appropriate deities.

5. Worship: (*a*) salutation; (*b*) taking refuge in the deity invoked as the embodiment of the Triple Gem; (*c*) offerings; (*d*) confession; (*e*) rejoicing in the work of Liberation; (*f*) urging that the Dharma-wheel be turned, i.e. that the work of spreading the Dharma to sentient beings go forward apace; (*g*) the offering of the adept's body and the renewal of his resolution not to enter Nirvana before other beings.

6. Taking empowerment.

7. Dedication of merit.

Each detail of the principal deity visualized during the sadhana has a symbolical significance, of which the following are a few examples:

one face:	the Dharmadhatu or realm of void seen as a spherical drop;
two arms:	the working in union of wisdom and means (compassion);
two legs crossed with the soles of the feet upturned:	the Trikaya or Three Bodies of the Buddha inseparably united;
elaborate ornaments:	the objects of the senses perceived as the five qualities of desire corresponding to the five wisdoms, not as things to be abandoned;
Yabyum figures:	all pairs of opposites in union, especially form and void, means and wisdom.

The Sadhana of the Essence of the Profound Meaning

Many sadhanas can be practised at four levels in turn; or, if the adept has been given the four kinds of initiation and mastered the four ways of understanding, he can practise them at all

such objective forms as human beings or natural objects, since all of them are in fact mental creations.

four levels simultaneously. These levels correspond with the four main divisions of the Tantras, the lowest of which is for those unable to grasp abstract concepts and likely at first to conceive of the deities as independently existing gods and goddesses. At the highest level, the mind is exalted from the start and the techniques used are 'the techniques of the void'. The sadhana described in considerable detail below is one performed to free sentient beings from rebirth in the various sub-human states of existence. Its full title is 'The Essence of the Profound Meaning, Being the Undiffuse Mudra of He Who Annihilates Avicci'.[1] It is a Nyingmapa sadhana containing the gist of a much longer and more widely known sadhana, the Mayajala or Web of Brahma—which means the Realm of Illusion. Containing elements of the four principal divisions of the Tantras, it requires the invocation of all the mandala deities in their wrathful guise, but combined in the person of Vajrasattva who himself appears first in the terrible Heruka form and later as a tranquil deity.

The fact that a few complete texts of sadhanas have been published in English[2] has emboldened me to give the Essence of the Profound Meaning in rather more detail than I should otherwise have ventured to do, because the sadhanas have much in common as regards method and the essence of that method is already well known among people interested in the subject. I sincerely hope there is nothing in my version which the Lama who gave it to me could regard as a betrayal of his confidence; as he does not read English, I have had to trust my own judgement.[3] The translation from the Tibetan is closely based on one made by John Driver, my fellow-initiate or 'Vajra-brother' whose fluent Tibetan made it possible for the rest of the initiates (an English and a Chinese monk, a Chinese layman and myself) to follow the Guru's exposition easily. If all that has been set forth in the previous chapters is kept in mind, even those parts of the sadhana which, without explanation,

---

[1] Avicci in this particular case connotes all three of the sub-human states.

[2] See Dr Conze's *Buddhist Meditation* for the complete text of the Arya Tara sadhana.

[3] For reasons already made clear, I have presented it in a form which cannot be made use of without a teacher.

might be mistaken for magic will be seen in their true perspective as part of a lofty spiritual technique for exploring and bringing into play the psychic powers stored in the depths of the adept's consciousness. One of my purposes in revealing more than I have withheld is to help combat the ignorant supposition that the secrecy surrounding the sadhanas guards something reprehensible. Whether the technique appeals to mystics of other faiths remains to be seen, but no one can have reasonable cause for not esteeming the sadhana as a rite fully consonant with the doctrines of Mahayana Buddhism.

THE ESSENCE OF THE PROFOUND MEANING

The Obeisance

'Ourselves we fervently prostrate with all that we possess
Before the All-Pervading Lord[1] who conjures up the Sphere
Of Tranquil and of Wrathful Ones, where changing dharmas
    blend
Existence and Quiescence in Sahaja[2] unity
Of single taste, from outflows free, the Vajra of Great Bliss.'

The devotee now seats himself comfortably in an agreeable and auspicious place, whereupon he adopts the mudra of evocation and prays the sacred throng—Buddhas, Bodhisattvas, Gurus, Devas and Dakinis, etc., to appear before him.

The Refuge

'Ourselves and all those sentient beings who fill the endless
    void
Salute the glorious Vajra-Host, Buddhas of Triple Time!
Transcending dualistic thought, for refuge we have come
To the Triple Gem which now appears within the mandala.'

The Offering

'Accept these pure offerings of all that we call "ours"

---

[1] Vajrasattva.
[2] Sahaja is the ultimate nature of everything—void.

Transmuted into precious gifts by the wondrous power of
   mind.'

Confession

'Those dams which stem the mighty flood of supernormal
   powers—
Our countless crimes of thought and deed we now confess in
   full.'

Rejoicing

'All deeds of pure dispassion, all dharmas throughout space
When void of Three False Elements[1] call forth our deepest
   joy.'

Generation of Bodicitta

'We now commence to generate the perfect Bodhi-mind
Possessed of four pure qualities,[2] forever undefiled.'

The Offering of the Body

'We offer to the Blessed Ones ourselves now purified
Of all the foul defilements of body, speech and mind.'

The Dedication of Merit

'The merits gained in countless lives past, now and yet to
   come
We dedicate to sentient beings—may *all* gain Buddhahood!'
   (All these verses are to be recited thrice with deep sincerity
and with the reflections appropriate to each.)

THE PRELIMINARY VISUALIZATION

The adept reflects that all those Beings to whom he has just

---

[1] Dualistic notions, such as those of 'giver', 'gift' and one to whom something
is given.
[2] i.e. transcending the categories of existence, non-existence, eternity and
cessation.

offered his accumulated merits and mind-projected aggregations have come pouring into his body from every direction and, for a little while, his mind purified of all that must be discarded enters into the sky-like state of void.

The Circle of Guardians

Now do syllables of power spring forth from that state of void and the adept himself is instantly transformed into the body of Vajra Heruka[1] (dark blue in colour, grasping a vajra-sceptre and a human skull brimful of blood),[2] whereupon he adopts the appropriate posture (asana) and gesture (mudra). The Heruka is manifested in Yabyum, the exact posture being specified.

Next the adept recites words of power whereat a shower of Wrathful Ones armed with every kind of weapon emerges from the Yabyum figure, spreads out and fills the sky.

Incited by another mantra, these Wrathful Ones filling the sky strike, drive off and destroy all hindering forces.

In response to the next mantra, the throng of Wrathful Ones coalesces to form a vast vajra-pavilion composed of the own-nature of the transformed Wrathful Ones. Beyond it is a fierce fire like that which rages when the universe is periodically destroyed at the end of kalpa,[3] encircled by a black wind like that which rages when an aeon draws to its close; and this in its turn is encircled by an ocean of huge, violently agitated rollers. These circles of fire, wind and water fill the void in all directions, isolating the adept and making him impervious to destruction.

THE MAIN BODY OF THE SADHANA

The Generation of Relative Bodhicitta
The Generation of Absolute Bodhicitta

(The two sets of verses to be recited here were given on pages 159 and 186).

[1] Vajrasattva in wrathful form.
[2] Blood: the Guru's nectar of compassion which is stirred by the mudras that follow. [3] 432,000,000 years.

The Meditation on the Three Kinds of Samadhi

1. The adept reflects that in none of the seemingly substantial objects is there the smallest hint of substance. In their true form, each of them transcends discursive speech and thought. Their thusness is one with the realm of void and their apparent solidity very far from real. Thus all dharmas which give rise to appearances are of unimaginable nature, free from duality and utterly void. This realization is the samadhi pertaining to Suchness.

2. Though their thusness is a single whole—world-mani-festing space, from pity for sentient beings, sky meditates on sky. Towards sentient beings (themselves illusory) the vast (but illusory) compassion of the Blessed Ones, devoid of attachment, is as extensive as the sky. This realization is the samadhi pertaining to the manifested universe.

3. The clouds of transient dharmas rise amidst the substance-less, each rooted in that rootless mind which is the root of all—its substance is now to be manifested as written syllables seen as wish-fulfilling gems,[1] of which the syllable from which they spring must first be visualized. Our original Mind, at once manifest and uniformly void, now takes the form of a white *Ah*.[2] This realization is the samadhi pertaining to causation.

(It is not sufficient merely to reflect that those three samadhis are thus and thus. It is essential to enter into the states in which what is said about each is experienced as vividly as the warmth of fire, the feel of wind against the skin and every clearly recognizable sensation.)

Generating the Mandala of Container and Contained

From Original Mind now appearing as a spotless-white *Ah*, six syllables spring forth and the adept recites the mantras for sending forth and recalling.

---

[1] Magic gems that will turn themselves into whatever is desired.

[2] *Ah* and all similar seed-syllables, dharanis, etc., must appear perfectly alive and real. They are not just letters, but 'beings' imbued with a mysteriously living force.

During the issuing forth, contraction and transmutation of the syllables: The first of them expands to fill the Dharmadhatu (Realm of Void) and then contracts to form the triangular sky mandala. In it and arising from the next of the syllables, appears the green mandala of the wind element marked by waving pennants. From the third syllable arises the round white mandala of water; from the fourth, the square yellow mandala of earth; from the fifth, the sharp-edged mandala of Mount Sumeru composed of precious substances. From the sixth appears an encircling ring of fire blazing beyond the outermost limits of the sky. And from the top of Mount Sumeru, the syllable *Bhrum* splits off from the causal *Ah* which is the seed from which the whole magnificent panorama arose.

The adept then recites a mantra which can be interpreted: 'By opening up the Void, the mandala is produced.'

The *Bhrum* now condenses into a hall of enormous proportions blazing with jnana-jewels[1] and extending to infinity in all directions. To symbolize its immeasurable virtues, it is in the form of a square adorned with portals of precious substances created by Supreme Jnana;[1] and its pinnacle is identical with the Jnana of the Buddhas of the Ten Directions and the Four Times —all of them, without exception, not seen separately but as being of the same pure essence. Excellent indeed is that hall with its five walls composed of precious substances of the five colours ornamented with pearls and precious stones, its Chinese roof and richly decorated gates—a place of beauty, lovely to behold. Perfect are its proportions, shape and form, its embellishments and the colour of its jnana-jewels which are peerless on account of the all-surpassing nature of Jnana. Moreover, that great hall is filled with every sort of object of outflowless desire,[2] limitless as the sky in number and lacking nothing.

In the midst of all is a magnificent throne of precious jewels and substances, supported by eight lions (the symbols of Buddha-supremacy), two to each edge holding it up with their fore-paws.

---

[1] Jnana, pure void and, here, the 'wisdom-substance' of the void.
[1] Objects of stainless, i.e. dispassionate, desire—things we may enjoy to our heart's content if no hint of attachment arises.

Now does the adept intone a mantra containing the words lotus, sun and moon, whereat three syllables appear, from the first of which springs a lotus; from the second comes a solar-disc above the lotus and, from the third, a lunar-disc which tops them both. Then his own Original Mind, after remaining for a little while in a state of voidness, appears as a stainless-white *Ah* and drops upon the lunar-disc where it is transmuted into a clear, blazing *Hum*.

Two words of power cause rays of light to issue from the *Hum* and these rays, falling upon all beings, establish them in Buddhahood.

At the words of recall, the rays are withdrawn and merge into the *Hum* which, in response to a mantra, is transformed into the adept now in the peaceful guise of the Blessed Vajra-sattva. The Body (of the adept in Buddha-form) is a mass of deep sapphire blue blazing with light-rays like the rising sun. One-faced and two-handed, he radiates tranquil smiles whose changes indicate the play of Void and Bliss in union. His figure shines with the sacred Buddha-signs. Grasping a vajra-sceptre close to his heart and a vajra-bell above his hip, he prepares to manifest himself in Yabyum form.

From his heart comes forth a *Mum* which pours forth light-rays which are then, in response to a mantra, withdrawn into the *Mum*; this straightway becomes the Yum, Vajra Dhatisvari, whose body is of lighter blue. She too grasps a vajra-sceptre and vajra-bell. Their white upper garments are of divine silken stuff ornamented with bold designs in gold. (There follows an elaborate description of ornaments and garments.) Soft of hand, supple of body and limbs, sleek of skin, sinuously waisted, youthful, shining, pure of form, they possess countless sorts of excellence and splendour.

Seated as the essence of non-dual bliss and voidness, within a sphere illumined by red, yellow, white, blue-green, silver and purple light, they now appear as a cloud-like mass of Buddhas spreading forth and blazing gloriously. Each band of colour splits into a further six, and so on again and again until sixty million separate beams shine forth.

Now in the hearts of Yab and Yum (who are one with the

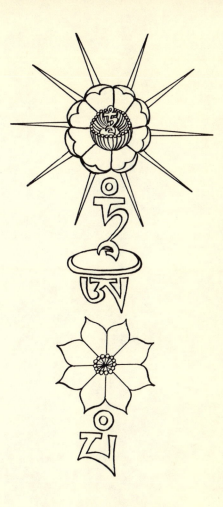

11. A visualization diagram

adept) appear two Jnanasattvas[1] with a tiny white *Hum* in the heart of one and a tiny white *Mum* in the heart of the other, each resting upon a lunar-disc.

Such, then, is the mode of visualization.

The Conferment of Power and the Transmutation

Light-rays now emerge from the little Jnanasattva forms in the hearts of the Yab and Yum. By words and a gesture of power, the adept invites the Buddhas of the Ten Directions and Four Times, who now appear as the divinities of the initiation mandala arranged in their five classes, all in Yabyum form. The adept prays them to fulfil their bond of ardent compassion, whereat streams of nectar born of non-duality rain down upon the adept conferring power. To obtain this power, he pronounces the mantras pertaining to the five Buddha-wisdoms and attracts it to himself by five appropriate mudras.

By the power thus conferred, the stains of the five klesas are cleansed and the five skandhas or aggregates of the adept's body, speech and mind now abide as the Buddhas of the five circles in the core of the mandala. The excess of nectar remaining at the crown of his head is transformed into the Buddha Aksobhya. The adept now glories in the transformation of his purified aggregates into the Five Jinas.

In the centre of his skull at forehead level appears a white *Om* resting upon a lunar-disc; its rays move the mind-stream of all the Buddhas, and the Body-Vajras of the whole great assembly of deities fill the sky. These now merge into the *Om* which thus becomes identical with the Body of all the Buddhas, whereat it is transformed into a white Vairocana Buddha, whose symbol is a wheel. The adept presses his hands joined in the Vajra-mudra against the top of his head and recites a sacred mantra, whereupon a white *Ah* appears at his throat resting upon an eight-petalled red lotus and the Speech-Vajras of the whole great assembly of deities fill the sky. These now merge into

[1] Small figures without garb or ornaments because they represent the Dharmakaya of the Yab and the Yum, through whose transparent bodies they are visible. The white *Hum* and *Mum*, being in the hearts of these inner figures, are of minute proportions.

the *Ah* which thus becomes identical with the Speech of all the Buddhas, whereat it is transformed into a Red Amitabha Buddha, whose symbol is a lotus. The adept presses his hands joined in the Vajra-mudra against his throat and recites a sacred mantra, whereupon a blue *Hum* appears outside his heart resting upon a solar-disc and, in a way similar to what went just before, the *Hum* becomes identical with the Mind of all the Buddhas and is transformed into a blue Aksobhya Buddha whose symbol is the vajra-sceptre. Accordingly, the devotee recites the mantra whereby he acquires the Buddha-Mind. Now he glories in becoming one with the Body, Speech and Mind-Vajras of all the Buddhas.

The Four Processes for Achieving Identity with the Mandala of Wisdom-Void

The adept visualizes the life-essence at his heart in the form of a blue *Hum* of the own-nature of the five wisdoms ever dawning. The rays emanating from it stimulate the Buddhas of the Ten Directions and Four Times to emerge from the Dharmakaya and take upon themselves the Yabyum form. Thus thinking and forming the hook-mudra, he cries:

> '*Hum!*
> Ye Blessed Ones, sky-like yet holding the bond,
> By Void itself and that High Yoga which o'erleaps
> All opposites, I conjure Ye! Deign to descend!
> Ha! Diamond-Being, how radiant is the state we share!
> Come here! Look down on us! The time has come!'

The Invitation

> '*Om!*
> Compassion's hook now moves the Yidam;[1]
> The noose of kindliness constrains him to appear,
> Likewise the iron chain of sympathetic joy.
> The Perfect One[1] comes forth and sits in joy serene.'

Having pronounced this invocation, the adept recites a mantra and employs mudras which constrain the Void One to appear.

[1] Vajrasattva.

Now the adept reflects: 'I am seated in the Mandala of the Samaya with the flames of its fire-mountain mingling with those of the Mandala of Wisdom-Void in which Vajrasattva appears before me.'

The Casting of the Flowers of Consciousness

Reciting five brief mantras, the adept casts a flower each time, while reflecting: 'The Body, Speech, Mind, Qualities and Actions of myself and the Void Ones are identical.'

Imploring the Gift of Supernatural Powers and Dissolving the Mandalas

'*Om!*
How wondrous the Body, Speech and Mind,
The Qualities and Deeds of Void-Wisdom's King!
Ah that my own may flow into his, for thus
Is union with the Mahamudra[1] gained!'

Thereupon, using appropriate mantras and mudras for soliciting the blessing of Vajrasattva, he thinks of the flame mandala in which he is seated and the Mandala of Wisdom-Void in which the deities appear before him as merging like water into water and becoming one and invisible.

The Recitation

The adept sees at his heart a Void-Being resembling himself but who is really Vajrasattva as the Being united with him by the Samaya-pledge, in whose heart is the syllable *Hum* surrounded by the Hundred Syllable Dharani of Vajrasattva; the syllables are white in colour and blaze with light. The rays they emanate stir the Mind of all the Buddhas and Bodhisattvas of the Ten Directions and Four Times. From the adept's own mouth and from the mouths of that assembly of divinities vast as the sky, pour forth the sounds of the Hundred Syllable Mantra accompanied by light-rays of compassion which illuminate the Triple World,[2] purging the realms of evil rebirth and

[1] Supreme Attitude, a synonym for the consciousness transmuted into void.
[2] Universe.

211

releasing into the Bodhi-Sphere all sentient creatures (whom the adept now visualizes). Then he watches the light-rays dissolve into himself,[1] so that the Triple World and all the deities and other sentient beings are contained in Vajrasattva's shining mantra, which the adept now repeats a hundred and eight or a thousand and eighty times.

To ensure that this mantra will benefit other beings, after each recitation he should repeat a short mantra that will some-what mitigate their miserable state despite their evil karma[2]— but only an accomplished Lama cleansed of fault can perform this part of the rite successfully.

Closing the Rite Before Getting Up from the Seat

From the syllable *Hum* in the adept's heart emanate purifying light-rays; his body becomes a great hall which dissolves back into himself, that is to say into the body of Vajrasattva. There-upon, the Yum dissolves into the Yab, the Yab into the tiny Jnanasattva or Wisdom-Void Being in his heart and that small Dharmakaya figure merges into the minute *Hum* within its own heart. The miniature *Hum* dissolves into itself until even the tip has vanished and the adept enters with perfect equanimity into a spontaneously produced state of void that is wholly free from intellection.

(The end)

The Fruits of the Practice

Performing a lofty sadhana of this kind cleanses the adept from karmic hindrances, greatly helps to calm the passions and negate the ego and opens the mind to the inflow of intuitive wisdom. The advanced adept fully experiences the phenomena

---

[1] Since adept and Vajrasattva are now one, the syllables emitting the light-rays are in his own heart.

[2] It is generally held that one's bad karma cannot be mitigated by others; but some believe that an accomplished adept can take a part of other people's load of karma onto himself. This seems to accord logically with the widely held conviction that merit (i.e. good karma) can readily be transferred to others merely by voicing an intention to donate it.

visualized and the resulting states of consciousness which rise step by step to the state of pure void—that marvellous, shining void which, so far from being a dreary waste, is the container and the source of a myriad myriad objects. Knowing of it from books and teachers avails nothing; it is the untrammelled experience of it that liberates. Adepts who send forth their minds to dwell in those high places day after day, night after night for years on end cease to be as other men. Their personalities, thoughts, words and actions are permeated through and through with the brilliant, objectless, attachment-free consciousness of men approaching the holy state of Liberation. Into them wisdom flows like pure white milk pouring into a shining crystal vessel. Theirs is the fruit of mighty achievement, provided of course that their practice is well done and properly conjoined with the conduct and attitude which constitute its basis. Mystical communion with the divine forces of the universe requires as concomitants conduct steeped in compassion and unerring skill in transforming the passions which drive men further and further downward into delusion so that the direction of their force is reversed and their whole being united in a swift progression upwards in the direction of Enlightenment.

It would be easy to misunderstand the nature and purpose of such a sadhana. It is, in Christian terms, not a just rite but a sacrament in the sense that power and purification are conferred. Yet, since Buddhism denies the existence of a supreme deity, it may be asked by whom these benefits are conferred. As I suggested much earlier in this book, the difference between god-based religions and those such as Buddhism and Taoism which are, to coin a term, god-free is to some extent a verbal one.[1] In the former, supreme divinity is conceived as a being, in the latter—as a state. Now, where space and form are transcended and we are considering an invisible, omnipresent source of blessedness, the difference between a being and a state of being is obviously hard to define. The link between the two concepts is provided by the Christian mystics' recognition

[1] There is a fundamental difference, though not one that concerns us in this context, namely that the theists take God to be the *creator* of the universe, which is a concept quite foreign to Buddhism.

that even God (as a being) is subordinate to the Godhead (a state). In the sadhana, the empowerment and purification come from the union of the individual (temporarily drawn out of his puny egohood) with the divine Source which is the shining Void.

Two points must be emphasized, even at the cost of repeating what has been said in earlier chapters. First, Vajrasattva and the hosts of deities who spring from and return to him are not really regarded as gods; they are personifications of the divine forces which pour through the adept's being at the time of union. Even the name Vajrasattva, which means Adamantine Being, connotes not a person but a state of being. It is this state which the adept enters and takes upon himself when their two bodies are visualized as becoming one. The adept *is* Vajrasattva, i.e. he has temporarily achieved the state which, in permanent form, is the very goal of all his practice—the conversion of his ordinary human body into a Vajra-body, an adamantine being impervious to ill and ready for Liberation.

Second, the liturgical part of the sadhana, the visualization of mystic syllables and so forth are not ritualistic in intent. There is no suggestion that these are pious actions (like singing a psalm) and that by doing them we shall earn commendation and blessings from on high. Each of those syllables and everything else that is visualized has a precise correspondence with a psychic reality existing within the adept. Thus the sadhana is no ordinary religious ceremony but analogous to an exercise carried out in a laboratory during which certain substances are heated, mixed, separated and so on in the proper sequence in order to achieve a foreseen and inevitable result. In the West, where the sciences of the mind lag far behind the others, the point has not yet been reached at which so much is known about all the psychic entities and forces that experiments can be conducted to achieve results as precise as those achievable in chemistry and physics. It is in this respect that the Tibetans, so backward in the physical sciences, are our mentors. There would be no difficulty in proving this, were it not that adepts sufficiently advanced to perform spectacular feats such as modifying the shape and size of material objects, making them vanish, or moving them in space solely by power of mind are strongly averse to giving demonstrations. Instances can be seen only by chance or by dealing with persons who, having acquired some limited powers, have left the path and no longer feel bound by the rules

People unfamiliar with the Vajrayana might think it wonderful enough if the adept merely saw and experienced all that is described in the sadhana text as clearly as he sees the walls of the room where he is sitting and the view from the window. But of course he does very much more than that. To train one's mind merely to see such things for the sake of the experience would be pointless. It is because everything he sees and experiences corresponds to a psychic reality and brings about the desired results that the sadhana is of inestimable value. Producing a vision of the great ring of fire, for example, is not an end in itself but a means to achieving an infinitely more worthwhile purpose. If the sadhana is looked upon either as a pious ritual like matins or evensong, or as a fascinating exercise in creating mental projections rather like a cinema show, then the whole of this chapter (indeed, the whole of Tantric practice) loses ninety-nine per cent of its meaning.

The Essential Core

This sadhana, besides resembling other sadhanas in its general form—the seven branches (eight in this case) and so forth—shares with them three vital points which are: the pouring of light-rays and of the white nectar of non-duality into the adept's body, the union and perfect identification of worshipper and worshipped, and the final contraction into a single syllable which dissolves into itself and thence into a state of pure void. If mystics of other faiths adopt this potent method of achieving the mystical experience at will, they will doubtless make wholesale changes to ensure that the new sadhanas are consonant with their own beliefs; but, whereas all the detail and symbolism can be reconstructed, the conferment of power through the light-rays and nectar, the union with the deity worshipped and the ultimate contraction into the void cannot, I feel sure, be omitted without robbing the practice of its miraculous results.

The Arya Tara Sadhana

As Dr Conze's work, *Buddhist Meditation*, includes a more or less complete and beautifully worded version of the Arya Tara Sadhana, I have decided not to include another version here. For the sake of comparison, however, I have selected some parallels which demonstrate that the Tara Sadhana, though more simple, includes the same essential practices.

The Arya Tara Sadhana opens in much the same way as the Essence of the Profound Meaning; but, as it is a form of Guru-yoga, Arya Tara appears as the embodiment of the Guru and the Three Precious Ones, just as in the other Vajrasattva in Heruka (wrathful) guise embodies all the deities of the man-dala. When the preliminary sections of the rite have been performed, Tara's heart reveals the syllable *Dham* surrounded by her special mantra from which light-rays shine in all directions. The adept draws these rays 'like nectar or rain' through the crown of his head and down into the heart, whereupon his body becomes 'pure as a crystal vessel filled with spotless-white curd'. Thereafter he recites her mantra which revolves round the seed-syllable in her heart a hundred and eight times. Next Tara gazes at him with great joy and, gradually diminishing to the size of a thumb, enters his body through the crown of the head and comes to rest upon a solar-disc atop a lunar-disc and lotus in his heart. Now the adept's own body begins to diminish in size, getting smaller and smaller until it is coextensive with the diminutive figure of Tara. 'Tara, Guru and adept are truly one with no distinction whatever.' Possibly because the rite is meant for less advanced devotees, nothing is said about their unified body melting into the syllable contained in the heart which then contracts into its apex and vanishes into the void, although this is a common feature of Tantric sadhanas.

The Suitability of the Sadhana Practice for Western Adepts

It is likely that some people's reaction to the sadhanas described will be that they are unnecessarily complicated; that it would be better to sit down Zen-style and get right to the heart of the matter by entering into the pure state of void without intermediate steps. This is a reasonable viewpoint and one that would surely commend itself in principle to Tantric Buddhists themselves, but with a proviso. They would probably answer: 'By all means get directly to the heart of the matter without the assistance of psychic forces visualized as deities—*if you can!*' Indeed, that is precisely what Tantric adepts do when they have transcended the need for supports.

My own experience and that of a number of Zen followers among my Chinese and Western acquaintance incline me to think that, even after long years of effort, relatively few people using the direct approach manage to get beyond the elementary stage of stilling the mind for a little while. Undoubtedly there are some who succeed in entering deep samadhi, reaching the state of bliss and going beyond that, but there would seem to be many more who do not. Now the Tantric method with its exacting preliminaries and elaborate techniques may intimidate people not willing to cope with so much 'extraneous detail'; yet it can be said that, of those who carry out the preliminaries faithfully and then perform the sadhanas with zeal and regularity, very few fail to make notable advances. However, I do not want to be led by my own predilection into making false comparisons, so I hasten to add that most of my successful Tantric friends are Mongols or Tibetans. It could be argued that Tibetans, a people who have for a thousand years been ardently pursuing the mystic's goal, do not constitute a fair comparison with Westerners or with modern Chinese and Japanese. That may indeed be so.

In any case, it is obvious that each man's choice between the more and the less complicated forms of mystical endeavour must depend on his personality and on whether or not he is irrevocably committed to the view that rituals are cumbersome. It is true that mysticism by its very nature suggests simplicity. Union with the pure, undifferentiated void is a concept according well with absence of formalism. And yet? The history of most mystical sects includes accounts of initiations and elaborate symbols; this seems to bear out the Lama Govinda's contention that a special imagery based on psychic correspondences is needed for cutting through the barriers separating everyday consciousness from the states lying beyond discursive thought.

This would seem to be corroborated by the users of mescaline. However much we may feel that the use of such drugs leads to results that are uncertain and perhaps of no lasting value, no one can reasonably deny that some of the drug-induced insights amount to profound yogic experiences. If that evidence is anything to go by, the attainment of advanced mystical states is indeed attended by situations in which light-rays, brilliant colours (like those of the dharanis) and elaborate patterns (like those of the mandalas) appear of themselves and have a vital part to play. In evaluating the Tantric methods, it may be well worth taking account of the many experiential similarities discovered by Tantric adepts on the one hand and by mescaline users on the other during their voyages into those brilliant states of consciousness which have for centuries been a closely guarded secret known only to initiates.

Chapter V

ADVANCED PRACTICE

The Divisions of Tantric Practice

At this point I step out of my depth, having never had the opportunity to stay close to one of my Lamas for more than three months at a time. If they taught me precious truths, that was due to their compassion and not to my deserts. Certainly they did not teach me much that is meant for advanced mystics, for I was not qualified to receive it.[1] Yet this book would not be complete without some mention of the further stages of the path and I have tried to supplement what I learnt from my Lamas by reading the works of Western scholars. For part of the subject matter of this chapter I am indebted to those modern pioneers of the Adamantine Way, the Lama Govinda, Evans Wentz, Edward Conze and Herbert Guenther. Though I have not had the good fortune to share with them an initiation, as I did with John Driver, they are all in a sense my 'Vajra-brothers' and will, I am sure, generously accept my apologies.

What I term advanced practice covers:

1. Techniques for transmuting the emotional forces into spiritual power;

2. Yogic techniques pertaining to the body, especially the breath, the sexual vitality and the psychic centres and channels;

3. Techniques pertaining largely to mind.

All three categories overlap. Though there are meditational practices in which the part played by the body is limited to

[1] To be more accurate, one of my principal Gurus did confer on me the necessary initiation and 'lung' to cover all the higher Nyingmapa practices, but I did not stay long enough to learn them either from him or from my co-initiate, John Driver, who could, had there been time, have given me at least the theoretical or textual explanations that would have obviated my having to borrow from the works of others.

postures and mudras, there are no psycho-physical practices that are divorced from meditational techniques or that do not utilize the force of the emotions where that is desirable.

The Tantras can be divided into four or six classes, but there is some disagreement among the sects as to the boundaries between them and many Tantric works contain elements of several classes. The classification given here is that of the Nyingmapas. It is said that the Gelugpas do not use the term Atiyoga, but divide Annuyogic works into Father Tantra, Mother Tantra and Non-Dual Tantra, of which the third category perhaps corresponds more or less exactly to Atiyoga.

The Nyingmapa classification is:

LOWER

Kriya Tantra	in which the deities are visualized as external.
Carya Tantra	in which the deities are visualized as identical with the adept.
Yoga Tantra	in which the power of deities is recognized as arising from non-duality.

HIGHER

Mahayoga Tantra (also called the basis of all dharmas) — to which entrance is gained by the three siddhis (supernormal powers) and the defilements of body, speech and mind are cleansed *through* body, speech and mind. The three samadhis obtainable by this form of Tantra are those of jnana(innate reality) and sunyata (void); of manifestation or unwavering compassion towards all phenomena; and of cause, which is meditated by a special symbol. This is the yoga used for opening up the psychic channels and for the visualization of deities.

Annuyoga Tantra (also called the path) — in which the adept comes to realize and honour the true meaning of the Mantrayana (Vajrayana), never breaks the stream of compassion for the beings of the Triple World, and reveres his Lama as one who has discovered jewels in the infinite ocean of Samsara. This yoga is used for the sacred breathing; the deities appear of themselves.

Atiyoga
(also called the fruit)

which is devoid of distinctions of depth, extent and difficulty, and resembles a spontaneously achieved state of unity in which no rules remain to be kept. This yoga is for certain mysteries.

This description is incomplete and even what has been said contains meaning within meaning, but as a rough guide it will serve.

Supernormal Powers

Like all Buddhists, followers of the Vajrayana hold that Enlightenment cannot be achieved even by the gods, but only when the quest is commenced in the human state. The body, which cannot be considered apart from mind by those who think in terms of non-duality, is the sacred vessel into which liberating wisdom can be made to flow. The psycho-physical exercises are not aimed at achieving strength, grace or poise, but at purifying the vessel of Liberation. Principally they are concerned with breath control, the control of some of the body's fluids and the cleansing of the psychic channels which link the chakras or psychic nerve centres to all parts of the body. The force which passes along the psychic channels is sometimes called Vayu (wind) but, like the Ch'i or K'i of Chinese Taoist adepts, it is of a kind much more subtle than the air we breathe. These Tibetan yogic exercises, though applied in a strictly Buddhist context, are generally not of wholly Buddhist origin but can be traced back to their Hindu and Taoist counterparts.

By many adepts, the physical techniques (embodied in special sadhanas) are practised day after day for months or years at a time. Those who wish to make them their main practice and perhaps to acquire psychic powers as a means to rapid progress live apart as togdens (yogis) who wear their hair very long and dress eccentrically as though to emphasize their unconventional approach. They are not monks, but generally remain chaste to conserve the whole of their energy to assist in their arduous practice.[1]

Before outlining the yogic practices in their spiritual context, it may be of interest to mention some of the psychic powers that incidentally (or more rarely by design) result from them. Deliberate pursuit of such power is generally frowned upon by the more advanced adepts who, if they happen to acquire them, take pains not to display them except in circumstances which fully warrant their immediate use. By far the most common is telepathy; one cannot have close contact with Tibetan Lamas without discovering so many instances of it (in widely varying degree) that it ceases to astonish.

Another common kind of extrasensory perception is the ability to predict—before illness or danger strikes—the day and place of one's own death and, in some cases, the locality and surrounding circumstances of one's rebirth.[2]

Two of the powers gained incidentally from psycho-physical yogas aimed at wholly spiritual ends are specially welcome to

[1] I know several people who have witnessed some extraordinary feats by yogis and other advanced adepts. An English girl living in the foothills of the Himalayas wrote to me describing how she was awakened every day in the small hours of the morning by tremendous bumping noises coming from a neighbouring room inhabited by yogis. On investigation, she discovered that her neighbours were practising levitation—not always with maximum success! I have never seen Tibetans engaged in levitation, but in Thailand I once saw a Miao tribesman who, seated on a bench in a state of trance with the upper part of his legs parallel to the ground, kept bobbing several feet into the air without using muscular power— the lower and upper parts of his legs remained at right angles throughout. Another English friend, during a visit to Sikkim, met a dying Lama who, while seated on the ground during the rites preparatory to death, temporarily lost control and, to his huge embarrassment, could not prevent himself from levitating although the occasion was so inopportune!

[2] The English friend referred to in the previous footnote wrote recently: 'One of the monks died about this time. Do you remember the monk of about twenty-seven who was tiny like a child? He knew he was going to die because about three days before, when leaving the wood-carving section in the evening, he bade farewell to the lay carvers saying that he would not be seeing them again.' This example is perhaps not striking as the monk may have known he was ill, though I do not think that was implied. There have been many other cases of very accurate prediction of time and place of death made several months or years in advance of the event by Lamas in good health. Apparently such predictions are accurately fulfilled.

the adepts because of conditions in Tibet and may therefore be, to some extent, cultivated for their own sake. They are the effects of *lung-gom* and *tum-mo*. The former enables people in a state of trance to cover great distances at amazing speed, leaping like a ball and negotiating obstacles with supernormal dexterity. In a country devoid of vehicles and telegraphs, this must have been extremely useful for sending messages between monasteries situated far from one another. *Tum-mo* is a practice of the Hathayoga type described later in this chapter; it is aimed at engendering psychic heat as a special means of hastening Liberation, but physical heat also is incidentally engendered; a naked adept seated in the snow in a sub-arctic temperature can melt thick ice by contact with his body. For Kargyupa hermits meditating in icy caves year after year without intermission, this side-effect is most convenient. Powers much more difficult to acquire result from the practice of *pho-wa*, which aims at transferring the consciousness at the moment of death and thereby exercising some choice as to the circumstances of the next incarnation. The incidental fruit of this practice is the ability to transfer the consciousness during the adept's lifetime when and where he wishes. (There must be C.I.A. officials who envy those proficient in this art!)

Some of the sadhana texts have attached to them lists of the supernormal powers they generate, but it is difficult to know whether they are to be taken literally, whether the abnormal phenomena are manifested but only subjectively, or whether the terms used are mystical 'code names' for spiritual developments of a more subtle kind. As the matter is not of much importance, it did not occur to me to ask my Lamas about them. According to the texts, they include the powers: to shrink or hugely enlarge objects (including one's own body) at will, to make them light as a feather, to make them appear in a chosen place, to be one or many, to transform the five elements one into another, to pass unscathed through fire, water or solid objects and so on. It is hard to pass judgement because a man so spiritually advanced as to wield powers remotely resembling these would not be inclined to demonstrate them merely to satisfy curiosity. However, accounts written during the last two centuries or so (some of them recently) by Christian missionaries and others living on the fringes of Tibet speak of weird phenomena, such as the waxing and waning in size or sudden vanishing and reappearance of small objects in response to mantric commands, so perhaps the hidden meanings contained in the lists of powers are not as far removed from the ostensible meanings as might be supposed. After all, natural phenomena are, like ideas, mentally produced. Those who have thoroughly grasped this principle may be able to manipulate the one as easily as the other.[1]

Despite the disinclination to demonstrate unusual powers or even to discuss them, unless to warn pupils to dismiss them as being of no importance, some powers (such as telepathy) manifest themselves under quite ordinary circumstances and are hard to conceal; and others (the rapid covering of great distances and the engendering of bodily heat) are so useful that they are used commonly enough to have drawn the attention of many reliable witnesses. There is abundant evidence that most advanced adepts develop at least *some* powers which verge on being supernormal, although it is more likely that they are natural faculties of the human body and mind acquirable, like human speech, by anyone with the knowledge and patience to fulfil the necessary preconditions. It is also likely that Tibet used to provide a physical, social and spiritual environment which peculiarly favoured their development. Since on the one hand there were many people prepared to spend long years in solitary confinement to promote their spiritual advancement

[1] Some eerie tales come from the Himalayan region—tales hard to believe even though, if one accepts that the universe is a mental creation, there is no valid reason for rejecting them out of hand. For example, men skilled in giving palpable form to their thought-creations are said to send forth semblances of themselves on journeys during which the wraiths behave and talk so convincingly that everyone supposes their creator is present in the flesh. In other words, palpable ghosts are sent forth by men alive and well. Easier to credit is another type of power, that of sending the consciousness to distant places where, unperceived, it perceives what is said and done. There are authenticated cases of comparatively inexperienced adepts being able to leave their bodies asleep in bed and look down on them from the ceiling or elsewhere in the room; and there are cases of advanced yogins who can correctly relate what has just transpired a hundred or more miles away; from these it is clear that a living man and his consciousness can be separated for a while without fatal results.

and on the other hand communication facilities were undoubtedly the most backward in the world, it is not surprising that some adepts did develop and could make valuable use of various means of speeding up communication, e.g. telepathy and *lung-gom* travelling. In the modern world of telephones and super highways, who would care to spend, say, sixteen hours a day for five years on end acquiring the power to cover distances at the pace of a fleet horse?

The reason why supernormal powers are not held in high esteem is that deliberate efforts to cultivate them would distract devotees from the infinitely more rewarding quest for Liberation. Furthermore, once such powers are acquired, they can be turned to profit and people wielding this means of gaining wealth and fame might be deflected from the quest altogether. An exception is made in the case of healing power, which is quite another matter because not the healer himself but others benefit. I am not well acquainted with the subject of miraculous healing in Tibet, but I have observed that, quite apart from the medical Lamas who can be described as herbalist doctors, there are many Lamas who compound pills from simple non-medicinal substances and imbue them with power during night-long vigils by transferring to them some of the psychic force from their minds and, perhaps, some of their accumulated stock of merit. I doubt if such pills are intended to cure purely physical ills; whether they have any medical effect other than helping to accomplish faith cures, I do not know.[1]

---

[1] I know personally of only two cases of spiritual healing by Tibetan Lamas. The first occurred many years ago in Hong Kong. A young Cantonese suffering from an eye disease was treated in my presence by a famous Lama on his way from Nanking to Tibet via Hong Kong and Calcutta. The Lama intoned a mantra and blew into his eye with, from what I heard a few days later, excellent results; but I never learnt the details of the disease or the extent of the man's recovery. In the second case, I was the patient. While gardening in Bangkok a few months ago, I managed to get a drop of poisonous cactus juice in my eye. The pain was frightful and I was sure that my sight would be seriously affected. Strangely enough, Bangkok's one and only Tibetan Lama, who had not visited me for two years, dropped in the very next day. He too uttered a mantra and blew into my eye. In a few days, the symptoms of poisoning were gone and my sight completely recovered. However, I was under daily treatment by an English doctor and there is no way to know whether my very rapid recovery was wholly, partly or not at all due to the Lama's healing power.

Transmutation of Passions and Desires

Apart from the detailed psycho-physical and meditational exercises shortly to be described, advanced practice also covers skill in dissolving passions or transmuting them so that their force can be applied to serve the highest end. I have received only brief instruction and do not know the details of the more potent methods. It is not likely that a Lama learned in this technique could be persuaded to teach it merely to satisfy a foreigner's curiosity; nor, even had I been specially eager to acquire it, would it have been imparted to me unless I had been able to stay near my instructor for some years so that he could first gauge my sincerity and, later, guide my progress; for using techniques of this sort is like playing with fire or juggling with high-tension wires. It is doubtful whether, outside the select circle of Tibetan, Mongol and Chinese Vajrayana adepts specially instructed in these techniques, there are in the whole world more than one or two people qualified to describe them. Tibetan and Sanskrit texts on the subject are available to scholars with a knowledge of those languages, but—as with other important Tantric texts—the essential keys are withheld and laughable misunderstandings result.

In talking of advanced practice, we are of course speaking of sages far beyond the stage of people governed by passions and inordinate longings who have to make the best of an unsatisfactory situation by turning their failures into sad object lessons for their future benefit. Advanced adepts are those who have eradicated not just the rash behaviour resulting from passion and desire, but the passions and desires themselves. Mere abstinence from gratifying desires as opposed to getting rid of them altogether is psychically and, in some cases, physically dangerous. From the first, the aim must be to uproot the desires and not to hack at their branches thereby causing the foliage to grow all the more luxuriantly. Abstinence leading to severe frustration is a sure way to spiritual destruction.

However, there comes a time when a distinction must be made between unbridled passion which cannot but be harmful and forces within the psyche which, though of a passionate nature, can be directed to assist in the achievement of an egoless state by breaking down the illusory barriers which reinforce our feeling of being individual entities. Adepts who have not taken monastic vows are not debarred from sexual intercourse, although it is generally discouraged because the frequent emission of the vital fluid is a waste of the psychic force and because wrongly directed sexual emotion is a fruitful source of karmic hindrances. So it is recommended that, when sexual activity takes place, the vital fluid should if possible be restrained. Whether or not this is possible depends upon various circumstances not the least of which is the extent of the adept's power of control. What is much more important is that the emotion and the resulting bliss should be made to contribute to his realization of not being an individual cut off by his envelope of skin from the rest of phenomena. During enjoyment, he must visualize his desire as 'a companion to voidness-bliss, that is to say as an integral part of the universal play of void functioning through him but not belonging to him. Recognizing all beings, including himself and his partner, as the mandala divinities, he resolves to generate the Jnana[1] of bliss-voidness and either to restrain the vital fluid or to allow nature to take its course while visualizing the object of desire as the mandala of the Yidam. Meanwhile he converts his passion into an overpowering ardour that is replete with the holy power of adoration not for his partner *per se* but for the immaculate bliss-void which she represents. The offering must be attended by joy followed by serenity; remorse or disgust would pollute the offering, the partner and the adept with gravely injurious results.' To quote Dr Herbert Guenther:[2] 'Since love proceeds from the concrete person to that which is unfathomable, co-existent in or co-emergent with the concrete, the "lure of the flesh" turns out to be "transcending awareness in and through discrimination and appreciation" as a transcending function.'

Sexual desire is a component of one kind of love and all love is a manifestation of Compassion in its highest sense as one of the co-progenitors of Enlightenment, the other being Wisdom.

[1] Union of void and manifestation or the fruit of that union.
[2] *The Life and Teaching of Naropa.*

Therefore, although Compassion need not and often does not express itself through sexual love, the latter can generally be deliberately elevated to become an expression of Compassion that embraces much more than sexual love's immediate object. Love is felt by individual sentient beings; yet it does not belong to them or originate from them, for it is part of the universal force of Compassion working through them; hence even passionate men given to over-much sexual indulgence are less remote from perfection than loveless men who, by loving nobody, dam the stream of Compassion. To quote Guenther[1] again: 'stimulation, from whatever source it may come, tears the individual out of his withdrawal from man . . . The more man comes out of his solitude, the more he will observe that his sense of egoness dwindles in proportion to his growing intimacy with others. Particularly when there is the reality of love as the fundamental actualization of the sublime in man . . . egoness quickly loses its hold over him and, in a corresponding way also, the idea of the other as an isolated entity disappears.'

The Tantric aim in utilizing sexual love for an exalted end, in cases where that is thought desirable, is to draw upon its power to destroy feelings of isolated egohood and erroneous belief in there being any distinction between subject and object· Even people wholly ignorant of Tantric teaching and uninterested in spiritual endeavour lose themselves in one another at the moment of fulfilment and, very probably, lose the sense of being one or even two. At such a moment their two bodies become for them the entire universe, which is precisely the aim of every sort of yoga. It is to be assumed that an advanced Tantric adept is not in need of a simple object lesson; no doubt the methods taught aim at enlarging the experience of at-oneness in such a way that a profound and perhaps prolonged mystical realization of the identity of microcosm and macrocosm is experientially achieved.

[1] Ibid.

Yogic Practices Pertaining to the Path of Form

The Tibetans divide advanced spiritual practice into the yogas pertaining to the Path of Form and those pertaining to the Formless Path. They are of equal worth, since both aim at full experience of the void by beings still within the realm of non-void. Nirvana which is formless and Samsara which has form are twin aspects of the one reality—namely the transcendental void which, so far from being mere emptiness, combines the attributes of formlessness with the potentiality of producing a myriad myriad forms. Which of the two approaches will be taken by the adept must depend upon his Lama's assessment of his character and abilities. Though the Formless Path may seem to be the higher—as Zen followers clearly suppose—it is beset with deeper pitfalls; just because of the absence of a diversity of means and the difficulty of conveying in words the steps to be traversed, it is easier for those whose practice is formless to confound success with a sort of 'mental woolliness'—a vague happy feeling that 'everything is one' and 'all's right with the world, amen'.

In practice it is perhaps less difficult to acquire the tremendous energy required for transforming an unenlightened man into a Liberated Being from the yogas constituting the Path of Form.

Most of what has been said so far in this book is based on knowledge acquired from Nyingmapa Lamas. Now I am compelled to make use of those texts on advanced practice which are available in the languages I understand. For some reason, Kargyupa practice has received more attention than the other Tantric schools. Accordingly what follows is derived largely from Kargyupa sources. Fortunately the Kargyupa and Nyingmapa practices are close enough for there to be no cleavage between them.

Among the innumerable yogas of the Path of Form there are six outstanding ones concerning some or all of which Evans Wentz, Herbert Guenther and the Lama Govinda have all had enlightening things to impart. They are:

1. The Yoga of Psychic Heat or Inner Fire, pronounced Tum-mo, whereby a tremendous psychic force is produced; it also has a valuable side effect, the generation of physical warmth.

2. The Yoga of the Illusory Body, pronounced Gyu-lü, whereby the adept comes to realize that his own body and all natural objects are illusory.

3. The Yoga of the Dream State, pronounced Mi-lam, whereby the adept learns to observe and control his dreams and to equate the equally illusory waking and sleeping states.

4. The Yoga of the Clear Light, pronounced Öd-sal, whereby the adept comes face to face with the Suchness of phenomena and achieves the state of thought-transcending bliss otherwise called ecstatic illumination.

5. The Yoga of the Bardo, pronounced Bar-do, whereby the adept learns to traverse dying, death, after-death and rebirth with no break in his stream of consciousness.

6. The Yoga of Consciousness Transference pronounced Pho-wa, whereby the adept learns how to transfer his consciousness from body to body or place to place, and to enter upon a state of rebirth of his own choice.

The Yoga of Psychic Heat: Though this yoga is sometimes valued for its subsidiary effect which is a great advantage to hermits suffering the rigours of a Tibetan winter in unheated caves, the real purpose is to achieve a state of unequalled unity and completeness in which all the forces of the adept's being are concentrated and integrated. At the outset, he must accustom himself to doing without thick clothes or a fire to keep him warm; and he must also observe strict sexual continence as the transmuted sex energy is one of the main sources of psycho-physical heat. The practice often takes years to master and is usually perfected in solitude. The method used is a form of Hathayoga combined with a sadhana involving visualizations and breathing exercises. The prime object of visualization is the letter *Ah* which the adept, by controlled respiration and intense mental concentration, causes to blaze with heat and turn into a flame that fills his body and then expands to fill the universe before contracting and disappearing into the void. When he has become proficient, the adept can break his solitude and practise tum-mo where and when he likes. To test his success, his Guru may require him to sit naked on the mountainside throughout a cold winter's night, during which he must dry sheets dipped in icy water one after another by wrapping them around himself and subjecting them to the blaze of his inner heat. Madame David-Neel speaks of competitions among newly qualified adepts who vied with one another to dry as many icy, dripping sheets as possible between late evening and sunrise. Another test is to measure the quantity of snow that melts under his body.

The Yoga of the Illusory Body: The purpose is to recognize the illusory nature of the adept's own body and of all objects in the universe.[1] The practice begins with contemplation of an image in a mirror. Mirrored images are remarkable in that they have every appearance of depth, though they are in fact perfectly flat. Contemplating them is an excellent means of undermining faith in the trustworthiness of perception and thus in the individual reality of physical objects. Next, the image is contemplated as standing between the adept and the mirror and finally the difference between adept and image is abolished in an act of pure sensation. Next he contemplates the image at length and in various contexts until he ceases to regard it as admirable or reprehensible, an advantage or disadvantage to himself, a cause of fame or obloquy, or a source of pleasure or pain. Regarding himself as in no way different from the mirrored form, he thinks of them equally as being like a mirage, clouds, reflections of the moon in water, the substance of dreams and so forth. Then a picture of Vajrasattva or the Yidam is reflected in the mirror and its image meditated upon until it becomes animated. If the adept is highly skilled, the image, now regarded as standing in front of the mirror, presently becomes substantial enough to touch, whereupon the adept must visualize all visible forms as being the body of that deity. As a result, all phenomena are recognized as being the play or emanations of the Yidam,

[1] This does not mean that they do not exist but that their existence is not at all as it appears to our faulty sense perceptions.

i.e. of the void. Next, the adept, freeing his thoughts from past, present and future, fixes his mind one-pointedly on an empty space in the sky; and, having caused his vital force to enter the median psychic channel in his spinal column, he perceives such signs as flaring heavenly bodies or the outline of a Buddha-form like the reflection of moon in water. Ultimately, by viewing the moving (Samsara) and the unmoving (Nirvana) as a unity he attains to a state of non-duality and, when the yoga has been thoroughly mastered, the full realization of final Truth dawns in his consciousness.

The Yoga of the Dream State: In this yoga, the adept is taught to enter the dream state at will, to explore its characteristics and return to the waking state without any break in his stream of normal consciousness. Thereby he discovers the illusory[1] nature of both states and learns how to die, traverse the bardo and be reborn without loss of memory, in the same way that he passes back and forward between dreaming and wakefulness. This practice is an excellent way of coming to recognize that the apparently substantial universe and everything contained in it are of the subtle nature of thought and wholly lacking in objective reality. However, mere comparison made during waking hours between dreams and the phenomena of waking life is of rather limited value. For the yoga to be effective, it is necessary to remain fully conscious while dreaming and thus experience the identical nature of the two states.

The Yoga of the Clear Light: It is held that, shortly after death, every being beholds the Clear Light of the Void, which is none other than reality in its pure, fundamental state—the pure Nirvanic Consciousness of a Buddha! It appears just before the dead man's karmic propensities burst forth and cause him to stray into rebirth with its attendant sufferings. A very advanced adept, able to recognize the Clear Light for what it is and not terrified by its radiance, is sure to escape rebirth, but most people *are* terrified and flee as fast as they are able from what, did they but remember, would ensure their instant Liberation!

[1] Not non-existent!

Therefore, if the Clear Light can be beheld from time to time during this life, the benefit is incalculable, for after death such people are more likely to gaze upon it unafraid and thereby swiftly attain their goal. Moreover, the ecstatic experience while it lasts will enable the adept to enter into the feelings and perceptions of a Buddha! The unobscured, primordial condition of the mind which shines between the cessation of one thought and the birth of the next is 'the Mother Clear Light'. That which dawns in the mind when imagining, thinking, analysing, meditating and reflection cease, thus leaving the mind in its natural state, takes the dual form of voidness and phenomenal appearances—it is called 'the Offspring Clear Light'. The blending of these two is called 'blending the Nature of the Clear Light and of the Path into Oneness'. The same experience can be made to occur at the moment that divides waking from sleeping by performing a short sadhana after going to bed. Again the Clear Light can be made to dawn in the 'Mother' form during deep sleep. Finally, the highly skilled adept can, at the moment between sleep and awakening, perceive 'the Resultant Clear Light' the experience of which is generated by the blending of the 'Mother' and the 'Offspring'. This results in the attainment of a state of illumination as to the nature of reality from which no relapse into unenlightened views of man and the universe is possible. Like the Yoga of the Illusory Body, this yoga can, by itself, lead to Liberation if it is mastered perfectly.

The Yoga of the Bardo: This practice is based on the Bardo Thodol.[1] According to its doctrine, when, as usually happens, a newly dead man flees the opportunity of Liberation afforded by the dawning of the Clear Light of the Void, karmic accretions from the life just ended begin to stir. As the consciousness wanders through the bardo, it sinks downward stage by stage until the last lingering ray of the Clear Light has faded. Immersed in hallucinatory delusions arising from his karma, the wretch rushes about in terror until he runs at last to the shelter of a womb and thereby destines himself to yet another rebirth, one of a seemingly endless chain of existences. On the other

[1] *The Tibetan Book of the Dead*, edited by Dr Evans Wentz.

hand if, while still alive, he has grown proficient in the Yoga of the Bardo, at the moment of death he will enter deep samadhi and, retaining his consciousness, prepare to hold fast to the experience of the Clear Light's dawning. Thus liberated from the necessity of rebirth, he will await a favourable opportunity for incarnation in a form consonant with his Bodhisattva's vow to work for the Liberation of all beings. Thenceforth he will continue from life to life with his stream of consciousness unbroken, always choosing forms of incarnation that suit his purpose well. Thus this yoga can lead directly to Bodhisattvahood.

The Yoga of Consciousness Transference: This yoga is practised for a time by nearly all initiates. At death, in accordance with their skill, they will be able to transfer themselves to realms of radiant light, into an apparitional existence or at least into a desirable incarnation. For, if they are fully successful in mastering this yoga, they will succeed in transferring the consciousness through an aperture which can be opened in the crown of the head at the sagittal suture where the two parietal bones come together or, if less skilful, from various other parts of the body, of which the mouth, anus and penis are the least desirable. The practice is performed daily until success is signalled by lymph or blood oozing from the crown of the head at the spot just mentioned. That this indeed occurs and that a small hole spontaneously opens there as a result of the yoga has been attested by numbers of reliable witnesses in China and in the Indo-Tibetan border regions. Furthermore, when the newly opened aperture is first touched by kusa-grass, the adept feels himself pierced from top to bottom of his frame. Sometimes, when this strange sensation ceases to occur, a stalk of kusa-grass is planted in the aperture, which is deep enough to give the stalk sufficient support to remain erect. It is not left there forever, but worn in that position by newly successful adepts as a sign of their success. These extraordinary physical results, to which should be added a rather painful sensitivity of the top of the skull for several days after the aperture appears, indicate that the yoga is dangerous and should not be attempted except under the guidance of a fully experienced Guru.

The yoga takes the form of a sadhana in which a certain deity is visualized above the head; psychic force is gathered from the chakras (psychic centres) in the lower, middle and upper parts of the body, forced upwards through the median psychic channel and driven to the top of the head. This median channel is contained in (or runs parallel to) the hollow of the spinal column and is connected with the other channels at the chakras which are situated at the base of the spine, at the centre of the sex organs, at places near the navel, heart, throat and forehead, and at the top of the head. The psychic force, starting as moon-fluid or transmuted sex-force, meets and blends with a force generated in the head; the result of this union is bliss which, like heavenly ambrosia, feeds all parts of the psychic body from head to toe. It coalesces in the form of a fluffy ball about the size of a pea and can be made to ascend and descend rapidly time after time. Once skill has been acquired, the technique can be used for various purposes besides preparation for death. The consciousness can be transferred anywhere at any time the adept chooses.

Yogic Practices Pertaining to the Formless Path

Treading the Formless Path involves performing yogas of the mind without the support of detailed visualization or the manipulation of the psychic centres and channels. Because no specific physical changes are looked for, there is a danger that adepts will delude themselves into exaggerating their progress. However, an accomplished Lama can, by subtle questions, gauge it accurately, phrasing his questions so that no one less accomplished could divine the expected answers.

The texts of two important yogas of this kind are available in English—the Mahamudra[1] and the Great Liberation;[2] as their practice is by no means confined to any one sect, they will serve as good examples of the formless method.

Formless Vajrayana practice is, like Zen, rooted in the knowledge that all beings possess the Buddha-nature and, in a

---

[1] Evans Wentz: *Tibetan Yoga and Secret Doctrines*, Book II.
[1] Evans Wentz: *The Tibetan Book of the Great Liberation*, Part II.

profound sense, are already Buddhas. When an ordinary man is considered apart from the karmic accretions built up during life after life of bondage to Samsara, there is no distinction between his 'reality' and the reality of the Buddhas. The Dharmakaya or void being of the Buddhas is not something to be won; from the first, it has never been lacking. Liberation consists in becoming experientially aware of it. The Buddhas may be likened to dazzling jewels shining in the void and ordinary men to jewels of no less loveliness whose brilliance is cut off by wrappings of mud-clotted leaves—except that they are not really separate but emanations of that great Vajra-Jewel which is the void itself. Even during the last stages before Enlightenment, they may appear separate, since they are glimpsed through the lingering mists of delusion; but during profound meditation the sense of separation vanishes.

Based on this same doctrine, Zen differs from the formless aspect of the Vajrayana only in two ways. As one would expect, its outward trappings lend it a Chinese-Japanese fragrance instead of a Tibetan one; and it is less clearly graduated to suit people of varying capabilities. Not everyone will agree with Dr Evans Wentz that the Mahamudra transcends all other paths. Indeed, that could not be; of the many paths leading all the way to Liberation, none can be loftier than another, only longer or shorter, more or less direct. Perhaps Dr Wentz shared the Western predilection for methods of realization that dispense with elaborate detail—an attitude that does not commend itself to many orientals. If, even in Tibet, the Mahamudra is one of the yogas most widely practised, the reason is probably not a distaste for magical aids, but a conviction that the Mahamudra practice is relatively less difficult and attended by less danger. On the other hand, even its warmest protagonists assert that the Path of Form is a surer way to Liberation in this life, because the psycho-physical and visualization techniques are particularly effective in building up vast reserves of psychic power.

The Yoga of the Mahamudra: 'Maha' means 'Great', 'Mudra' commonly means sacred gesture, but its Tantric connotation embraces the idea of an aid to practice. (For example, in the case of Nyingmapa Lamas married to lady adepts, the latter are sometimes referred to as Mudras.) Here, Mahamudra means the *experience* of non-duality, that is to say of the Dharmakaya which, in this context, Guenther felicitously renders 'authentic being'. It also connotes the bliss experienced when Samsara's ties are broken; above all, it points to the actual merging in the adept's mind of the relative and of (what comes nearest in Buddhist terminology to being) the absolute—the merging of the manifold and the indivisible, from which results *the unimpeded consciousness of things as they really are* which constitutes Supreme Unexcelled Enlightenment.

The text of this yoga begins with instructions regarding posture and the achievement of mental tranquillity, followed by one-pointedness of mind attained with or without the help of an external object. Next come the complementary techniques of inhibiting thought, letting the thoughts wander freely but without reacting to them, and alternating tension with relaxation. These lead up to the very subtle technique of abandoning both cognizer and cognition—of substituting objectless awareness for 'knowing something' and, at a higher level, experiencing the oneness of knower, knowing and knowledge. If visions result from these exercises, they must neither be clung to nor inhibited; instead, the practice must be effortlessly continued until the mind of its own accord prevents thought from arising. By these means, moving and quiescent mind—observed and observer—are investigated and found to be identical.

Now a higher stage of consciousness is entered; the adept, while doing no more than take note of the arising of his thoughts, comes to perceive their voidness. By meditating upon the yoga of uncreate mind; by observing that the past is past, the future not yet come and the present ungraspable; by reflecting also that mind is neither material nor otherwise—being void of singleness and multiplicity—he comes face to face with reality. (Zen followers will recognize the passage about past, present and future, which is found in the writings of all schools of Mahayana. Only the present is real and even that is ungraspable because, as we stretch out our hands to it, it passes. Reminiscence and speculation are both time-wasting hindrances to immediate liberating activity. The present is the time to act but even that is fluid. Realization that the mind abides not in the past, nor in the present or the future, brings the adept nearer to understanding its true condition, which is timeless and non-abiding.)

The next step is to bring phenomena and mind into a state of perfect unity by discovering the identical nature of waking and dream experience and by seeing that objects and mind, bliss and voidness, the Clear Light and voidness, wisdom and voidness are related to each other like ice to water or like the waves to the sea. Phenomena are now recognized as the off-spring of mind. Non-cognition permits everything to be transmuted into the Dharmakaya by Immaculate Mind, otherwise known as Mahamudra.

The adept sets himself face to face with Immaculate Mind by attaining quiesence and by utilizing past experience gained during aeons of existence. (Very advanced adepts can by yogic means recover memory of what transpired during their previous lives—not necessarily in the form of a detailed recollection of each incident, but in essence. That is to say, the essential lessons drawn from numberless incidents become present to the mind. Moreover, there have been numerous reports of specific incidents from the immediately previous life being remembered in detail, and at the time of his Enlightenment Sakyamuni Buddha is believed to have remembered what took place in many incarnations, both human and animal.)

Now the adept is able to distinguish clearly between the various yogic states and knows the fruits of each. Impediments are cleared away by reflecting that they are void. The four errors in meditation—going astray in the void, dogmatic thoughts, inhibition of thought and over-fondness for yogic exercises—are remedied by employing the remedial technique for each of them. The adept now makes the proper distinction between mere theoretical knowledge[1] and actual experiential

[1] Theoretical knowledge leads many a would-be yogi astray. In China and in the West, there are numbers of people who have read so much on the subject that

knowledge of the true nature of mind—hearing about it and pondering its implications belong to the realm of theory; being conscious of mind free from duality is experience.

The Yoga of Great Liberation: This yoga begins with the knowledge imparted by the Lama that mind is the only reality— the container of Samsara and Nirvana in inseparable unity. The adept is advised to reject all dualistic attachments and beliefs, especially belief in the existence of an ego, for it is these which have caused his wanderings in Samsara. He must recognize mind as the originator and container of the cosmos; as one with the ultimate wisdom he is seeking—as immaculate, clear, non-dual, timeless, uncompounded, the unity of all things and yet not composing them. (A widely used Buddhist analogy is to liken mind's functioning to that of a mirror. The images cannot exist without the mirror and yet the mirror remains itself, neither composing nor sullied by the images. Yet, were there no images, the existence of the mirror could not be detected—except by reference to its surroundings, which are excluded from the analogy. Mind is the container of all things, none of which could exist apart from it, but it is imperceptible *per se.*)

The adept is then taught to perceive that his own mind and the minds of all sentient beings are inseparably one. (This concept presents difficulties. What I know and think does not correspond exactly to what you know and think, so it is natural to suppose that our minds are separate entities. However, the science of psychology has demonstrated that our minds contain vast stores of knowledge that cannot be summoned to conscious thought in the absence of suitable stimuli; and some psychologists have gone so far as to suggest that at least a part of the unconscious area of our minds is common property. These two reflections, coupled with the difficulty of envisioning the separate existence of entities not governed by the laws of space,

they can hold audiences spellbound by their eloquence; among them are many who do not practise meditation for as much as an hour a day, if at all. That is well enough provided their mastery of theory does not lead them to suppose that their reading will carry them far along the path to Liberation. Knowing how to drive a car does not help a man in an armchair to get as far as the next room.

may make it easier to grasp the Buddhist concept of all the knowledge in the universe being present—though the individual may not be aware of it—in our common mind. When the karmic accretions responsible for the illusion of separate egos have been dissolved, what remains is pure, indivisible mind.[1]

Now looking deeply into his mind, the adept perceives that all appearances are his own preconceived concepts, and this knowledge makes them vanish like clouds. He finds that the very Dharma exists only in his mind; where else could it be? Continuing his introspection, he becomes aware that mind shines neither internally nor externally, being omnipresent. Not subject to life, death or defilement, possessed by all beings, it is not recognized by them, so they engage in their fruitless search for values elsewhere. (This is a cardinal Mahayana teaching. Illusory bodies live and die; illusory persons defile themselves; but the reality that is mind remains unaffected, just as the surface of a mirror is unaffected by events occurring to the images it reflects.)

His meditation gradually becomes all-embracing, devoid of mental concentration and imperfection. Recognizing his mind as the unfaltering light of unique wisdom, he relinquishes past and future, dwelling in mind's quiescence.

Availing himself of the experience recollected from aeons of past lives through introspection, he ceases to stray. He discovers that there is nothing to cognize and therefore no knower and no cognition, hence nothing to go astray and therefore no straying. Hitherto he has been using the method of exhaustive contemplation; now at last cognition is replaced by wisdom, which is free from such distinctions as knowledge, knower and the act or state of knowing. With attainment of the goal comes

[1] Experience with mescaline tends to bear this out. Under the influence of such drugs, many people have become aware that they possess 'all knowledge'. This does not of course mean that they can tell you what happened to your Aunt Jane on Thursday afternoon; the concept is much more subtle and rather difficult to convey. If knowledge is regarded as a great wheel, when Yogis or mescaline users claim to have 'possessed all knowledge' what they are saying is that their minds encompassed the hub of that wheel—the essence of all knowledge. This, pretentious or deliberately mystifying though it may seem, is no empty boast. It expresses what they feel to be a profound truth, but one which perhaps cannot be conveyed to those who have yet to achieve the same experience.

awareness that nothing remains to be sought, nor a need to seek, no performer and nothing to perform. Uncreate Wisdom dawns —self-radiant, quiescent, immaculate and beyond acceptance or rejection. This is the true negation of the ego whereby the Trikaya is made manifest in self-cognizing mind.

Together with this practice, the adept learns to seek the Buddha in his own mind, the true self being undiscoverable by those who seek outside the mind. (Seeking the Buddha in the mind is another Mahayana saying familiar to Zen followers. The Buddha—as the principle of Enlightenment and urge thereto—proceeds from the void and will presumably exist as an emanation of mind for as long as there are beings to be Enlightened. It is a principle that exists nowhere but in the mind. Therefore Enlightenment must come from within and it is folly to seek it elsewhere.)

Mind is primordial consciousness and liberation results from allowing it to abide in its own place. Introspection leads the adept to discover that dualistic error arises, persists and vanishes nowhere but in his mind. In truth, the one mind—omniscient, immaculate, void as the sky—is the Suchness, hence the need to cultivate a state of voidness. (Since reality transcends the categories of existence and non-existence, it cannot be conveyed by any epithets or concepts whatsoever. Phrases like 'the Absolute', 'Ultimate Reality' and so on are all inappropriate because each of them has an opposite or counterpart and therefore limits what it describes—hence the useful term 'Suchness'. 'Mind is the Suchness' means that mind is what may for convenience sake be called reality—the only reality.)

Since the delusion of there being multiple objects arises from the concept of multiplicity, introspection coupled with control and understanding of the thought process constitutes the sole way to Liberation. Everything—the doctrines of the Buddha, gods, demons, the perfections required of a Bodhisattva, the passing of beings in Nirvana, existence and non-existence, create and uncreate, all concepts used by the Buddhas and our Lamas to guide us towards Enlightenment—every one of them is a mental concept to be discarded, being nothing more than skilful means that must be relinquished as Enlightenment draws near. (This passage is found almost word for word in certain Zen texts. Since nothing exists but pure, undifferentiated mind, even the Dharma is ultimately void. It was evolved by the Buddha as a network of skilful means for emancipating sentient beings lost in delusion. There comes a time when even these teachings must be discarded. Clinging to them would be to cling to the notion of plurality, to the various pairs of objects such as Buddhas and beings yet to be Enlightened, virtues and impediments, a Samsara to be escaped from and a Nirvana to be attained. Until all dual and pluralistic concepts are discarded, Liberation remains a dream.)

The adept is next taught that mind is knowable, that there is nothing conceivable which is not mind, but that its Suchness is unknowable. (Mind, formless and invisible, is known through the forms reflected in it. The two are not separable and cannot be known apart. To suppose that pure mind can be known in essence involves a dualistic view of reality and delusion as separate states or entities.) Therefore mind can be experienced only through the myriad forms; there is no *underlying* reality, nothing *separate* from the cosmic flux.[1] The realization of the one mind is the sole means to Liberation; hence there must be indomitable control of all mental processes to inhibit further error. If the mind is not known, meritorious action may lead to heaven and evil conduct to hell, but nothing can release men from Samsara.

> 'Therefore seek thine own Wisdom within.
> It is the Vast Deep!'

These brief summaries of two works setting forth the Formless Path may at first sight look out of place in a chapter on practice,

---

[1] Here indeed is the crux of the matter. The Hindu doctrine that the universe is an illusion postulates an underlying Reality. Buddhists never accept this view. The universe is held to be illusory, but not in the sense of not existing. It does exist. It is mind. It is illusory only in the sense that we do not see it as it really is. It follows that there is no state of perfection underlying illusory phenomena. The two are identical though, owing to our ignorance, we fail to see them so. We have to grasp the difficult concept that, though what we see of the universe is the result of very faulty perception, it is our only means of seeing mind. Mind in the abstract, i.e. apart from phenomena, is ungraspable and imperceptible.

but it is not so. Every single paragraph, each sentence almost, represents a fact which has to be *experienced*. Any reasonably intelligent man can understand what is taught here, but understanding unsupported by experience will avail him next to nothing. Being knowledgeable and intelligent is far from enough. Only a great Yogin can experience each facet of the teaching as vividly as we perceive the warmth of the sun upon our skins or the bitterness of strong tea on our palate. When a burning coal falls upon my hand, the onlookers know it is hot; I do not have to know, I experience the burning quality of heat. All Mahayana Buddhists recognize that mind—uncreate, imperishable—is the only reality, yet most of us are as far from Liberation as the moths that fly across the writer's lamp. Not until I perceive the nature of my mind as clearly as I now perceive the light of my desk-lamp shining on this paper have I the right to suppose I am approaching Liberation.

The Prajnaparamita

This is the title given to a large section of the Tibetan canon which corresponds to the Abidharma of some other schools of Buddhism. As its name implies, it deals with the Perfection of Wisdom (prajna). It is not specifically Tantric but, as the whole of the Vajrayana is rooted in its teaching, it demands an honoured place in all books dealing with Tibetan Buddhism. The great Madhyamika school which developed in ancient times around the Prajnaparamita doctrines[1] was the forerunner of all the Mahayana Buddhist sects now in existence both in and outside Tibet. It is from there that Tantric Buddhism's central theme of voidness was derived.

What has been said about the yogas of the Formless Path brings us very close to the Prajnaparamita scriptures, for those yogas set forth the essence of the teaching of the Prajnaparamita in yogic form, that is to say in a form suitable for staged meditations. Tibetan Buddhists have always held that Enlightenment can be attained in two (overlapping) ways—by the various

[1] Dr Edward Conze has devoted many years to translating the voluminous Prajnaparamita texts, but, as far as I know, they are most unfortunately not yet available in published form.

yogic means of experiencing voidness in the mind, the Tantric way; and by the wisdom method, which consists of making a profound study of the Prajnaparamita scriptures and realizing their full meaning during ecstatic meditation. There is, to most Tibetans, no question of the Tantric experiential approach being superior or inferior to the wisdom approach. Which one is selected will depend upon the personality of the adept— whether he is more inclined to mysticism or scholarship[1]— and upon the Guru who accepts him as a pupil.

Meditation upon teachings which have first been intellectually mastered is of course very different from the Tantric approach with its emphasis on visualization and manipulation of psycho-physical processes; that they overlap is due to two circumstances, the first of which is that the ecstatic introspection that follows upon study is itself a kind of yoga. The second is that many followers of the wisdom school attach a special significance to a mantra which is held to contain the whole essence of the hundreds of volumes comprising the Prajnaparamita section of the canon. They find that the repetition of this mantra induces a state of profound meditation in which the true meaning of the teaching can be realized. Some of them have gone even further and personified Transcendental Wisdom as a goddess[2] who fulfils a function similar to that of Arya Tara and the other female deities on whom the Tantrists meditate. The power of the mantra, and therefore of the goddess, resides in its being able to confer yogic insight and its being the root from which springs forth a complete categorical chain of vast logical deductions which, taken all together, comprise the Doctrine of the Void.

[1] Not the arid scholarship of one who learns but does not experience, for the followers of the wisdom school use their studies as the base for their meditations.

[2] As Dr Conze points out, the authors of the Prajnaparamita sutras were aware that the pursuit of perfect wisdom could easily assume the character of a love affair with the Absolute, to which wisdom's elusiveness would lend unfailing interest. Adepts are instructed to think of perfect wisdom with the intensity and exclusive-ness that characterize a young man's thoughts of a young and lovely girl. This is a purely Tantric technique which has often proved effective in stimulating adepts to unflagging zeal.

Conclusion

How truly sublime has been this reaching up to lofty heights by a people whose long isolation in their grim mountain fastnesses, intensified by a guarded attitude to strangers, has kept them so much apart from the rest of the world that one might well have expected to find them savages. Beset by intimidating hardships unsoftened by such basic conveniences as vehicles, roads, hospitals or a postal service, these extraordinary people have bent their powers of mind and spirit to the task of self-conquest. Their mastery of psychological processes and the profundity of their studies are such that, given a common language, Tibetan scholars could debate on at least an equal footing with Europe's most highly trained philosophers and psychologists. Western men of learning, whatever their attitude to the content of Tibetan scholarship, cannot fail to admire the amazing feat of the Tibetans in reaching so high an intellectual level, especially when comparisons are made with the cultures of other mountain and island kingdoms isolated for centuries from the main stream of progress.

In all history, no other people, hindered by comparable difficulties of climate and terrain and cut off from the wellsprings of world civilization, has advanced to such heights. The systematic destruction of their age-old culture by the invaders is doubly tragic in that it was the very last to survive more or less unmodified from the ancient world.

If the Tibetans had originally been a highly civilized people like the Chinese or the ancient Egyptians, one could explain their present standard of learning and intellect as a survival from a glorious past. In fact, this was not so. When Buddhism reached Tibet from India and China in the middle of the eighth century of our era, the Tibetans were a primitive people forever engaged in feuds among petty rulers. From India and China they took relatively little besides Buddhism. Even their adaptation of an Indian script to suit their own tongue was dictated not by the wish for a written language *per se* but by the desire to have a means of perpetuating Buddhism in their country. So it seems to have been Buddhism alone which has raised them to their present stature.

Whether, if Buddhism had not appeared in their land at about that time, they would have responded to some other cultural stimulus and progressed as far cannot be known, but it is certain that the Vajrayana has suited them most admirably. Some idea of its breadth can be gleaned from this book. Its followers include simple illiterates content with concentrating on the mantra *Om Mani Padme Hum*; scholars capable of debating the most delicate of metaphysical subtleties; mystics able to visualize whole universes of shining deities and to perform elaborate rituals in which every sound and gesture is calculated to produce a particular psychic response; thinly clad hermits living in desolate caves on a diet of nettle-soup, with no possessions but a cooking pot and a heap of rags to shelter them from the arctic cold of Tibetan winter nights; yogis with powers that transcend what are generally taken to be natural limits; and several other categories of adept, each with special forms of practice.

Indeed advanced adepts are to be found among monks, nuns, recluses, yogis, married Lamas, lay disciples, government officials, busy householders and housewives. To all of them, the Vajrayana offers appropriate paths within their capacity. No one is too intelligent or too deluded, too wise or too stupid to find within its system a method of spiritual advance suited to his abilities. No aspect of life is omitted from the practice, which can be performed in a shrineroom blazing with light and colour or on the bare hillside, in bed or even in a bus, until the time comes when practice is abandoned and the accomplished adept emerges from his state of bliss solely in response to a heart-felt urge to communicate his joy to others.

In the Tibetan view, people by and large are like the Rajah in the Buddhist fable who spent his time searching high and low for the wish-fulfilling gem that shone from an ornament bound upon his brow. Traversing the kingdoms of India, he never thought to look for it on his own person. Men pursue wealth or knowledge or seek Enlightenment or God, without dreaming that true happiness is to be found nowhere but in their own minds.

The Lamas teach that the only pure, unfailing happiness is

the jnanic bliss generated from within; that discursive know-ledge pales beside this wisdom; and that Enlightenment is wholly a function of the mind. Whether mystics call the object of their search God, Wisdom or Enlightenment, what they will find in the end is none other than the immaculate, uncreate mind of the cosmos itself that is reflected in every constituent atom.

We in the West may well pause to wonder whether the Tibetans have much reason to envy our fantastic progress in conquering the external world. It is now apparent that each step of progress made in the pursuit of happiness and well-being outside the mind adds to our distress. To take just two examples, in the underdeveloped countries that comprise three-quarters of the world, recent successes in exterminating the chief causes of early death have resulted in a population problem that threatens millions with starvation. In the advanced countries, science the great healer and ameliorator of the human condition, is being used to forge weapons that turn living human beings into pillars of flame, to say nothing of those other weapons which may soon exterminate all life upon this planet.

Perhaps the followers of the Vajrayana are right to regard us as pilers of delusion upon delusion, forever strengthening the grim palisades of our ego-prisons. This is a viewpoint which has been held throughout the ages by certain individuals of all faiths. It could be urged that people with the mystic's gift of finding joy within themselves are rare and that the rest must make the best of the world as they find it, were it not that the Tibetans furnish an example of an entire nation bent on developing their inner resources to an extent comparable with Western man's mastery of his environment. How pleasant the world would be if all human beings were taught to concentrate their destructive energies on rooting out the ego and if they took wisdom and compassion as the only guiding forces of their lives. May the wisdom of the Lamas flourish!

TASHI SHOK![1]

[1] Most Tibetan religious works end thus—'May these blessings prevail!'

GLOSSARY

(Some of the special terms used only in contexts where they are explained are omitted. Unless otherwise stated or implied, non-English words are Sanskrit.)

Abhidharma, the division of the Buddhist canon which deals with metaphysics and philosophy.

Acharya (Ācārya), a person deeply learned in spiritual matters.

Ahga, a ritual word meaning 'light'.

Amida (Amita), the name of one of the five Jinas or principal aspects of the Buddha-wisdom, a manifestation of 'Boundless Light'.

Ārya Tārā. *See* Tara (Arya means 'noble').

Aśoka, the great Indian Emperor who, some two centuries after the Buddha, did much to propagate Buddhism.

Avalokiteśvara, the Bodhisattva embodying the principle of boundless compassion who, under the name of Chenresigs, has become the principal deity of popular Buddhism in Tibet.

Avīcci, the name given to the lowest of the Buddhist hells, none of which are permanent.

Avidhyā, primordial ignorance or delusion, which is held responsible for the unsatisfactory form of the universe that is apprehended by sentient beings.

Bardo, a Tibetan term meaning the disembodied state between death and rebirth.

Bīja-mantra, a syllable corresponding to a particular psychic force, the 'seed' from which a particular visualization springs.

Bodhi, Enlightenment, the full perception of transcendental wisdom.

Bodhicitta, the mind of an Enlightened Being or 'Enlightened-mindedness'.

Bodhisattva, an Enlightened Being who postpones his Nirvana in order to assist other sentient beings to enter before him.

Buddha, the, (1) the historical founder of Buddhism; (2) the principle of or urge to Enlightenment; (3) any fully Enlightened being.

Ch'i, a Chinese word equivalent to the Sanskrit 'prāna', meaning the vital breath or psychic energy.

Chorten (chöten), a Tibetan term meaning a sacred tower.

Dākinī, a symbolic being in female form required for certain kinds of meditation, a bestower of secret knowledge.

Devī, a goddess.

Dhāranī, a mantra in written form, often visualized as a series of shining syllables revolving in a circle.

Dharma, (1) the Doctrine of the Buddha; (2) Universal Law; (3) plural and spent with a small 'd', the brief impulses of energy of which the perceptible universe is held to consist.

Dharmakāya, the body of a Buddha at one with the uncreate void.

Dhyāna, deep meditation, the term from which the Japanese word 'Zen' is derived.

Duḥkha, literally 'suffering' but the term embraces every kind of unsatisfactory sensation from boredom to grief and agony.

Gelugpa, the Tibetan Buddhist sect which puts less emphasis than the others on Tantric practice.

Guru Rimpoché, the Precious Teacher, a Tibetan title of honour given to Lama Padma Sambhava who introduced Buddhism into Tibet (A.D. 747).

Hathayoga, yogic practice involving the psychic centres and channels, as well as physical exercises.

Heruka(s), the wrathful forms of the deities of the mandala.

Jina, Conqueror, a title given to the five main manifestations of the Buddha-wisdom, but also used collectively for all Buddhas, Bodhisattvas, etc.

Jñāna, the essence of wisdom and of the void, the non-material of which the universe is constructed.

Kalpa, the vast period between the creation of a universe and the destruction which precedes its re-creation.

Kargyupa, a Buddhist sect which places a high value on asceticism.

Karma, the force generated by thoughts, words and deeds which to a great extent fashions the circumstances of this and future lives.

Khadroma, see Dākinī.

Kesar (Kesara), a yellow flower symbolic of perfection.

Kleśa, karmic defilement, any of the hindrances to Enlightenment caused by desire, passion and delusion.

Lama, a Tibetan or Mongolian monk or layman deeply learned in Buddhist doctrine and/or Tantric practice.

Mādhyamika School, the progenitor of Mahayana Buddhism.

Mahāyāna, the Greater Vehicle, the school of Buddhism prevalent in all Buddhist countries except Burma, Cambodia, Ceylon, Laos and Thailand.

Maṇḍala, an intricate pattern of decorated squares and circles used as a support for instruction and meditation.

Mantra, (1) a formula composed of syllables the sounds of which produce psychic effects; (2) sacred sound.

Milarepa, the most famous figure in the history of Tibetan Buddhism, a poet, philosopher, ascetic and master of psychic powers.

Mudrā, a gesture which produces psychic responses.

Nirvāṇa, the state of perfect at-onement reached as a result of Enlightenment, so subtle that it defies description.

Nyingmapa, a Tibetan Buddhist sect which gives emphasis to Tantric practice and does not require that its Lamas be monks.

Prājña, supreme, liberating wisdom.

12. Three Guardians of the Nyingmapa sect

Rimpoché, a Tibetan title meaning 'the Precious One' which is accorded to high Lamas and to Tulkus or recognized incarnations.

Śākyamuni, Sage of the Sakyas, the title given by Mahayanists to Gautama Buddha, the founder of Buddhism.

Samādhi, a state of deep concentration in which the void nature of existence is experienced.

Samaya, a bond entered into at the time of initiation, which includes numerous pledges regarding conduct and discretion.

Saṃsāra, the universe as perceived by the senses, a state inherently unsatisfactory.

Saṅgha, the sacred community of Enlightened Beings and of monks now on the path to Enlightenment.

Sufi, a Persian word used to denote a sect of Moslems whose beliefs, being mystical, are in essence not very different from those of Mahayana Buddhists.

Sumeru, a mountain which forms the centre of the universe as conceived of by Hindus and Buddhists, metaphorically used to denote ascent towards Enlightenment; also the abode of the gods.

Sūtra(s), sermons said to have been delivered by Sakyamuni Buddha to gatherings of monks and/or Bodhisattvas and supernatural beings.

Tantra, a word connoting action, used to denote a series of books and methods concerned with special yogic practices for swiftly attaining Enlightenment

Tārā, any of a group of twenty-one female deities or symbolic figures used as supports during meditation, two of whom (the Green and White Taras) also figure in Buddhism at the popular level as the patron deities of Tibet and Mongolia respectively.

Theravāda, the Vehicle of the Elders, also known as Hinayana or the Lesser Vehicle, the school of Buddhism prevalent in south-east Asia.

Trikāya, the three Bodies of a Buddha, namely the Transformation Body used for teaching sentient beings; the Bliss Body in which the Buddhas appear in dreams, visions and the divine realms; and the Dharmakaya in which they are at one with the void.

Triple Gem, The, the Buddha, Dharma (sacred Doctrine) and Sangha (sacred Community), also known as the Three Precious Ones.

Tulku, a Tibetan term for a person recognized as the present incarnation of an exalted being.

Vairocana, the name commonly given to the central Jina or supreme manifestation of the Buddha-wisdom at the very heart of the mandala.

Vajra, adamantine, an adjective or noun referring to all that is pure and indestructible.

Vajrasattva, (1) the name of one of the five Jinas or aspects of the

Buddha-wisdom; (2) the state of being achieved as a result of success in yogic practice by someone close to Liberation.

Vajra-sceptre, a symbolical object standing for adamantine power, also for compassion and skilful means.

Vajrayāna, the Adamantine Vehicle, a name given to the Tantric school of Buddhism.

Vijñānavāda, an ancient Mahayana sect which emphasized voidness.

Vinaya, the Buddhist rules of conduct.

Yabyum, a Tibetan term meaning literally Father-Mother, a representation of wisdom and compassion or wisdom and skilful means locked in embrace.

Yama, the judge of the dead, a deity belonging to popular Buddhism.

Yidam, a Tibetan term meaning a male or female symbolic deity required for certain meditational purposes.

Yinyang, a Chinese concept of the passive and active aspects of existence interlocked.

Yoga, the practice of achieving union of the individual with the divine Source.

Yogacharya (Yogācārya), the school of Buddhism which developed yogic practice.

Yum, see Yabyum.

Zen, the Japanese translation of 'dhyana' (deep meditation) now applied to a school of Buddhism which emphasizes meditation above all other practices for achieving Enlightenment, of which the Chinese equivalent is Ch'an.

List of Useful Books Containing Material on Tantric Buddhism

BLOFELD, J., *The Wheel of Life* (some chapters), London, Rider & Co.

CONZE, E., *Buddhism*, Oxford, Bruno Cassirer.

— *Buddhist Meditation* (one chapter), London, Allen & Unwin.

— *Buddhist Texts*, Oxford, Bruno Cassirer.

— *Buddhist Wisdom Books*, London, Allen & Unwin.

CHANG, C. C., *Hundred Thousand Songs of Milarepa*, New York, University Books Inc.

— *Secrets of Tibetan Yoga*, London, Humphrey.

DASGUPTA, S. B., *An Introduction to Tantric Buddhism*, University of Calcutta.

— *Obscure Religious Cults*, Calcutta, F. K. L. Mukhopadhyaya.

DAVID-NEEL, A., *Initiations and Initiates in Tibet*, London, Rider & Co.

GOVINDA, Lama A., *Foundations of Tibetan Mysticism*, London, Rider & Co.

— *The Way of the White Clouds*, London, Hutchinson & Co.

GUENTHER, H. V., *The Life and Teaching of Naropa*; and several other books, Oxford, Clarendon Press.

SNELLGROVE, D., *Buddhist Himalaya*, Oxford, Bruno Cassirer.

— *Buddhist Texts*, Oxford, Bruno Cassirer.

— *The Hevajra Tantra*, London, Oxford University Press.

TUCCI, G., *The Theory and Practice of Mandala*, London, Rider & Co.

WENTZ, E. (in collaboration with KAZI DAWA-SAMDUP), *The Tibetan Book of the Dead*, London, Oxford University Press.

— *The Tibetan Book of Great Liberation*, London, Oxford University Press.

— *Tibet's Great Yogi Milarepa*, London, Oxford University Press.

— *Tibetan Yoga and Secret Doctrines*, London, Oxford University Press.

INDEX

Passing references to terms explained elsewhere have been omitted.
Most references to Bodhisattva, Buddha, Buddhist, Dharma, Enlightenment, Liberation, Tantra, Tantric and Vajrayana have been omitted,
because these concepts form the warp and woof of the entire work;
however, references to them in certain contexts are given.